Dear Reader:

The book you are about to read is the latest bestseller from the St. Martin's True Crime Library, the imprint *The New York Times* calls "the leader in true crime!" Each month, we offer you a fascinating account of the latest, most sensational crime that has captured the national attention. St. Martin's is the publisher of John Glatt's riveting and horrifying SECRETS IN THE CELLAR, which shines a light on the man who shocked the world when it was revealed that he had kept his daughter locked in his hidden basement for 24 years. In the Edgar-nominated WRITTEN IN BLOOD, Diane Fanning looks at Michael Petersen, a Marine-turned-novelist found guilty of beating his wife to death and pushing her down the stairs of their home—only to reveal another similar death from his past. In the book you now hold, THE DATING GAME KILLER, Stella Sands uncovers the dark and twisted life of a one-time TV bachelor.

St. Martin's True Crime Library gives you the stories behind the headlines. Our authors take you right to the scene of the crime and into the minds of the most notorious murderers to show you what really makes them tick. St. Martin's True Crime Library paperbacks are better than the most terrifying thriller, because it's all true! The next time you want a crackling good read, make sure it's got the St. Martin's True Crime Library logo on the spine—you'll be up all night!

Charles E. Spicer, Jr.
Executive Editor, St. Martin's True Crime Library

Titles by Stella Sands

Behind the Mask

Murder at Yale

The Good Son

The Dating Game Killer

From the True Crime Library of
St. Martin's Paperbacks

For

Jill Barcomb
Charlotte Lamb
Jill Parenteau
Robin Samsoe
Georgia Wixted

who deserved so much better.

And for their families and friends, whose love endures.

And for those victims who escaped—and those not yet known.

Acknowledgments

The victims' families and friends have lived with the nightmare of what happened to their loved one for decades. However, even in their enduring sorrow, they have graciously shared their memories with me. Thank you Carolyn Adkins, Marianne Connelly, Bruce Barcomb, Anne Michelena, Dedee Parenteau, Taranne Robinson, Tim Samsoe, Robert Samsoe, and Mike Wixted. I am humbled by your faith and generosity.

The book could not have been written without the help of many people. A heartfelt thank you to all:

Matt Murphy, who took the time to walk me through his involvement with the case and gave me the opportunity to sit with a skilled, artful prosecutor.

Matt's assistant, Dena Basham, who verified accounts, supplied photo credits, and sent along much-needed documents. Everyone should have a Dena in his or her life.

Gina Satriano, whose attention to detail in the manuscript was unparalleled.

Detective Steve Mack, who supplied key information and put me in touch with many witnesses—and whose work as a detective never stopped at 5 p.m.

Marilyn and Art Droz, who explained their decades-long involvement and individual roles in helping solve the case.

Vernon Geberth, forensic expert, and Mark Safarik, former senior profiler with the FBI, who offered their invaluable professional analysis and opinions.

Aaron Mintz, who walked me through the often over-looked expertise of the court reporter.

Charlie Spicer and Allison Strobel, for once again giving me the wonderful opportunity to write for St. Martin's, and copy editor par excellence David Chesanow.

Marjorie Frank and Jennifer Dixon, who are, quite simply, the best friends a girl could ever have.

Jess and AF, for being who you are.

And a special thank you to Sass, for watching over us all.

PART
I

Chapter One

Nineteen sixty-eight was one hell of a year.

Martin Luther King Jr. was fatally shot at the Lorraine Motel in Memphis.

Robert F. Kennedy was gunned down at the Ambassador Hotel in Los Angeles.

Nearly seventeen thousand U.S. armed forces died fighting in the Vietnam War.

In the face of such real-life violence, dark currents began to flow through American culture. The horror movie *Rosemary's Baby*, directed by Roman Polanski, was a surprise success in Hollywood—both with critics and at the box office. It was about a group of Satanists who trick a young newlywed into carrying and giving birth to the devil's spawn. (In a disturbing real-life twist the following year, the sociopathic cult leader Charles Manson ordered the brutal slaying of Polanski's pregnant wife, Sharon Tate, and four others in the Los Angeles hills. Charles "Tex" Watson, who was the Manson Family disciple in charge of committing the murders, told one of the victims, "I'm the devil, and I'm here to do the devil's business.")

As images of carpet bombings and body bags from Vietnam dominated the airwaves, young Americans increasingly began to challenge authority and "the Man." As cars cruised up and down Hollywood Boulevard and the Sunset Strip, radios blared edgier, angrier rock and roll: "Masters of War" by Bob Dylan, "What's Going On?" by Marvin Gaye,

"Eve of Destruction," by Barry McGuire. Musicians from bands like the Doors, the Byrds, Cream, and the Animals played the Whiskey-a-Go-Go on the Sunset Strip—and partied with abandon at the Chateau Marmont Hotel up the street. Los Angeles became a mecca for the most hedonistic aspects of this emerging counterculture: psychedelic drug use, sexual freedom and experimentation, smoking grass.

Amidst all this turmoil and social upheaval in 1968, an event occurred that is not well documented by the era's historians: "Tali S.," age eight, was abducted on her way to school.

Chapter Two

On September 25, 1968, at a little past eight o'clock in the morning, eight-year-old Tali was skipping along Sunset Boulevard on her way to Gardner Street Elementary School in Hollywood, California. Tali was living temporarily at the Chateau Marmont Hotel in West Hollywood with her brother, sister, mother, and music-industry executive father because their home had recently burned down in a fire. No doubt, the Chateau Marmont (known as "the castle on the hill" and located at the top of a short, winding road above the Sunset Strip) held plenty of intrigue for the curious girl as she wandered through a Hollywood legend: plush carpeted hallways; invitingly cushioned velvet couches; exquisitely furnished bedrooms; luxuriously large living rooms and formal dining rooms; balconies overlooking the shimmering sheen of Tinsel Town; and lush gardens wending their way through arbor-draped pathways. The outdoor swimming pool, grand reception area, and open-air dining room rounded out the idyllic picture, offering guests the transient belief they were experiencing the grandeur of a French castle. If Jean Harlow, Greta Garbo, Bette Davis, John Wayne, Marilyn Monroe, or James Dean meant anything to the young girl, she probably felt like a princess among the ghosts of queens and kings.

The hotel was beloved by Hollywood's elite for its intimate charm, and the management was appreciated for its discretion. "If you must get into trouble, do it at the Chateau

Marmont," one Hollywood mogul in the 1930s had famously advised. By the end of the 1960s, "getting into trouble" had become an art form at the Chateau Marmont, particularly among the rock-and-roll legends who stayed there. Jim Morrison of the Doors was injured while (unsuccessfully) attempting to leap from the roof of the hotel into his room, and the drummer from Led Zeppelin rode his motorcycle through the lobby as onlookers cheered. The director Roman Polanski once commented about the Chateau Marmont that "you can almost get stoned from sniffing the haze that seeps through the various keyholes."

As a child, Tali had little knowledge of what might be happening behind closed doors at her temporary home. She was more concerned with the problem of getting to school. Each morning she would wake up extra early and, without telling her parents, walk all the way to Gardner Elementary instead of taking the public bus. For some reason she felt unnerved on the bus and did anything to avoid it. As she strolled along Sunset Boulevard that sunny Wednesday morning, her skirt fluttered in the breeze and her pigtails flew this way and that. Her step was lively as her white Mary Janes tap-tap-tapped on the sidewalk. Tali thought about all the fun she would have at recess playing dodgeball and spending time with her new friends. She had memorized her multiplication table the night before and felt confident that, if called upon, she could say "three times nine is twenty-seven" without a moment's hesitation. Tali had no reason to doubt that this would be another lovely day.

While quizzing herself, "Three times seven is twenty-one; four times three is twelve," a car pulled up alongside her, momentarily interrupting her calculations. A nice-looking man peered out of the driver's window. "Come on in," he said kindly. "I'll give you a ride to school."

Knowing she was never *ever* to speak to someone she didn't know, Tali immediately responded, "I'm not allowed to talk to strangers." And with that, she walked quickly on.

"I'm not a stranger," said the soft-spoken man as he moved apace with the young girl. "I know your parents."

Tali heard what the man said, but she decided not to pay him any attention. She continued on her way. "I have a beautiful picture to show you," he called out cheerfully.

Hmm, thought Tali, *he knows Mommy and Daddy* and *he has a pretty picture. . . .*

"Come on," said the man congenially. "It'll be fun!"

"Well . . . okay," Tali said haltingly, and then lightheartedly hopped into the nice man's car.

Once settled, the soft-spoken man asked, "What time does school start?"

Tali thought for a moment, looked at her watch, and then responded, "In about an hour." She felt proud that she could tell time as quickly as she could. She wondered if the man was aware of her accomplishment.

"Good. There's time for you to see the poster. It's psychedelic. Of forests and trees."

Tali was excited. She was not only getting a ride all the way to school but was also about to see something beautiful.

As they drove along, Tali enjoyed the breeze from the open widow. She felt lucky, too, that she didn't have to walk the long distance. But after a few minutes she had the strangest sensation that something wasn't quite right. The man kept looking over at her but saying nothing.

She thought about what she had done and wondered if maybe she had made a mistake. However, she knew she could always trust an adult—she really believed that—so she tried to bury her anxiety right then and there.

On September 25, 1968, at a little past eight o'clock in the morning, Donald Haines was driving along Sunset Boulevard on his way to work. While pausing at a stop sign, he casually glanced out his window. There, on the other side of the street, he watched a scenario unfold. A car was inching along, apace with a young girl. The driver leaned out his window and said something to the girl. The girl stopped, said something back to the driver, and then walked quickly on. The car continued trolling alongside the girl.

A thought immediately popped into Haines's head: *Something weird is happening.*

The vehicle behind Haines beeped, momentarily halting his rubbernecking activities. Forced to move, Haines drove forward but pulled over to the curb to continue observing. After a few moments he saw the child get into the car.

In his gut Haines knew something was not right, but his rational mind flexed its muscle: *Don't I have anything better to do than create sinister scenarios about random people? I should have my head examined.*

In spite of his doubts, Haines decided to follow the vehicle. He wondered if this was what people called having a sixth sense or, perhaps, and more likely, "going off one's rocker."

Haines made a U-turn and began to shadow the vehicle. Within a few minutes the car pulled into a parking space in front of an apartment complex on De Longpre Avenue. The building was located in a lovely, seemingly safe neighborhood and flanked by exquisite blossoms.

No doubt about it, thought Haines. *I've lost my marbles.*

Nevertheless, he kept his eyes peeled. The driver, perhaps in his twenties, and the little girl exited the car and walked toward an apartment in the complex. It seemed that the child was hanging back a bit, not quite comfortable with what she was doing. The two entered an apartment and disappeared from sight.

The whole thing gave Haines the heebie-jeebies.

Relying on his gut but prepared to be belittled, Haines walked to a pay phone nearby and dialed the police. "You may think I'm a little screwy," said Haines, "but I just witnessed something that doesn't look right. I think a man just lured a little girl into his car, so I followed them, and now he and the girl went into this apartment together. I may be wrong. I may be right. But maybe you could just check on it so I can sleep tonight?"

"Okay, sir," said the police officer. "Why don't you give me your name and where you are and I'll send someone over. You stay there, okay? Better safe than sorry."

Haines felt relieved. Even if it turned out that nothing the least bit alarming was taking place, he had done his civic duty.

Within minutes a patrol car pulled up and an officer walked up to Haines's vehicle. The man introduced himself as Los Angeles Police Department (LAPD) officer Chris Camacho. He asked Haines which apartment the girl and the man went into, and Haines pointed it out. Camacho thanked Haines and assured him that he had done the right thing, even if it turned out to be something totally aboveboard.

That day was Camacho's first day back at work. While on duty in August, he had been shot and had taken a short leave. He was hoping for a nice, calm morning; he'd seen enough action for a while.

While waiting for backup, Camacho took a quick glance around the apartment complex. Everything looked perfectly normal. He walked up to the front door of the apartment Haines had pointed out and knocked. "Police officer. Open the door."

No answer.

He knocked again. "LA police. Open the door. I want to talk to you."

A man appeared at a window, pushing the venetian blinds off to the side. "Hey," the man called out. "Give me a sec. Just got out of the shower."

To Camacho, the guy looked like he was nude—and he wasn't wet. Something in the man's voice bothered Camacho. It seemed too excited, or maybe even panicked. *But then again,* thought Camacho, *most people are anxious when confronted by police at their front door.*

As Camacho stood waiting, he thought he heard a faint sound coming from inside. It sounded like someone moaning. Concerned, Camacho yelled, "Open the door now or I'm kicking it in."

No answer.

Without waiting another second, Camacho broke open the door. With backup officers now arriving on the scene, Camacho entered the apartment. Guns drawn, the cops split up to check all the rooms.

The officers immediately noticed a large amount of photographic equipment, including a tripod, in the living room. And in piles all over the apartment were photographs of young girls. A trail of bloodstains led from the living room into the kitchen.

Camacho entered the kitchen. And then he gagged.

On the floor in a pool of blood lay a nude child on her back. Her head was bashed open.

A large, heavy metal bar—like a dumbbell—lay horizontally across her neck.

Her legs were spread apart.

A massive amount of blood, coming from her vaginal area, was pooled between her legs.

White Mary Janes, a dress, and little girl's socks lay in a heap on the floor.

To Camacho, the child looked like she was dead—her face was white and drained of color—but instinct told him to remove the bar from her neck and check her pulse. Grabbing a towel so as not to compromise the crime scene, he lifted the bar and saw the slightest pulse in the child's neck. Immediately he called for an ambulance.

The backup officers reported to Camacho that there was no sign of anyone else in the apartment. In the short time it had taken to kick in the door, the perpetrator—the *monster*—had slipped out the back.

As he waited for the ambulance, Camacho reflected. He had served four years in Vietnam as an infantry squad leader, and he had seen his share of atrocities. But this tiny child laying in a massive pool of blood . . . this child who had been grotesquely violated and brutalized . . . it was almost beyond anything. *She's so innocent,* he thought.

In Vietnam, Camacho had once attempted to save a soldier from drowning, but the man had died in a relentless, raging river. The memory still haunted him. Maybe, he thought, God was giving him a second chance with this little girl. Would she live? He prayed for her to hold on, and he wondered, *What kind of sicko would do something like this?*

Chapter Three

Siren blazing, an ambulance sped to the De Longpre Avenue apartment. Emergency Medical Service workers dashed inside. Seeing a barely alive, unconscious, nude child covered in blood, they immediately administered CPR. As soon as they could, they placed the girl's limp body on a stretcher, lifted her into the ambulance, and raced to the hospital.

When Tali arrived at the emergency room, doctors looked at each other, stupefied. Sure, they had seen their share of god-awful injuries—stabbings, gunshot wounds, broken bones, even mutilations—but this was off the charts. Here lay a little girl with dark bruises on her neck. Her face was bashed in. She had angry welts all over her body. And she was bloodied from head to toe.

The doctors took the girl into the operating room and began sewing up the fissure in the back of her head. It took several hours and twenty-seven sutures to close the gap.

Even after the operation, the doctors could not say for certain whether she would live or die.

At a little after nine o'clock that morning, the officers who had backed up Camacho began combing through the De Longpre apartment, where an as-yet-unnamed man had nearly bludgeoned a little girl to death, strangled her with the weight of the dumbbell, and viciously raped her. They realized that the perpetrator had fled out the back door, so

several detectives began inspecting the area behind the building and asking neighbors questions.

Who was this monster?

The following days passed achingly slowly for Tali's parents
and siblings, who were distraught beyond consolation. Never
in their wildest dreams could they have imagined that something like this could happen to their beloved daughter and
sister. *Who would do such a thing to anyone, let alone a small
child?*

After a few days, little Tali slowly regained consciousness.
She recognized her family. She smiled. She was just beginning to be able to move her limbs. The doctors felt cautiously
optimistic. They informed officer Camacho that if he had not
removed the weight from Tali's neck that had been cutting off
her air supply, she would have died on the scene. The attacker's intent had been to kill Tali. But Donald Haines, the Good
Samaritan, had been there to prevent that, and so had the
quick-thinking Camacho. Plus, the child was a fighter. She just
might make it.

Day by day, Tali grew stronger. However, because she
had been so brutally attacked, she remained in the hospital
for nearly a month, all the time under intense scrutiny from
the doctors. *Would she have permanent physical damage?
Would she be able to walk again? Would she have brain
damage?* No one could say for sure. However, there was one
thing everyone knew: Little Tali would suffer major emotional damage for the rest of her life.

When it was clear that Tali was firmly on the path to re-
covery, she was released from the hospital and brought back
to the Chateau Marmont hotel. During the next several weeks,
her family didn't leave her side for a second.

Several months later Tali was finally able to get out of
bed, but it was still many more weeks until she was strong
enough to return to school. By then it was the middle of the
school year.

One saving grace was that Tali could not remember the
most terrifying parts of the assault. The last thing she re-

membered was going into her attacker's apartment and looking at a picture. After that, everything was a blank. She had blacked out, presumably when her attacker struck her in the back of the head.

However, the trauma proved so devastating and all-consuming to Tali's family that they could no longer bear to live in the neighborhood—or even the country—where the unspeakable tragedy took place. Tali's father quit the music industry and moved his family to the resort city of Puerto Vallarta, Mexico, in the hopes that distance might help them heal.

Unfortunately, the family came to understand that they would never, *ever* be free of this monstrous event, no matter how far away they traveled. The perpetrator had not been caught. He was still out there, and no one had the faintest clue where.

Chapter Four

The definition of a pedophile is someone who is sexually attracted to a child or children. A fuller description appears in the 2000 edition of the *Diagnostic and Statistical Manual of Mental Disorders IV*, or *DSM-IV*, the accepted guide for diagnosing psychological disorders, published by the American Psychiatric Association.

According to the *DSM-IV*, pedophilia involves "sexual activity with a prepubescent child (generally age 13 years or younger). The individual with pedophilia must be age 16 years or older and at least 5 years older than the child. . . . Some individuals with pedophilia are sexually attracted only to children (Exclusive Type) whereas others are sometimes attracted to adults (Nonexclusive Type)."

According to experts who specialize in this category of mental disorder, pedophiles in general do not stand out in society in any significant way. They easily blend in as, possibly, the clean-cut guy next door. (Most pedophiles are male.) They are often good-looking, charming, intelligent, and cultured. Usually they are polite and well-spoken and often have excellent interpersonal skills with children, enabling them to facilely gain a child's trust. Pedophiles may have respectable professions, which they use in the commission of their deviant behavior. For example, they may be teachers, counselors, photographers, coaches, or even members of the clergy.

However, whatever else a pedophile is, he is always *somebody's* next-door neighbor. And he is a predator.

Meanwhile, at the LAPD, Detective Steve Hodel had been put in charge of tracking down the fugitive. Hodel had joined the force in 1963 and served nearly six years on uniform patrol before transferring to the Hollywood Division Detectives, where he worked "all the tables": burglary, robbery, crimes against persons. Rising quickly through the ranks, Hodel was considered energetic and tenacious. Now it would be up to him and his team to bring the perpetrator of this unspeakable crime to justice.

By talking to the escaped man's neighbors, the police learned that the fugitive was considered a quiet person, not a troublemaker. In fact, they learned he was a student at the University of California at Los Angeles (UCLA). A student ID left behind in the apartment said his name was Rodney Alcala.

On the UCLA campus, no one seemed to have anything bad to say about Alcala either. In fact, most people said they liked the guy. When Hodel questioned one of Alcala's professors, the professor told him that Alcala "wouldn't harm a fly."

Could *this* be the man they were looking for?

Chapter Five

Rodrigo Jacques Alcala-Buquor was born on August 23, 1943, in San Antonio, Texas, to Anna Maria Gutierrez and Raoul Alcala-Buquor Sr. Rodney, as Rodrigo was called, lived there with his two sisters, one brother, mother, father, and maternal grandmother until he was around eight years old. Raoul, nicknamed Roy, was the oldest child, born in 1941. Next came Marie Therese, known as Paqui. She was born in 1942. Then came Rodney, and the youngest was Maria Christine, called Christine or Krissy. She was born in 1947.

The Alcala-Buquor family lived in a middle-class home in a middle-class neighborhood. No doubt, they had the time and means to enjoy the offerings of historic San Antonio. With the Alamo just a short distance away, and River Walk and the San Antonio Zoo nearby, the family's weekends were always filled with plenty of things to do and see.

Rodney Alcala spent most of his schooling attending Catholic institutions. In kindergarten in San Antonio, he first attended St. Joseph Catholic Elementary School, the stated goal of which was to "educate our students in moral and ethical values as taught by Christ and in keeping with the dictates of the Roman Catholic Church"; then he moved on to Mount Sacred Heart, a private Catholic school sponsored by the Sisters of the Sacred Heart of Jesus, "which evangelizes youth within the mission of the Church, proclaims and witnesses to its Catholic identity, fosters a community of faith, and celebrates the value and dignity of each person."

Throughout his school years, Alcala maintained consistently excellent grades. According to school reports, he was of above-average intelligence and took his studies seriously. He was considered respectful and kind. None of his teachers nor anyone in his family ever reported that Alcala was a problem child in any way.

Around 1951, Alcala's maternal grandmother became ill, and she told her daughter that she wanted to spend her final years in Mexico. In response, Anna Maria, who adored her mother, agreed to move the family to Mexico to fulfill her mother's wishes. Although life south of the border was far different from life in San Antonio, the Alcala children embraced the rural lifestyle and soaked up the love and support of their large extended family. For the first time since he began school, Alcala attended a private non-Catholic school, the American School, where he once again excelled.

While living in Mexico, two key events took place in young Alcala's life: His grandmother, whom he adored and who adored him, passed away; and his father left the family and moved back to the States. Although both events were no doubt deeply troubling, on the surface, Alcala seemed to take them both in stride.

Soon after Alcala's grandmother passed away and after three years living in Mexico, the now-smaller-by-two Alcala family headed to Los Angeles to put down new roots. It would be a fresh start and everyone looked forward to life in the big city.

In 1954, Alcala enrolled in St. Alphonsus in East Los Angeles, which he attended for about two years. After completing eighth grade in 1956, he attended high school at private Cantwell–Sacred Heart of Mary, owned and operated by the Archdiocese of Los Angeles. However, during his last semester of high school, Alcala felt he had had enough of religious education and desperately wanted to attend public school instead. After pestering his mother nonstop, Alcala was finally given permission to change schools. For the next

six months Alcala attended nonsectarian Montebello High
School, from which he graduated in 1960.

According to those who knew him then, Alcala had many
friends. He also had plenty of dates. He enjoyed piano lessons,
lettered in cross-country, and was on the yearbook planning
committee. He was tops in his class.

After Alcala graduated from high school, he decided to
join the Army, on June 19, 1961. It was a natural choice. At
the time, his older brother was attending West Point, so the
tradition of serving one's country was already a part of the
family's history.

Alcala entered a program in North Carolina to become a
paratrooper. While there, he served as a clerk and, according to reports, performed his duties well. Alcala kept in
touch with his mother by mail; rarely did they speak on the
phone.

In 1962, while Alcala was in the Army, his father passed
away in Tulare County, California, around 140 miles from LA.
An obituary, which appeared in the *Porterville Evening
Recorder* under the heading "Services held for Raul [*sic*]
Alcala, 55," stated that a funeral had been held for the elder
Buquor-Alcala, who had lived in Porterville for the past year
and whose occupation was Spanish-language instructor. He
passed away "unexpectedly" in a Tulare hospital on January
8. According to the article, attending the service was "a son,
Raul [*sic*] Jr., who will be graduated from the United States
Military Academy at West Point in June," as well as "another
son, Rod, stationed in North Carolina with the Air Force
[*sic*]; two daughters, Marie Theresa and Mary [*sic*] Christine, and his widow, Virginia."

Even though Alcala Sr. hadn't lived with the family for
years, and even though he had remarried, the death deeply
saddened his children.

After the funeral, Raoul Jr. returned to West Point and
Rodney returned to North Carolina, both to continue their
service to their country.

One day around two years after Alcala first joined the
Army, while his mother was cooking dinner at home in Los

Angeles, Alcala showed up unexpectedly at her door. Flabbergasted, she asked him what he was doing there. He told her he had hitchhiked from Fort Bragg, North Carolina, some three thousand miles away. He said he had gone AWOL.

AWOL? That can't be! Rod had never been in any trouble. He was always polite and so intelligent. Mrs. Alcala couldn't imagine what had gotten into her son to cause him to do such a thing.

After some lengthy discussions in which Mrs. Alcala urged Rodney to turn himself in—telling him not only that was it the right thing to do but also that he had no choice if he didn't want military police coming to the house to arrest him—her pleas prevailed and Alcala went to the local recruiting station. After being interviewed by various people, including an Army psychologist, Alcala was hospitalized and told that he was in urgent need of psychological care. When Alcala's superiors were contacted in North Carolina, they said that during his last weeks there, Alcala seemed to have been suffering a nervous breakdown and had been unable to perform his duties as required.

Mrs. Alcala had never seen her son so anxious and upset, but no matter how many times she asked him what was the matter, he was unable—or unwilling—to articulate his feelings.

Alcala was first taken to a hospital in San Francisco but was soon transferred to one on the Marine Corps base at El Toro, near Irvine. When it appeared that he would be there for some time, his mother began to visit him every day. She was convinced that her son had some serious emotional problems, but she held on to the belief that the doctors would be able to give him the help he needed.

Several months later, when it became clear that Alcala would not be able to perform his military duties to the standards required, he was discharged from the Army. It was early February 1964.

A military psychiatrist handed down a diagnosis of Alcala: "antisocial personality disorder, chronic, severe."

Chapter Six

According to the *DSM-IV*, a person with antisocial personality disorder displays the following traits:

A. There is a pervasive pattern of disregard for and violation of the rights of others occurring since age of 15 years as indicated by three (or more) of the following.

   1. failure to conform to social norms . . . as indicated by repeatedly performing acts that are grounds for arrest;

   2. deceitfulness, as indicated by repeatedly lying, use of aliases, or conning others for personal profit or pleasure;

   3. impulsivity or failure to plan ahead;

   4. irritability and aggressiveness, as indicated by repeated physical fights or assaults;

   5. reckless disregard for safety of self or others;

   6. consistent irresponsibility, as indicated by repeated failure to sustain consistent work behavior or honor financial obligations;

7. lack of remorse, as indicated by being indifferent to or rationalizing having hurt, mistreated, or stolen from another.

B. The individual is at least 18 years.

C. There is evidence of Conduct Disorder ["a repetitive and persistent pattern of behavior in which the basic rights of others or major age-appropriate societal norms or rules are violated"] with onset before 15 years.

The *Psychodynamic Diagnostic Manual* (*PDM*) prefers the term "psychopathic personality" disorder to "anti-social" personality disorder because they believe that not all those who suffer from psychopathic personality disorder are anti-social people who cannot conform to social norms.

The range of severity of people with psychopathic personality disorders is broad, the manual states, but some characteristics of people suffering from this disorder are:

- an "orientation towards expressing power for its own sake"
- taking "pleasure in duping others and subjecting them to manipulation"
- feeling "anxiety less frequently or intensely than non-psychopathic individuals"
- having "higher than normal physiological threshold for stimulation and therefore seek it addictively"
- notably "lacking the moral center of gravity that, in people of other personality types, tames the striving for power and directs it toward socially valuable ends"
- being "charming and even charismatic"
- being able to "read others' emotional states with great accuracy"
- being "indifferent to the feelings and needs of others"

- showing "lack of remorse after damaging other people."

After Alcala was released from the Army hospital, he returned to his mother's home in Monterey Park, where he soon began to feel more like his old self—the curious, inquisitive, purposeful self he was before he entered the Army. In time, he decided to apply to California State University, with the goal of one day transferring to the more prestigious UCLA. He had no doubts about his ability to succeed academically. The Army had measured his intelligence on an IQ test and the results showed him to be in the "genius" range, with a score over 140.

After being accepted and taking courses at Cal State, where he earned excellent grades, Alcala applied to UCLA to enter their art program and pursue his dream of becoming a photographer. Not surprisingly, with his top-notch grades, he was accepted right away. Once he gained a solid footing in college, he moved in with several other UCLA students. Alcala was consistently on the honor roll, and in 1968 he received his bachelor of fine arts degree.

It seemed that his singular nervous breakdown was a distant memory.

What would be next for this promising young man?

Time would tell.

PART
II

Chapter Seven

Greenwich Village in the 1960s was where Jimi Hendrix, Bob Dylan, Simon and Garfunkel, Joan Baez, the Velvet Underground, and Richie Havens, among others, entertained nightly at Gerdes Folk City, the Bitter End, the Bottom Line, and Café au Go-Go.

It was where beat poets Allen Ginsberg and Gregory Corso showcased their poetry at the subterranean Gaslight Cafe.

It was where jazz played by Herbie Mann, Chick Corea, and Miles Davis and belted out by Betty Carter and Nina Simone streamed into the streets from the Village Vanguard, the Blue Note, and the Village Gate.

It was where beats, hippies, and alternative culture seekers of all kinds experimented with music, art, sex, and drugs.

And it was where, in 1968, just a short time after Tali S.'s near-fatal assault, that a John Berger walked into the admissions office at New York University (NYU) and applied to the undergraduate School of the Arts. Although the semester had already begun, Berger thought that perhaps he could still be awarded a spot in the prestigious program.

Chapter Eight

In 1968, R. Lee Mauk held the dual position of chairman of admissions and assistant dean at New York University's School of the Arts. As such, she interviewed all prospective students to the program and then served as the admitted-students' administrative contact. In these roles, Mauk came to know many undergraduates not only as an academic advisor but also as a surrogate parent and trusted friend.

After spending some time interviewing John Berger, Mauk was impressed. Here was a charismatic, articulate, and bright young man who was also among the most open and approachable of the prospective students that semester. He would certainly be an asset to the program.

Although the semester was a few weeks old, Mauk believed that Berger could easily make up the work he had missed, and he was formally accepted to the undergraduate School of the Arts. It was quite an honor, not only because admission to the program was highly selective, but also because one of the instructors was Roman Polanski, the acclaimed and much-sought-after director of *Repulsion* and *Rosemary's Baby*.

As soon as Berger was accepted, he began the registration process and soon became mired in the convoluted task. Mauk came to his rescue—as she did to many others—guiding him through the maze of course requirements as well as helping him sort out the various housing possibilities. The two quickly became friends.

As Berger's first year unfolded, Mauk became aware of Berger's unusual ambition and initiative as he proudly showed her each of his projects. "There was a quiet determinism that seemed to pervade everything he did," she said.

While attending NYU, between 1968 and 1971, Berger worked as a security guard so he could afford his tuition. He was courteous and well liked, had plenty of friends, and enthusiastically shared in group projects and on film crews. He saw several girls socially and was considered a "catch." One secretary in the department recalled that he was a real pleasure to deal with.

Many evenings after work and school, Berger hung out in the Village, rubbing shoulders with performers and others in the music and art scene. It was a heady time for him, and the charismatic young man never wanted for companionship. In spite of his heavy work-, school-, and playload, Berger was still able to maintain a grade-point average as high as 3.5.

However, Berger's frenetic lifestyle soon started taking its toll, and he decided he needed a respite from his round-the-clock activities. After coming across an ad for a counselor at an arts and drama camp in rural Georges Mills, New Hampshire, he decided to apply, eager to show off his skills as a photographer and moviemaker and equally as eager to breathe some fresh country air—at least for the summer.

Berger sent off his résumé and letters of recommendation to the camp, which was nestled between the shores of Lake Sunapee and Otter Pond. After a lengthy phone interview, Berger was hired. The director was impressed with the brilliant young NYU student.

In early July 1969, after Berger arrived at the charming village of Georges Mills, he began his role as arts counselor. Almost immediately, the director realized that Berger was even more of an asset than he had hoped. The counselor related well to the campers and staffers, plus he was a natural-born teacher. He always had an interesting story to tell—especially about bohemian life in the Village and the famous people he knew—as he confidently demonstrated techniques of filmmaking and photography to the eager young campers.

After successfully completing his first summer, Berger was asked to come back the following year, and he happily accepted. After that second summer, he was once again asked to return the following year.

In late June 1971, after twenty-seven-year-old John Berger received his college diploma and a final sterling report from NYU, he was ready to return to Georges Mills for his third stint as a counselor. And when the summer was over, he planned to start on the road to becoming a famous photographer.

The sun shone brightly.

Chapter Nine

That same June 1971, the sun also shone brightly for Cornelia Crilley. While John Berger was photographing people all over Manhattan to enhance his already impressive portfolio before heading off for camp, Crilley was starting out on her own road to independence. She was just beginning to spread her wings, literally and figuratively, also in New York City.

Michael, as her friends called her, had grown up in Woodside, Queens, one of the five boroughs of New York, with her mother, father, two sisters, and two brothers. She had enjoyed an idyllic childhood in the predominantly Irish neighborhood, even if she was sometimes creeped out by the enormous Calvary Cemetery on Queens Boulevard right across from her family's apartment building. The seemingly endless miles of stark grey tombstones could raise the hair on anyone's neck.

The Crilleys were a close-knit family who attended church at nearby St. Sebastian, played touch football with one another, and supported one another's dreams. And Michael's dream since childhood was to become a stewardess for an international airline. She wanted nothing more than to travel around the world and see all the places she had only read about in books.

After graduating in 1965 from All Saints Commercial High School in Brooklyn, New York, Michael took a variety of clerical jobs in order to save enough money to attend flight attendants' school. In one, the law office of Jacobs, Persinger, and Parker, where she worked in late 1969, she met a young lawyer, Leon Borstein. In time they began dating, although it was not an exclusive alliance. Soon, however, they settled into an "only-you" relationship and fell deeply in love.

To Borstein, Michael Crilley was every man's dream come true. She was "funny, vivacious, had a jaunt in her step and a real joie de vivre," he said. But not only that. "She was also gorgeous. She had long, beautiful Irish brown hair, great eyes, and a tremendous body." And on top of it all, she was confident and poised. Crilley knew who she was and what she hoped to achieve.

Although the two spent nearly all their free time together, both knew that Michael's goal would eventually take her away from him, if only for a short while. And indeed it did. After Crilley saved up enough money, she decided to follow her dream.

With Borstein's blessings, Crilley headed off to the twenty-five-acre Trans World Airline (TWA) flight attendant campus in Overland Park, Kansas, to begin her training. Breech Academy was considered the gold standard. In fact, other airlines sent their budding flight attendants to attend school there.

Training at the academy included learning about almost all aspects of flight, including emergency procedures, such as shimmying down a deflated ramp from thirty feet from the plane's emergency door hatch to the ground; the interiors of airplanes, such as 747s and L-1011s; as well as food and beverage service. One of the subjects studied was "personal development," in which students were trained in voice and diction, walking, grooming, and hairstyling. Diet control was also studied. In fact, to make sure they paid attention to their figures, the young air hostesses were required to attend weekly weigh-ins.

Crilley and the other young women loved their home in Kansas, where they lived in state-of-the-art facilities that contained thirty different "pods," each with a different theme: Mediterranean, African, English, Far Eastern, French. A communal living room served as a meeting place where new friends talked about their courses and the routes they hoped to fly once they graduated.

On graduation day, proud parents and siblings came from all over the country to celebrate the momentous occasion. The graduates felt an enormous sense of achievement, having "gotten their wings" from the top flight-attendant school in the nation. At that time, TWA air hostesses served as unofficial ambassadors of the United States in countries all over the world. Wearing tailored blue or red double-breasted jackets, white mock turtlenecks, blue skirts, and perky square hats—and carrying, if need be, a red overcoat or raincoat—these young women served as walking (or flying) advertisements for the American way of life: Proud to be American!

After graduating the academy, Crilley moved back to New York City with two fellow flight attendants. The three rented an apartment on Forty-third Street, in the heart of the city and not far from where Borstein lived. Crilley mainly flew the New York to Los Angeles route, but she also worked flights to countries all around the world. Whenever she returned home, she would regale Borstein with stories about the passengers and the places she had seen. One story, which Crilley considered "harmless fun," detailed how passengers would ask her and the other stewardesses to reach for things overhead "just so they could look at our legs." At that time, said Borstein, "they wore minis."

When their lease ran out, the three air hostesses decided to move farther uptown, to Eighty-third Street. However, because there was some time between when they had to leave one apartment and when they could take possession of the next, they needed a place to stay. Without a moment's hesitation, Borstein said they could stay with him, which was just perfect with everyone. Borstein's apartment immediately morphed into a stewardesses' dorm, with beautiful young women coming and going at all times of the night and day, depending on their schedules. Most of the time, Borstein would sleep on the couch in the living room; the girls, often three or more, would crash in the bedroom.

When Crilley and her two roommates chose their new

apartment, they picked one that was located in the Yorkville section of Manhattan, known as the "girl belt" because secretaries, stewardesses, and other working women gravitated there. Theirs was a $225-a-month, second-floor, three-room apartment at 427 East Eighty-third Street, between York and First avenues. The five-story brick building with twenty apartments had an intercom and buzzer system but no doorman; it was nice but not a high-end type of place.

Heavily German and Hungarian, the restaurants and stores of the area offered "old-country" treats such as raspberry and apricot linzer cookies at Bauer's Bakery; duck at Czardas; and pork and potato pancakes at Mocca on Second Avenue and Eighty-first Street. Of course, no one could be a self-respecting resident of the neighborhood without becoming a regular at Paprikas Weiss, where the young and old, hoping to replicate their remembrances of homemade meals, went for their supplies. It wouldn't be easy for the three roommates to watch their figures in *this* neighborhood.

Finally, the big moving day arrived. It was Thursday, June 24, 1971, and Michael Crilley and her roommates would be taking possession of their new place. Crilley had been designated as the receiver of goods, since her two roommates, Pamela Brown and Linden Brauer, were both on flights that day.

That morning, neighbors in the building saw a stunningly beautiful auburn-haired young woman moving furniture and clothes into an apartment on the second floor. In the early afternoon, after receiving three beds and two dressers, Crilley called her mother to tell her how great her apartment was looking. The two were extremely close, sometimes speaking five or six times a day. When they finished the conversation, Mrs. Crilley told her daughter that she would phone her back in an hour or two, just to get an update.

Crilley then spoke to her sister Katherine, twenty-two, a year younger than Michael, and asked her if she'd like to come to the apartment and help arrange the new furniture. Katherine was eager to, but because she was in the middle of studying for exams—soon to graduate as a nurse from the New York Foundling Hospital—she asked her sister if she could take a rain check and come by in a day or two. Michael said that would be great.

As promised, a few hours later, Mrs. Crilley called Michael. No one picked up the phone. She tried again half an hour later, but again received no answer. She kept trying for several more hours, but each time the phone kept ringing and ringing. (At that time, there were no cell phones.)

By around five p.m., Mrs. Crilley had become so concerned about her daughter that she called Borstein at the Brooklyn district attorney's office, where he was working as an assistant DA. She had never called him there before and was hesitant, but she was becoming increasingly more uneasy, unable to fathom where Michael could have gone for so long without phoning her.

As soon as Mrs. Crilley heard Borstein's voice, she apologized for bothering him at work but wondered if he would mind checking on Michael as soon as he got home. Mrs. Crilley said that she hadn't been able to reach her daughter for many hours and was beginning to get nervous.

Borstein assured her that he would be leaving work soon and would check on Michael when he got back to the city. He also told her that he was certain that there was nothing to worry about.

When Borstein arrived home, he changed his clothes and immediately walked over to Crilley's new place. He went upstairs and knocked on her door, but nobody answered. He thought that she had probably gone shopping, but maybe she was sick in bed or had fallen down and needed help. He decided to go back downstairs and try to climb up a fire escape to her apartment. However, after a few attempts, he wasn't able to reach her window, so he decided he would walk over to the local police station and ask if someone there would come back with him to check out things.

Borstein knew the neighborhood police well. He had been riding homicide for the Brooklyn DA's office for the past year, so that whenever he got called in the middle of the night to come to Brooklyn to take statements at crime scenes, he would telephone the local police, who would then drive him to Brooklyn.

The cops on duty at the precinct said they'd accompany him on what was known as a "courtesy call." Everyone was certain it was simply a case of poor communication and everything would be cleared up shortly.

Everyone turned out to be wrong.

Chapter Ten

Bornstein and the cops arrived at Michael Crilley's apartment at around 8:45 p.m. on Thursday night, June 24. First, the officers checked that the intercom and buzzer system were working. Both were in good condition. They then went to Crilley's door and noted that there were no signs of a break-in. So far, so good. The police knocked repeatedly, but they, like Borstein, got no answer. They tried the door, but it was locked. They, like Borstein, decided to climb the fire escape; if successful, they would smash in a back window to gain entrance. They advised Borstein to stay put and wait to be let in.

As Borstein waited at Crilley's door, he tried to come up with different scenarios to explain what could have happened to her. If Michael wasn't sick or hurt or out shopping, perhaps she had been called to cover somebody's flight and had raced out of the apartment to arrive on time. Yes, one of those scenarios would turn out to be what had happened. Indeed, he told himself, there was no reason to be alarmed.

While waiting, Borstein heard a crash of glass shattering. Obviously the cops had broken a window and were now inside. He felt an enormous sense of relief. The mystery was one step closer to being solved.

Once inside the apartment, the officers entered the living room. Everything looked A-OK. There were no signs of a burglary.

The same was true for the kitchen.

Ditto for the first bedroom.

However, just as they were about to enter the second bedroom, they saw something that made them stop short. Inside
the room was a body.

It was a partially clothed, dead female, lying on her back.

A stocking was tied tightly around her neck.

Her upper garments had been stuffed into her mouth.

Saliva and bite marks were on her breasts.

Her face and body had undergone severe trauma.

It appeared she had been sexually molested.

After the officers regained their composure, one opened
the apartment door to let Borstein in. Borstein immediately
knew from the officer's face that something dire had taken
place.

"Come inside, please," said the officer somberly. Borstein
did as he was asked. "I don't know how else to say this," the
cop said and then paused. "There's a body that needs to be
ID'd."

For a moment Borstein thought that maybe the man was
joking. Cops often made off-color jokes, but if that was the
case, this guy was a real jerk. Cops *never, ever* told someone
that there was a dead body if there wasn't.

Going on instinct, Borstein replied, "I can't go in. If I do,
I'll never be able to forget it."

Fearing the worst, Borstein's mind was churning. It flashed
into his mind that there was still the possibility that the body
was *not* Crilley's. Not that he wished *anyone's* body to be in
there, but he didn't know how he could deal with it being
Crilley's. Besides, he was fairly certain it *couldn't* be Crilley.
She had no enemies. She was sweet and innocent, yet certainly not naïve. She had her whole life ahead of her. And
she was *his* girlfriend. Nothing bad could happen to her!

As Borstein stood frozen, one cop offered up a description
of the deceased, which Borstein heard as though it were being spoken from another universe. *I am not hearing this.
This cannot be.*

Because there was no sign of forced entry, the police felt that the victim must have known her murderer. And aware of the statistics, they believed that, more likely than not, a family member, friend, or boyfriend might have been involved in the killing. Considering this, they told the immobilized Borstein that they would have to take him down to the station. It was routine, they assured him. We just need some information. Sorry.

For several hours two detectives interviewed Borstein, asking him every detail about how he had spent the day, why he felt someone would want to kill Crilley, how stable their relationship had been, if they had recently had a fight, if he knew anyone who would want to harm her, and on and on. After they got all they could from him, they accompanied him back to his apartment and interviewed him some more, all the time looking around for anything that might point them in the direction of the murderer.

By midnight, as word got out, it appeared that all of New York City was enveloped in fear. *Murdered in broad daylight? A young, attractive stewardess?*

The NYPD made Crilley's murder a top priority and assigned fifteen investigators to the case. By the following evening, another ten investigators were added. Chief of Detectives Albert A. Sedman, who was put in charge of the case, spoke to the press. He tried to quell the fears of people in the neighborhood and the city in general, but he admitted there had already been sixteen rapes in Yorkville since January 1 and only seven arrests.

Sedman warned everyone to be vigilant.

After Michael Crilley's body was taken to the morgue, someone had to positively ID it. The members of Crilley's immediate family were too distraught, so Borstein volunteered, even though he had not been able to bear the idea of seeing her murdered body when it was first discovered. He felt it was only right to spare the heartbroken family.

"It was a terrible scene," he said later. "I will never forget it. Michael's mouth was wide open because rigor mortis had set in and the killer had put something in her mouth to prevent her from screaming. I couldn't tell it was Michael. She was so disfigured. I never saw anybody in such a state."

During the autopsy, the coroner collected DNA evidence—saliva from a bite mark to Crilley's breast—but because in 1971 there was no way to identify it, no match could be made or even attempted.

The day after Crilley's murder was reported, TWA offered a $5,000 reward for information leading to the arrest and conviction of the person or persons responsible for her death. A special telephone number was set up. All information would be treated as confidential, the police stated.

On June 27, an additional $1,000 reward was offered by the twenty thousand members of the Professional Airline Stewardess Association.

After word of the murder wended its way up and down the streets of the Yorkville neighborhood, apartment dwellers reflected on how the neighborhood seemed to have changed for the worse. "I guess you just learn that you have to take a risk if you live here," said one. Another, who had lived in the area for forty-five years, said, "This used to be a neighborhood. You knew other people and you helped them and they helped you. No more." The owner of Paprikas Weiss told police that he used to keep his store open until ten or eleven, but now he closed up at 6:30. "There is absolutely no safety here," he said.

New locks flew off the shelves at Abbey Locksmiths at Second Avenue and Eighty-fourth Street. An employee told reporters, "It sounds gruesome I know, but right now I feel almost like an undertaker."

Although some of Crilley's friends posited that she might have asked a passerby to help her move in the furniture, others said she would never have done that. Borstein agreed. "Michael would have to have recognized him or known him before she would have let anybody inside," he said.

For weeks, as the police searched for the murderer, Borstein was considered a person of interest. At the same time they fixed their sights on "Freddy," a handyman well known in the neighborhood but who hadn't been seen for a week. Described as stocky, blond-haired, around twenty-eight years old, and six feet tall, he lived on the same block as Crilley. However, after the police located Freddy, interviewed him, and checked out his alibi, he was ruled out as a suspect. In time, so was Borstein.

At the end of June, Michael Crilley's body reposed at the Walter B. Cooke Funeral Home, at 80-20 Roosevelt Avenue, in Jackson Heights, Queens. A funeral Mass was attended by over 1,500 people at the family parish, Saint Sebastian Roman Catholic Church, in Woodside. The Air Line Stewards and Stewardess Association sent a delegation to the service.

Borstein stood solemnly in line with Crilley's parents, sisters, and brothers to pay his last respects and to say his final good-bye. As he stood over Crilley, through tears, he told her to have a safe flight. He then took off his MIT ring and placed it lovingly on her chest: To him, they would be together forever.

Michael Crilley was buried across the street from her Woodside home, in Calvary Cemetery—the very same place that gave her the willies as a child.

Surviving in her immediate family were her parents, Mr. and Mrs. John G. Crilley, her sisters, Katherine Crilley and Mary Coffey, and her brothers, Jack and Michael.

In the weeks, months, and even first few years following Cornelia "Michael" Crilley's death, the police held out hope that the killer would be found. However, as the passing years turned into decades, with no new leads, that hope turned to resignation. Nobody believed that the murderer would ever be brought to justice.

At the NYPD, Crilley still remained on some detectives' minds, but officially the case had gone cold.

It was a coincidence—or was it? That same June, the month Crilley was murdered, John Berger was busy photographing young girls and women all over Manhattan. What none of them knew was that Berger was just one of many aliases for Rodney Alcala. And Alcala was at the very beginning of what would become one of the most heinous and infamous killing sprees in U.S. history.

Chapter Eleven

Just a month after Cornelia Crilley's murder in New York, detectives in Los Angeles were seeking new tactics in their search for Rodney Alcala. As of July 1971, Detective Steve Hodel and his LAPD team had been trying to locate Alcala for nearly three years. They had followed every lead that came their way about the man who had fled Los Angeles in 1968 after beating and raping Tali. It had been a frustrating and disheartening time for Hodel. He knew he had to try something unique, something that could potentially break the case wide open.

Hodel set up a meeting with the FBI at its LA office. He wanted to persuade the FBI to help the LAPD locate the fugitive Alcala.

After the FBI met with Detective Hodel in 1971, the bureau made the decision that Rodney Alcala qualified as the worst of the worst and added Alcala to their list. Now people all over the country who knew nothing about the man might recognize his face and give the authorities a new lead to go on.

Something *had* to break this case.

Chapter Twelve

In August of 1971, while Alcala was working for his third summer as a counselor in rural New Hampshire, two campers decided to take a walk to the local post office to mail home some letters. The director allowed that, since the post office was nearby and the short walk was a safe one.

After the girls arrived, it began to rain so heavily that they decided to wait it out before heading back. Wandering around the quaint post office, they scanned the walls and looked at the new stamp offerings, then at the envelope offerings, and finally at a notice on the wall: the FBI's Ten Most Wanted Fugitives list. As they perused the pictures, they had a word to say about each one: "A real psycho!" "Hey, he doesn't look *that* bad!" "Yuck, look at that one!" And then, as their eyes continued to alight on each person, they saw a face that looked oddly familiar. They looked at each other in disbelief.

"No way!"

"Are you thinking what I'm thinking?"

"Doesn't that look like John?"

"Yes!"

However, as they read the details about the man, they felt certain that the photograph must be of someone who just *looked* just like their counselor but who certainly wasn't *really* John Berger. Firstly, his name was Rodney Alcala. Secondly, the fugitive was wanted for a crime in California, and as far as they knew, John lived in New York and always had.

Thirdly, the poster said he had harmed a little girl, and they knew John would *never* touch a child—or anyone, for that matter.

Once the rain let up, the girls walked slowly back to camp, talking all the while about the bizarre coincidence of the man in the photo and their funny, smart, and popular counselor. When they arrived, they told the director about their adventure. Concerned but not alarmed—*Of course it couldn't be John!*—the director decided check out the poster himself. Supposedly everyone has a twin somewhere in the world, he was once told, and maybe this was John's.

After he got to the post office, he took a long, careful look at the poster. He read every word about this "Rodney Alcala," studied the picture again and again, and then asked the postmistress if he could use her phone. Straightaway, he dialed the FBI number on the poster.

The agent he spoke with urged the director to go back to camp and act as normal as possible. The next morning, the agent said, FBI officers would arrive at camp and everything would be sorted out. The agent asked the director to keep an eye on the counselor—but to in no way indicate that anything was amiss. He warned the director to speak to the girls and urge them not to say a word to anyone about what they had seen. He also told the director to make sure "Berger" was not left alone with any young girls.

The next morning, the FBI officers arrived at the camp and placed Alcala in custody. After comparing Alcala's fingerprints with those on the FBI's Ten Most Wanted Fugitives List, they knew they had their man. They arrested Alcala and put him in jail.

The FBI agent then contacted Hodel. Hodel was standing when he got the call but quickly sat down. He asked the agent to repeat what he just said. *Could Alcala finally have been found? Might they, at last, bring this monster to justice?*

Hodel scheduled a flight that night from LA to Boston and arranged for a car rental at Logan International Airport so he could drive directly from Boston north to the jail.

The plane and car trips went surprisingly smoothly, and by the next morning Hodel was driving through the lush landscape of rural New Hampshire.

After arriving at the jail and introducing himself to Alcala, Hodel told Alcala he would be taking him back to LA for booking.

Curious about Alcala, Hodel asked the prisoner why he sexually assaulted Tali. The question had haunted Hodel for years.

Alcala responded, "I don't want to talk about Rod Alcala and what he did." To Hodel, it seemed almost as if Alcala was talking about another person.

The day was August 12, 1971.

At last, the monster who had taken away the youth, dignity, and optimism of little Tali S. would get his just deserts.

Or would he?

Chapter Thirteen

After Alcala was extradited to Los Angeles, he was immediately taken to jail. But afterward, things did not go so smoothly. According to Detective Hodel, Tali and her family were out of the country. Rather than taking the case to trial, prosecutors arranged a plea. For kidnapping, raping, and beating Tali S. nearly to death, Alcala pled guilty to child molestation. After committing a crime so heinous that he was placed on the FBI's Ten Most Wanted Fugitives list, he received an "indeterminate" sentence of one to ten years. This was on May 19, 1972.

"Indeterminate sentencing" allowed a judge to give a range of time, instead of a specific amount of time to be served for a crime, and allowed the convict to one day try to convince a parole board that he or she had been rehabilitated and was ready for release. (With determinate sentencing, a judge can impose low-, mid-, or high-term sentences, but each is an exact or "determined sentence," not a range, and is based on a number of factors, including the judge's discretion, the past criminal history of the defendant, the severity of the offense, and other mitigating or aggravating factors.)

The philosophy behind indeterminate sentencing was that offenders could be rehabilitated by the state through therapy, education, and other means. Opponents of indeterminate sentencing argued that under this philosophy, rapists and murderers could go free after very short stints because of "arbitrary parole boards" that could deem the offenders rehabilitated.

And this is exactly what happened with Alcala.

In August 1974, a state prison psychiatrist noted that Alcala was "considerably improved" and recommended that he be released. Apparently the diagnosis of "chronic" and "severe" antisocial personality disorder assigned to Alcala by the Army ten years earlier no longer applied.

Alcala was paroled to Los Angeles County.

He was required to register with the Monterey Park Police Department as a sex offender.

He had served less than three years for the sadistic rape and beating of an eight-year-old.

And he promised to be on his best behavior.

Chapter Fourteen

Once free on parole, Alcala went back to live at his mother's house. Monterey Park was a far different place from the two state prisons where he had served his time: the Deuel Vocational Institution in Tracy and the California Medical Facility in Vacaville. At both of those prisons he was unable to make a move without someone watching over him. Here, at his mother's house, he could come and go as he pleased. He even had his own entrance and bedroom. He had the use of a car. He had his photography equipment. He had all the freedom in the world.

After taking a few weeks to get reacquainted with his newly found independence, Alcala decided to look for a job. He needed to earn an income to help his mother with expenses. As luck would have it, he landed one on his first day out. It was with a photographic company, and his job was to take photos in stores in south LA. It was right up his alley.

Alcala appeared faithfully at work every day for over nine weeks and performed his duties in an exemplary fashion.

On October 13, while cruising around in his station wagon, Alcala pulled his car into a shopping center in Huntington Beach. There he saw a young girl waiting for a school bus. She looked to be around eight years old. Her name was written in big letters on her books, so Alcala spoke directly to her: "Hey, Julie, I'll take you to school if you like." The girl ignored him. Then Alcala turned on the charm, promising her that he had some great posters to show her. It worked.

Julie came to the conclusion that it would be a lot more fun to ride to school in a car than to go on the rickety old school bus, so she hopped in, and off they went.

As they drove along, Julie hummed to herself, feeling lucky that she didn't have to spend another morning with the losers on the bus.

The man asked her how old she was. She told him that she was thirteen but that everyone thought she looked much younger. He said she would appreciate that when she got older. She nodded. She'd heard that before. He told her his name was John Ronald. She said she was Julie Johnson. The two chatted on.

As they rode on, the car breezed right past her school. "Hey, that's my school. I can get out now," Julie said. But the man didn't stop the car. He didn't pay her any attention. He continued driving toward the Pacific Coast Highway.

She said it again. "You can stop the car now. I want to get out."

Still the man wouldn't stop. But this time he spoke to her.

"Sorry. I've got to make a quick stop to check on an apartment. It won't take long."

Becoming increasingly apprehensive, Julie started fidgeting.

"Sit still!" he yelled.

Julie was shocked. She felt frightened. She began to scream.

"Shut up!" he demanded.

Terrified, Julie tried to get out of the car, but the man grabbed her arm and she couldn't budge. When the car finally came to a stop, Julie tried to make a run for it, but he wouldn't let go of her and began to firmly steer her on foot to a spot along the cliffs. They were now at the bluffs at Huntington Beach, about fifteen minutes from the bus stop.

"Ronald" then forced her to sit down on a huge rock and made her smoke marijuana with him. She had never smoked before but agreed to do it out of fear. Then, when she tried to escape again, he grabbed her by the leg. This time he put his arms around her and gave her a deep French kiss.

Julie was repulsed.

"Do you like boys?" he asked with a smirk on his face.

Julie couldn't answer.

"Are you passionate when you're loaded?"

Julie could barely breathe.

Meanwhile, down the cliff a few hundred yards, a park ranger was walking the trails. Looking up, he saw two people in such an isolated area that he felt they had to be up to no good. He decided to check things out—surreptitiously. As he came closer to the pair, the distinctive smell of pot penetrated the air. Walking up to them, he said, "What're you guys up to?"

Surprised by the intruder, the man responded, "Uh, we were just hiking and now we're taking a break." Immediately the girl blurted out that she had been forced to go there and wanted to go home.

To be on the safe side, the ranger arrested them both and drove them down to the police station. The man claimed that his friend, Julie, had supplied the marijuana and suggested that they smoke it, while Julie claimed that she had been taken to the cliffs against her will. The officer was aware that sometimes young girls who are caught with older men accuse the guys of "kidnapping" to avoid parental punishment. Truly, the cop didn't know who to believe.

The officers then performed a background check on both the man and the girl. Within a few minutes the results came in. Julie Johnson was clean. The man, who admitted that his name was Rodney James Alcala, was a parolee.

A short time later, Alcala was taken before a judge and charged with several criminal counts: sale of pot, kidnapping, and violating parole. He was taken to jail.

The day after Christmas 1974, Alcala was found guilty *only* of violating parole and providing a minor with drugs—a felony—and was returned to prison.

For this crime, Alcala spent two and a half years, serving time first at Chino, the Southern California reception center for new California Department of Corrections inmates and parole violators, and then at California's Men's Colony in San Luis Obispo, where "emphasis is placed on providing all inmates with programs for self-improvement."

It seemed that the programs for self-improvement were doing just as they were supposed to, because when Alcala came up for parole in June 1977, he was declared "re-reformed" and released on the sixteenth of the month.

The one condition upon release was that Alcala was required to report weekly to his parole officer, which he did faithfully.

During one visit, just a few weeks after being paroled, Alcala decided to try his luck and make an earnest plea to be allowed to go to New York and visit some relatives. It would be a short trip, he promised the officer, just to see his cousins, aunts, and uncles.

After giving the request some thought, the parole officer agreed. He even thought it was a good idea. After all, this man had been given parole, having been deemed rehabilitated; he seemed truly sorry for any wrongs he had done; and he appeared to be firmly on his way to a new, clean life. Alcala had spent some time in Chicago, Washington, D.C., and New York.

Was Rodney Alcala the luckiest man on earth, or what?

Within the week, Alcala set out for New York City.

Once again, the sun was shining brightly.

PART
III

Chapter Fifteen

In 1977, Elvis Presley died at Graceland at the grand old age of forty-two.

The Sex Pistols and the Clash released their first LPs.

Newly elected president Jimmy Carter granted a pardon to draft dodgers from the Vietnam War.

Star Wars opened and soon became the highest-grossing film to date.

The double disco album from the movie *Saturday Night Fever* became the best-selling soundtrack of all time.

Gary Gilmore was executed by firing squad in Utah.

The Commodore PET, the world's first personal computer, was revealed at the Consumer Electronics Show in Chicago.

Studio 54 opened in Manhattan, with Mick Jagger, Donald Trump, Brooke Shields, Cher, and Michael Jackson among the nightclub's first guests.

Ellen Hover, twenty-three, went missing in New York City.

Jill Barcomb, eighteen, was murdered in Los Angeles.

Georgia Wixted, twenty-seven, was murdered in Los Angeles.

Chapter Sixteen

July of 1977 in New York City was steamy. Temperatures hovered around the 90-degree mark and unusually high humidity caused tempers to flare. The stench of garbage was unbearable; the songbirds fell silent; even stoops crowded with residents looking for relief from the heat looked more like solemn prayer meetings than boisterous gabfests. The city was at a low point. The unemployment rate was at an all-time high. The city government was in deep financial trouble and had only narrowly avoided bankruptcy. The crime rate had soared, and now the heat had followed suit. People were weary. Then, as if all that weren't enough, an electrical blackout that lasted some twenty-five hours, from July 13–14, turned an otherwise sizzling city into a black hole where nothing worked and everyone was on edge. The blackout precipitated widespread looting and arson, particularly in the city's poorest neighborhoods. Crown Heights, Bedford-Stuyvesant, and Bushwick in Brooklyn were particularly hard hit.

In Manhattan, the blackout was a bit more celebratory. Free (melting) ice cream was passed out in Greenwich Village, and patrons walking out of suddenly dark theaters on Broadway were greeted by Times Square hookers with flashlights, saying, "Come on up! It's better in the dark."

New Yorkers were simultaneously weary and a little bit crazy that summer. But not Ellen Jane Hover. At age twenty-three, Hover wasn't fazed by the lack of electricity or even the dire economic straits the city had found itself in. A black-haired beauty, she was young and optimistic, and she was an heiress.

Having just graduated from Beaver College in Glenside, Pennsylvania, where she had majored in biology and minored in music, Hover was excited about being on her own in the big city. A young socialite and piano virtuoso, Hover also happened to be the daughter of Herman Hover, owner of the legendary Ciro's nightclub in Hollywood, where Dean Martin, Sammy Davis Jr., Mickey Rooney, Lucille Ball, Cary Grant, and anyone who was anyone in Hollywood hung out—until it was bought and closed in 1959. Ellen Hover was raised amid wealth and privilege. She grew up sheltered and even a bit naïve. She saw no evil the world. Why would she? Surrounded by sophistication and advantage—Sammy Davis Jr. and Dean Martin were her godfathers—she had no reason to believe that people were anything but good and kind.

Like many young women of her day, Hover started on her road to independence by renting an apartment in Manhattan. Hers was located at 686 Third Avenue in midtown near Forty-fourth Street. It was a stone's throw from the Empire State Building and the grand New York Public Library, and within walking distance of a dozen movie theaters and restaurants of every variety. Hover loved the hustle and bustle of the city life. She also felt lucky to be living near her mother and stepfather, who had bought a duplex penthouse some twenty blocks away in Gramercy Park, and divided their time between the city and their six-acre estate in Westchester, a twenty-minute drive north.

With long, straight hair simply parted down the middle and glowing tawny skin, Hover was pretty and unaffected. She liked parties and had lots of friends. Men were drawn to her, not just by her looks but by her openness, and guys were always asking her out. On July 13, 1977, the day of the blackout, Hover was enjoying a conversation outside her apartment building with a tall, thin man with a ponytail. A boyfriend of hers saw the two chatting and later asked her, "Who was the freaky-looking guy?"

"Oh, he's all right," Hover replied. "He is a photographer." More than that, he was flirty, flattering, and charming.

On July 15, Hover left her apartment as usual to explore the city. No doubt, she felt greatly relieved to find that things were relatively back to normal: Her refrigerator was humming, elevators were running, and streetlights turned green, red, and yellow, just as they were programmed to do. After a quick trip to the library, she returned home for lunch. At around noon a neighbor saw a tall thin man with a ponytail knock on Hover's door.

That evening Hover uncharacteristically missed a dinner date with a friend. She also failed to call her parents to report on her day's exploits, as she did every other evening. When her parents tried to reach her by phone, they received no answer. In fact, no one picked up the phone all through the night or the next morning. By mid-morning, after Hover still hadn't phoned her parents or answered any calls, her mother and stepfather decided to contact the police. Although they told themselves that most likely there was nothing to worry about—perhaps their daughter was sleeping at a girlfriend's apartment—they were nevertheless concerned that she hadn't checked in. It was unusual, to say the least.

A short time after the police received the call, they headed over to Hover's apartment to check on her whereabouts. They saw no signs of a break-in. After they gained access and looked around, they found no trace of anything untoward— but no trace of Hover, either. They took a closer look to see if there were any clues that might point them in the young woman's direction. One thing did, in fact, catch their eye. On her night table was a diary open to the preceding day, July 15. In it were the words "John Berger, photographer."

At least the cops had a starting point.

When the police reported their findings to Hover's mother, Yvonne, and her third husband, Ruben Schwartz, a wealthy garment-district lawyer, they immediately offered a $100,000 reward for anyone who knew anything about their daughter's whereabouts, When Schwartz learned that Hover had written "John Berger, photographer" in her diary, he hired a private investigator to locate the man. Maybe his stepdaughter had found the love of her life and was holed up somewhere with him. He could hope.

A few days later the private investigator reported back to Schwartz that the John Berger in Hover's diary was most likely a "ponytailed photographer," who had recently been spotted outside Hover's apartment. Seizing on this information, Schwartz placed ads in the *New York Times* asking anyone who knew anything about Berger to contact him.

No one did.

Hover's family posted homemade flyers around the city with a picture of the long-haired young woman, a number to call, and a large caption that read, MISSING AFTER BLACKOUT. Later in the month, a massive headline in the *New York Post* read, "Girl Missing; Fear Abduction." As days turned into weeks, it seemed less and less likely that Hover had gone off on a tryst or disappeared voluntarily. But that summer, as the New York City cops were investigating Hover's disappearance, they found they had far more on their hands than the disappearance of one socialite.

Chapter Seventeen

In spite of Ellen Hover's position in society, her disappearance was simply one of nearly seventeen thousand reported in the city annually. And looking for a guy with a ponytail? Now, that wasn't much to go on. Adding to the problem of locating Hover was the fact that there was no body. Plus, the police didn't have many resources available in the summer of 1977. That year the NYPD was embroiled in one of the most frightening serial killing cases in the nation's history.

An unknown assailant had unleashed a psychosis-infused reign of terror on the city, eluding police for over a year and leaving disturbing, taunting clues. On April 16, 1977, he struck again. Valentia Suriani, eighteen, and her boyfriend, Alexander Esau, twenty, had been making out in a parked car near Suriani's home in the Bronx. At three a.m. a car rode up alongside and four .44 caliber bullets were fired, killing both. In an envelope found by police at the crime scene, the killer had left a letter addressed to the detective in charge of the case. Handwritten in weird, choppy, block letters, it read:

DEAR CAPTAIN JOSEPH BORRELLI,
  I AM DEEPLY HURT BY YOUR CALLING ME A WEMON
[*sic*] HATER. I AM NOT. BUT I AM A MONSTER. I AM THE
"SON OF SAM." I AM A LITTLE "BRAT."
  WHEN FATHER SAM GETS DRUNK HE GETS MEAN. HE

BEATS HIS FAMILY. SOMETIMES HE TIES ME UP TO THE
BACK OF THE HOUSE . . . SAM LOVES TO DRINK BLOOD.

"GO OUT AND KILL," COMMANDS FATHER SAM.

BEHIND OUR HOUSE SOME REST. MOSTLY YOUNG—
RAPED AND SLAUGHTERED—THEIR BLOOD DRAINED—
JUST BONES NOW . . .

I FEEL LIKE AN OUTSIDER. I AM ON A DIFFERENT WAVE
LENGTH THEN [sic] EVERYBODY ELSE—PROGRAMMED TOO
[sic] KILL.

The closing and signature on the letter were, "Yours in
Murder, Mr. Monster."

Based on this bizarre letter, the killer immediately became known to police, the media, and the public as the Son
of Sam.

Since the first Son of Sam murder on July 29, 1976, when
two young women had been shot at while sitting in a parked
car in the Bronx, two hundred detectives had been assigned
to the case. Police had matched ballistics from a series of
six shootings to the same gun, a .44 caliber Charter Arms
Bulldog. The killer's primary targets were couples and attractive young women, usually stalked in the early morning
hours and attacked in their cars in deserted areas and lover's
lanes.

Many New Yorkers were scared and shaken. The police
warned residents to stay away from their windows at night,
lest they become targets. Discotheques across the city were
turning into ghost halls as young couples became terrified
of going out. Because it was believed the Son of Sam targeted women with long dark hair, many women fitting that
description cut their hair, dyed it, or tied it up under a scarf.

Under these conditions—with the city under siege and
the Son of Sam on the loose—it's hard to imagine that long-
and dark-haired Ellen Hover would have gone off willingly
with a total stranger. But she was a trusting soul.

Within ten days of Hover's disappearance, the Son of Sam
attacked again. On June 26, several shots were fired at Judy

Placido, seventeen, and Sal Lupo, twenty, as they left a disco in Bayside, Queens. Judy was hit three times; both survived.

Then, on July 31, the rampage continued. While parked at a lover's lane, Bobby Violante and Stacy Moskowitz, both twenty, were targeted with gunshots, this time in Brooklyn. Stacy died. Bobby lost most of his vision.

This last tragic attack was the Son of Sam's undoing. A man named David Berkowitz had received a parking ticket at the site of this most recent murder. When police went to question this Berkowitz at his home in Yonkers, just north of the city—after all, he might have witnessed something— they saw a gun in plain view on the seat of his car. When Berkowitz emerged from his apartment building, police promptly arrested him. Once in custody, Berkowitz quickly confessed to his crimes.

By the time Berkowitz was apprehended in August 1977, six young people had died at his hands and several more had been maimed for life. The citizens of New York were relieved that the monster was finally off the streets. They had been held hostage by fear for over a year.

Because of Berkowitz's strange notes and contorted explanations—"Sam" was purportedly a "demonic" Labrador retriever that had ordered Berkowitz to kill people—he was considered by many psychiatrists to be a paranoid schizophrenic. However, in spite of a report from a psychiatrist labeling Berkowitz paranoid and delusional, he was judged sane enough to stand trial, and after pleading guilty, he received a sentence of six consecutive life sentences for a maximum of 365 years.

When Berkowitz was interviewed by the FBI in 1979, he said that he had invented "Son of Sam" so that if he ever got caught, he could take an insanity defense. He admitted that the true reason he killed was resentment toward his mother and women in general. He confessed that he had become sexually aroused when killing.

The capture of the Son of Sam led to multiple promotions within the NYPD. The police had gotten their man, and the

city was safer. But Ellen Hover's mother didn't feel any relief. Her daughter was still missing.

In August 1977, the NYPD redoubled their efforts to
track down John Berger, the ponytailed man who Hover was
last seen with.

Meanwhile, at the same time that Hover's family feared
the worst, Alcala was just getting back to LA after a brief
trip to El Paso, Texas, to visit family there and was beginning to look for a full-time job.

Chapter Eighteen

After being paroled in June 1977 and returning from New York, where he "visited relatives" for a little over a month, Rodney Alcala returned to Los Angeles, and in September he began looking for a job. Feeling confident, he walked into the *Los Angeles Times* personnel office and applied for a typesetting position. On his résumé he claimed to have worked for Blue Shield in New York between 1969 and 1971 and as an office manager at Hill Enterprises in Middlefield, Connecticut, between 1971 and 1977. After an interview and review of his résumé, Alcala landed the position—in spite of the fact that the new hiree had been a fugitive for three years; had been on the FBI's Ten Most Wanted Fugitives list in 1971; had been arrested and convicted of the 1968 child molestation of Tali S.; had served nearly three years in prison for that crime; had been convicted of violating parole and providing a minor, Julie Johnson, with drugs; had served two and a half years for that crime; was a registered sex offender; was currently on parole; *and* had applied for the position under his own name—not an alias.

So much for background checks.

Eager to create a good impression at work, Alcala turned up the charm. He was even friendlier and more outgoing than usual, sharing stories about the famous people he knew when he lived in Greenwich Village and showing off his photographs. According to his bosses, he always performed his work diligently and often stayed late to finish up assignments.

Sharon Gonzales was a fellow employee. She and many of her colleagues were impressed with Alcala. "[He] would talk about going to parties in Hollywood. It seemed like he knew famous people." Not only that, he was more hip and open than most of the people who worked at the paper, and his avant-garde way of thinking intrigued his co-workers. "He was very open about his sexuality," said Gonzales. "It was all new to me." Gonzales reported that Alcala would show her photographs from his portfolio, most of young girls. When she asked Alcala how he came by taking their pictures, he said that the girls' parents asked him to.

Chapter Nineteen

Around the time that Alcala was spreading his wings at the *Los Angeles Times,* far away, in another part of the country, a young woman was also contemplating spreading her wings—leaving her hometown in New York State and heading out west.

Oneida, New York, is far way from anywhere, really. Located in central New York State, it's just east of Wampsville, north of Munnsville, south of Durhamville, and west of Sherrill. It is actually centrally located between Montreal, Toronto, Buffalo, Boston, and New York, seemingly a sweet spot. But to get to any of those bustling metropolises from Oneida, one needs to journey approximately two hundred miles.

And depending on which Oneida folks you speak to, that situation is just fine—as is the average winter temperature of 20 degrees Fahrenheit; the average snowfall of thirty inches (compared to a national average of around five); the fact that with a population of around 11,660 in 1970, it managed to lose some 7.3 percent of its residents by the end of that decade and today boasts a booming 10,700. One of the town's main attractions is that it is home to one of the smallest churches in the world, Cross Island Chapel, which sits in the middle of a pond. Such modest allures ensure that not a whole lot of strangers stop by there on their way somewhere else.

Many Oneidans are diehard fans of their city. They point

to historic Oneida Lake, the largest lake entirely within New York State; the Oneida Indians, the Iroquois tribe that lived in the region and gave their name to the city; Oneida Ltd., the international tableware company founded in 1880 and one of America's top flatware producers in the twentieth century; and nearby Chittenango, where yellow-brick sidewalks honor the home of the author of *The Wonderful Wizard of Oz*, L. Frank Baum.

But for certain other Oneidans—younger folks with perhaps two dominant alleles on their "risk-taking" gene—all that idyllic country hoo-ha is but a death sentence in disguise. If you are unfortunate enough to be born in Oneida, they believe, there is a certain inevitability to the fact that that is exactly where you will spend all of your days *and* end all of your days, most likely in the Glenwood, Sherrill Kenwood, or Saint Patrick's cemetery.

Such a fate would not be in the cards for young Jill Barcomb—at least, not if she had anything to say about it.

Jill was born on December 18, 1958, the fifth child in the seemingly never-ending line of Barcomb kids. They were a large brood, even by Catholic standards of the day. And with their numbers came the usual familial advantages and disadvantages: always having lots of people around, never being able to be alone; and always having to be patient, to share, and to be in lockstep.

From oldest to youngest, the six girls and five boys, all born between 1954 and 1969, were Alice, Debra, Marlene, Maurice, Jill, Bruce, Brian, Kimie, Kelly, Joseph, and Michael. The older kids, of course, had different experiences from the younger kids in terms of social values and norms, as well as differing degrees of parental involvement. Even in Oneida, a child of the *Leave It to Beaver* 1950s was far different from a child of the drug-addled and flower-powered 1960s or the "Me Decade" of the 1970s. Plus, nearly fifteen years between the youngest and oldest child meant different generational parenting styles, with, at various times, the younger kids becoming easier to overlook as changing attention focused on the older girls getting married and leaving home.

The family home on Park Avenue was one of the few houses present on the street on a bird's-eye-view map of Oneida in the 1860s, housed at the local Madison County Historical Society. It was a classic two-story house of that era, complete with a full cellar and coal chute, living room, den, foyer, kitchen, laundry room, dining room, and four bedrooms—two dorms, one for the girls, one for the boys; a small bedroom reserved for the oldest sibling living at home; and a master bedroom. With only one and a half baths to support thirteen people at its peak, the kitchen sink served as an alternate vessel in which to brush teeth or wash hair.

Maurice and Joyce were the parents. Maurice was a first-generation-born United States citizen of French-Canadian ancestry. In fact, Maurice was a French-Canadian Indian raised near Rouses Point, New York, even farther north than Oneida and only one mile south of the Canadian-U.S. border. Maurice graduated from the eighth grade and then left school to go to work. Joyce didn't graduate from high school, either, because as the oldest daughter in her family, she stayed at home to help raise her six younger brothers and sisters. At seventeen years of age, however, Joyce started working as a waitress in Rouses Point.

One day, in walked a dashing young Air Force man who had just returned to town for his father's funeral. The two struck up a conversation, and that evening, after Maurice offered Joyce a ride home in his car, the two began a loving relationship that lasted the rest of their lives.

Upon Maurice's humanitarian discharge from the Air Force to help out his family, he decided to settle around Oneida, where his other siblings had gone after leaving northern New York—a place "far" south of Rouses Point.

Maurice, nicknamed "the Beaver" from the saying "busy as a beaver," worked not only a full-time job but also a part-time one, as janitor in the evenings, as his ever-burgeoning family arrived. Sometimes, in order to spend more time with his children, he would take one of them to his evening job.

The Beaver was the primary breadwinner for nearly twenty years of the Barcombs' married life, which allowed Joyce to ride shotgun over the kids, making sure they were all accounted for, homework was done, clean clothes were available, and each and every one of them had a chance at whatever life had to offer.

Joyce was a nurturing soul, as was Maurice. Although they both believed in a hard work ethic and involved their kids when special projects arose around the house, they also had plenty of love and warmth to spread around. Boys did chores such as taking care of the lawn, chopping wood, taking out the trash, and shoveling snow, while the girls did the cooking, cleaning, and washing. Some of the kids had paper routes by the time they turned ten; others babysat for cash. They received no allowance but never lacked for the basics. Dinners were always big, noisy affairs, and holidays were even bigger and noisier, with cousins and aunts and nephews coming from miles around.

As practicing Catholics, the Barcomb kids would go to church on Sundays and sit attentively with their religious education group. Every night at home, they would get down on their knees and say their prayers together as a family. Usually, Joyce or Maurice would lead from the upstairs hallway and listen carefully to make sure every voice was heard in the recitation. After the kids finished their "Now I lay me down to sleep's," they would hop into bed and play word games both within and between dorms. Sometimes their parents would catch them and scold them, but everyone viewed that as one of the "fun" parts of being in a large family. Sometimes one or another child would drift off to sleep between answers, but that was just fine, because there were always plenty of other siblings to pick up the slack.

On Saturdays the Barcomb clan would often take in a matinee, with the older siblings watching out for the littler ones. In the summer they would go to the local pool, where they could ignore, for at least a short while, the hot central New York weather. The Barcomb kids played with other neighborhood kids, generally away from the house, because of the sheer number of bodies that would have run amok over their household. They played neighborhood games of kick the can, hide-and-seek, tag, baseball, football, and dodgeball. Older sisters would sometimes babysit younger ones, and, as the sixties rolled on, they'd all listen to the Beatles' "I Want to Hold Your Hand" or "Michelle" while the younger kids sometimes drifted off to nap in the den.

Music was a big part of the household life, whether it was singing, listening to records, or playing instruments. The Barcomb family musical talent "show" featured Debra on piano, Marlene on clarinet, Morris on trombone, Jill on trumpet, Bruce on drums, Brian on saxophone and vocals, and Kelly on violin. In 1976, Maurice joined a local drum and bugle corps, and Jill, Brian, Kimie, Kelly, and Joey all played in his corps against the drum corps that Bruce belonged to. Bruce was captain of the drum line for his corps, and there was hell to pay—or, at the very least, a great deal of chiding—whenever one corps lost to the other.

In the 1970s, a new TV show, *The Waltons*, featuring a large Depression-era family, captivated the country. At night the Barcombs would often repeat the "good nights" of the Waltons between their bedrooms for laughter, not unaware of the similarity.

Like all the other Barcomb children, as Jill grew older, she formed an especially tight bond with one sibling, a special ally in the ever-changing landscape of the Barcomb household. For Jill, that was Bruce, her younger brother by eighteen months.

During one family dinner when Bruce was just three years old, he took a bite of the gross green stuff that was put on his plate and immediately spit it out. He *hated* spinach! Sternly scolded, Bruce was asked to leave the table, sit down by the refrigerator, and think about what he had just done. Right away, five-year-old Jill got up from table, sat down beside him, put her arm around him, and told him that everything would be all right. Bruce could always count on Jill to make things better.

By age nine, when Bruce was firmly established as the middle child of the brood, there was a clear break between the older five and the younger five. Whenever the older kids wanted to push Bruce down with the younger kids, Jill would make sure that he was with her as part of the older group. When Bruce was a freshman in high school, Jill took Bruce to his first freshman dance.

Jill was a golden child, good at anything she tried. She excelled in French and took advanced French classes. She was gifted musically and sang and played the trumpet in advanced band class. She loved to roller-skate and even tried her hand at being an amateur disc jockey. She volunteered as a candy striper in the local hospital and considered nursing as a possible career. She wanted to help others.

In such a large family, there wasn't any real mentoring when it came to pursuing college or professional life beyond high school: Those kinds of conversations were simply not a part of the Barcomb children's upbringing. Each child was expected to do as the others before him or her had done: Jill would get married, have children, and settle down close to home; Bruce would find a trade or employment opportunity on his own.

As older siblings started moving out to pursue their own lives, they were not there to help enforce household rules, and the younger kids could more easily get away with things the older kids never dreamed of doing. In the vacuum between parenting, there were many opportunities in the mid-1970s for two teens like Jill and Bruce to pursue clandestine activities—opportunities that they took full advantage of. And, as in the past, they always came to each other's rescue, if needed, covering for the other when called on the carpet for sneaking out at night.

By that time Jill's world centered more on roller-skating at the old Kallet movie theater than on studying. It was at the rink that she came in contact with an older and more exciting crowd. They were kids who didn't go to school and came from places outside Oneida, which automatically gave them a certain cachet. They had cars and money—and they had drugs. It was under their influence that Jill began to step away from the traditional Barcomb family values and start living a more carefree, even reckless lifestyle. Among other things, she began smoking pot and drinking.

By the time Jill was 17, she was ready to *really* spread her wings, desperate to set out for some high adventure. She dropped out of high school in her senior year, and because of all the friction created by her rebellious ways, she moved out of her parents' house and in with her older married sister Debbie.

It was while Jill was living with Debbie that her plans to follow her dreams gelled. Three of her friends decided to drive a van out west to LA, where there was at least the *possibility* of a life. Jill didn't tell her family of her plans—yet.

In October 1977, Bruce Barcomb was seventeen, living at home, and a senior in high school. He had just gotten his driver's license and made arrangements a few days before to pick up his sister Jill at about three o'clock in the afternoon at their sister Debbie's house. He was so proud and excited: Here was Jill's little brother taking *her* somewhere. Besides, he had missed her, now that she was living away, and looked forward to spending some time with her.

After getting out of his car, he walked up to Debbie's front door, which was uncharacteristically unlocked. Yelling "Jill!" he walked right in and immediately saw that the TV was on but no one was watching. He checked out the house and the backyard, but Jill was nowhere to be found. Bruce was surprised: It was totally unlike Jill to bail without telling him. Bruce called his mother and asked if she had heard from Jill. She said she hadn't and suggested he lock the door and go about his business. Surely, Jill would call later.

However, as night fell and Jill didn't return to Debbie's, the family started to become concerned. When no one heard from her the next day or the day after, they tried to reassure themselves that Jill had probably just taken a short trip with her new friends and they'd hear from her in a day or two.

A week later, Jill did, in fact, finally call home to tell her mother that she was in California. The family was shocked but relieved. Jill apologized for not telling her mother about her plans ahead of time, but she said that she thought it would be easier that way. She had wanted to avoid getting in a battle with them about her wishes for more independence. Jill told her mother that she was excited about being in California. There were so many attractions that she hardly had time to take them all in. She said that she was searching for a new life, a new start, and was on her way to finding one. She hoped they would understand.

Bruce got on the phone and Jill immediately apologized again, this time for not being there on the big day he planned to drive her around town, but she was sure he'd understand. Of course, he did. She told him that she absolutely loved California and hoped that one day he'd come out and visit. He asked her if she was afraid, being so far away and in a "foreign" part of the country. She said she had absolutely no fears. And the weather! she exclaimed: She just couldn't stop talking about how warm and lovely it was, even in November. She told Bruce that shortly after she arrived in LA, the van that the group had driven to California was repossessed, and its owner and her boyfriend had returned to Syracuse. She said she was okay with that. Although her friends were no longer with her, she loved her new life there anyway.

Like other young people of her time, Jill was a free-spirited soul trying to find her way. And with her long brown hair, olive skin, and infectious smile, she was a magnet for people—all kinds of people.

When Bruce got off the phone, he said to his mother, "I'm so happy for Jill. Maybe she's finally found what she's been looking for."

Chapter Twenty

At seven a.m. on November 10, 1977, the temperature in Los Angeles was already in the low seventies. A few high, dark clouds pocked the sky as the sun began poking through. Wednesday promised to be another perfect day.

As a West Los Angeles patrol unit was cruising the still-sleepy streets, the officers received an "ambulance and dead body call." Immediately they turned on their sirens and headed to the location: the service road between Mulholland Drive and Beverly Ranch Road, not far from Marlon Brando's estate. They were to be the first on the scene and had no idea what to expect.

Mulholland Drive, a mostly two-lane road, snaked along the top of the Hollywood Hills, overlooking the San Fernando Valley on one side and the city of Beverly Hills and the Los Angeles Basin on the other. It offered breathtaking views. Beyond Mulholland was a more remote, less-traveled road called Franklin Canyon Drive. In 1977 part of it was paved, while other parts were simply dirt. A gate stopped cars from traveling its length.

After driving on the paved road, the cops headed onto the service road and then onto the secluded Franklin Canyon Drive. As they bumped along on the finely powdered dirt road, one cop called out:

"Hey, what's that on the side?"

Coming closer, next to a rugged area of dense brush and

trees known as California chaparral, they came upon a body. It took only a few seconds for the officers to take in the carnage.

The female was on all fours low to the ground.

Her knees were bent, with the tips of her toes on the ground.

Her inner thighs and knees were pointing outward.

She wore no panties.

Her buttocks were spread wide.

Her face was tucked so tightly against her breasts that it looked as if her neck were broken.

The top of her head was touching the ground between her knees.

Her right hand was pulled under her body.

The fingers of that hand were curled up directly under her lacerated anus, which was three or four inches off the ground.

The ring and index finger of her right hand were covered in blood that had dripped from her vaginal and anal areas.

Blood from her anus pooled in the dirt below her.

A blood-smeared light-green sweater with dark green and orange trim was pulled up on her back.

She wore no stockings or shoes.

The backs of her shoulders, her arms, and her legs were bloodstained.

One pant leg was smushed under her knee, soaked in blood.

Her other pant leg was tied around her neck.

The bottoms of her feet were perfectly clean.

Two footprints were in the soil, with the toes facing the buttocks of the deceased.

A circle of blood surrounded her head.

A seven-inch-long, five-inch-wide, three-inch-thick rock was found in the blood circle, with a bloodstained point.

The area on the ground around her body was splattered with blood.

The officers immediately called for backup. In the

meantime they secured the area. They did their jobs. But one of the young officers would not be able to eat, for three full days following the discovery of the body. It was to be the most horrifying crime scene he would see in his career.

After the body was photographed, it was brought to the morgue, but the victim had yet to be identified. A Dr. Breton performed an autopsy and filed a report for Jane Doe 95. The damage wrought on the body of the unnamed victim was as follows:

Massive face, head, and neck trauma, including deep cuts embedded with broken bone fragments into her skull.

Blood seepage all around her brain.

Small blood vessels in her eye and those around her heart ruptured from pressure and the deprivation of oxygen.

Three ligatures around her neck: a top ligature of her blood-soaked left pant leg tied into a granny knot up under her left ear; a middle ligature of two knee-high nylons, knotted together, and tied around her neck; a bottom ligature of a woman's belt cranked tight around her neck.

A deep bite mark surrounding the nearly severed nipple of her right breast.

Four blood smears, like four fingers, "where the offender was holding the breast while he was biting the nipple."

Blood smears all over the body where the assailant was "manhandling and twisting and pulling and doing whatever."

Deep scratch marks, indicating defensive injuries, on her arms, shoulders, pelvic area, and abdomen.

Multiple bleeding lacerations and cuts penetrating her anus.

Singed pubic hair.

In his report, Dr. Breton stated these conclusions:

The body was that of a female, four feet eleven inches tall, weighing around ninety-five pounds.

Almost all of her injuries were inflicted while she was still alive and blood was pumping through the body.

She was strangled with hands, then with ligatures, then

bashed on the head. The beatings to her head were antemortem (before death): She was definitely alive.

The impact of the blows to the head were consistent with that from a rock.

There were multiple causes of death: blunt force trauma to the head and to the neck, either of which could have killed her; with strangulation a contributing cause.

The coroner theorized:

The deceased did not walk into the crime scene because there were no barefoot prints. The offender picked her up to get her into the position where she could be sodomized.

Her anus was torn and the area bruised, so she was still alive, although it appeared to be a perimortal (just as the person was dying) reaction.

Two contusions/lacerations of the anus itself, just below the vagina, indicated that while she was being sodomized, the perpetrator's fingernails were digging into her skin.

The victim's pubic hair was singed up the left side, showing that a flaming instrument was placed between her legs and into her vaginal area.

The victim's final position was posed, with the assailant's bloodied hand manipulating her left leg and hip.

Swabs of fluid were taken from the genital area of Jane Doe 95.

Through microscopic examination, sperm was observed inside both her anal and vaginal cavities.

DNA technology was not available at that time to help solve the crime.

Investigators quickly focused their energy on trying to ID the body and looking for the perpetrator. LAPD detective Philip Vannatter, later a lead detective in the O.J. Simpson case, interviewed neighbors in the Hollywood Hills area, including Marlon Brando. All claimed to have known nothing about the death. After spending some time in the area, the officers believed that the neighbors were probably telling the truth because the body could not have been seen from any of the estates along Mulholland. The police department disseminated a description of the young woman and asked anyone with information, no matter how insignificant, to come forward.

Within a day the police were able to identify the body. Juvenile records from an arrest, which resulted in fingerprints on file, served as proof positive of who the young woman was.

Chapter Twenty-one

On Friday night, November 11, Bruce Barcomb was attending a party in Oneida. He was having a great time, so he decided not only to stay out later than usual but also to sleep over at a buddy's house. A dutiful son, he called his mother to say he wouldn't be coming home that night. In totally uncharacteristic fashion, his mother said he could not stay out, that he had to come home immediately. "No, you absolutely need to come home now!"

He knew he'd better do it, and right away.

He got into his car and drove straight home. When he walked through the front door, his mother moved unsteadily up to him. She couldn't speak. He saw his younger siblings huddled together on the couch crying.

What was going on?

That same evening, as Jill's oldest brother Maurice was driving on the highway, a state trooper put on his siren and pulled him over. Maurice was surprised and nervous. He knew he had not been speeding, so he couldn't understand why the cops were stopping him.

"You Maurice Barcomb?" asked the trooper.

"Yes."

"You need to turn around and go home. Go to the State Thruway."

Incredulous, Maurice asked why.

"We will escort you. You need to go home now, son."

"Can't you tell me—"

"Just do as we say, please."

Maurice had no idea what was going on and no way of contacting anyone. He drove some forty miles with questions swirling in his mind. *Was someone sick at home? Had there been a fire? What could possibly be the matter?*

When Maurice arrived home and walked in the door, he nearly collapsed on seeing his entire family in hysterics. Not an eye was dry. Not a person could speak. Not in his wildest dreams could he imagine what could have happened.

Jill Barcomb was laid to rest on Wednesday, November 16, 1977, in Saint Patrick's Cemetery in Oneida, in a closed casket due to the disfiguration of her face and body. The Barcomb parents didn't want any of their children to see the carnage in the casket, but Maurice went against their wishes. "I didn't want to live the rest of my life not knowing whether or not that was *really* Jill."

Nothing could fill the loss that Bruce and all his family felt, and none of their questions would be answered. They would live for many more years without knowing who had killed Jill or seeing justice for her depraved murderer.

In searching for the killer, the police looked to see if Barcomb's death could be linked to the string of killings taking place that summer in the LA area, particularly those being perpetrated by the person dubbed the "Hillside Strangler." It came to light that Barcomb had reportedly known fifteen-year-old Judith Miller of Hollywood, a Hillside Strangler victim, whose body was found on October 31, 1977, in La Crescenta.

Maybe this was the lead the authorities were looking for.

Chapter Twenty-two

On December 14, 1977, the LAPD received a call from the FBI. They were investigating the disappearance of one Ellen Hover, they said, which had taken place five months earlier in New York City. They were looking for a John Berger, because his name was in her diary on the last day she was seen or heard from. Their records showed that "John Berger" was an alias for "Rodney Alcala," who lived in LA.

The LAPD had no trouble finding the man, whose records showed he had been incarcerated twice for a total of five years and was now on parole. After doing some checking, the authorities discovered that Alcala was working at the *Los Angeles Times*.

At the request of the FBI, the LAPD brought Alcala into the Parker Center, LAPD headquarters, for questioning. They told him that a woman named Ellen Hover was missing from New York City and they wondered if he could shed any light on the matter. To their astonishment, Alcala admitted not only that he knew Hover but also that he was with her on the day that they said she went missing. Alcala said that the two had struck up a friendship when they met casually one day on the Upper East Side of Manhattan, where Alcala was taking photos. Hover had agreed to go with him to a spot in Westchester, about half an hour away, where he would take photos of her, which he promised would take her breath away. However, Alcala swore to the police, he had absolutely no idea what happened to Hover after the two returned to

Manhattan and he left her at the door to her apartment building.

The police asked Alcala if he would be willing to take a polygraph test. After all, they said, if Alcala had nothing to hide, why wouldn't he? However, Alcala refused and after several more hours of interrogation, the police were forced to let him go. Without a dead body or any evidence directly pointing to Alcala, they had no right to hold him.

Smiling, Alcala left the LAPD headquarters. He was a free man and was thrilled to return to the lifestyle he had come to enjoy so much since his return to LA: During the day he worked at the *Times*; in the evenings he partied at a bar or club; on weekends he took photographs, mostly at the beaches, and mostly of young girls and women.

Life was good.

Chapter Twenty-three

On December 16, 1977, Jeffrey Cannon, a reserve for the Los Angeles County Sheriff's Department, received a call that a Georgia Wixted of 22648 Pacific Coast Highway, apartment eight, in Malibu had not picked up a co-worker that morning, as she customarily did, nor had she shown up for work. Despite repeated calls to her apartment, no one answered the phone.

Cannon, along with Deputies Jack Nenninger and Mike Powers, responded to the call. The three pulled up to the two-story building, on the south side of the Pacific Coast Highway, directly on the ocean. On either side of the building were other apartment houses and fast-food restaurants. It was a busy area.

They entered the complex through a gate into a courtyard, then turned to the left and walked to the ground-level apartment. The first thing the officers noticed was that a screen was missing from one of the three large windows in the front. It was propped against a nearby wall. Then they saw a box beneath the unscreened window, as if someone had used it as a boost. Looking closely, they also noticed scuff marks on the outside of the sill.

The men repeatedly knocked on door but received no response. They tried the door handle and found that it was unlocked. The three walked in.

Upon entering, the detectives immediately felt the

overwhelming heat. It was at least 90 degrees in there. They turned on their flashlights because it was totally dark.

Scanning the room, they saw a dead body on the floor.

Guns drawn, they split up and checked out the rest of the apartment to see if there were any other victims or, maybe, a suspect. No one was there.

After the apartment was cleared, the police backed out, shut the door, and notified the homicide unit. They then secured the area and waited, making certain that no one else went in until homicide got there.

At that time, Phillip Bullington was a lieutenant in the homicide bureau in the Los Angeles County Sheriff's Department and leader of a team of approximately fifteen investigators. At 9:20 p.m. he responded to the call to supervise the investigation of a murder at the Malibu Surf apartment complex.

When Bullington and his men arrived, the other uniformed deputies got them up to speed. Then they entered the apartment.

It took only a few seconds for the officers to take in the carnage:

A naked female body lay on her back on the floor, her entire body covered with bruises, lacerations, and blood.

Her knees were splayed outward, forming a diamond shape.

There was blood between her legs.

A pair of panty hose was knotted several times around her neck.

Bloody sheets, a bloody pillow, a bloody bedspread, and a bloody nightshirt were strewn on the floor next to her body.

There was a large blood-soaked stain in the middle of the mattress.

Blood was splattered on the railing of the bed and over the four walls and the floor.

Blood was on the toilet, on a bar of soap, and on a towel in the kitchen sink.

A bloodstained claw hammer lay two feet from the victim's head, as did a pair of shoes.

On December 18, 1977, a Dr. Shipley performed an autopsy and filed a report for Georgia Wixted. He documented her extensive injuries as follows:

Massive face and head trauma, including circular bruises, skull fractures, and clawlike lacerations into her skull.

Tears inside the front part of her mouth and lower lip from blunt-force impact.

Cut marks on her neck from ligatures and broken bones inside her neck and under her jaw, which had pierced through to the back of her throat from the force applied to tightening the ligatures.

Ruptured blood vessels in her eyes from the pressure to her neck.

A fractured and dislocated arm.

Laceration of the lips of the vagina and labia.

Dr. Shipley wrote these conclusions:

Almost every injury was inflicted while she was alive and blood was still pumping through her body.

Ligature marks to the neck were consistent with strangulation, and a tear to the vaginal wall was consistent with forced penetration by an object.

The fracture to the left skull was consistent with being struck by a hammer.

A palm print from the brass railing of the bed was recovered, as was the sperm from inside her vaginal, anal, and oral cavities.

Two different types of blood were found at the scene.

DNA evidence was collected.

Technology in 1977 did not allow for authorities to make a determination as to who the murderer might be.

Chapter Twenty-four

Georgia Wixted was born on December 22, 1949, the second child of Mary Golden Wixted. Georgia had an older brother by one year, Michael (Mike). Their parents separated shortly after Georgia was born, and Mary and the two kids lived with their grandparents in a large Victorian-style home in the small town of Mechanicville, New York, less than twenty miles north of Albany.

When Georgia was five, the family moved to Los Angeles, California, for a job opportunity and to start a new life with their youngest sister, Anne, who was born in 1955.

Georgia and Mike spent many hours during elementary and high school helping watch over younger sister Anne, as well as sharing the joys of youth among a large group of friends. Their mother worked hard as a teacher in a local elementary school. Summers were spent back in Mechanicville among "cousins by the dozens," where the Wixted kids were always busy playing outdoors.

Anne and Georgia shared a room growing up in their small one-story house in west LA. Because there were not many kids living in the neighborhood, they became best friends. Older sister Georgia taught Anne how to roller-skate and ride a bike. Later, Georgia would babysit for Anne's friends when their parents were out.

The Wixted kids led a simple life. They played outside a lot. They attended Catholic church and went to Catholic high school. They enjoyed going to nearby Picwood Theater and sometimes to the theaters in Westwood. Georgia especially loved playing volleyball, going to the beach, and dancing. Among her favorite TV shows were Dick Clark's *American Bandstand* and *The Lloyd Thaxton Show*, both of which featured local high school students dancing on the soundstage. Mike remembers Georgia teaching him how to dance after they were both invited to appear on *American Bandstand*. In high school, Georgia was named "most humorous." She often had the family—and fellow classmates—in stitches.

The family watched *Bonanza* together on TV and often watched scary movies on the Friday night *Chiller Theater* show, which featured, among other films, *The Lost Missile*, *The Pharaoh's Curse*, *The Vampire Bat*, and *Supernatural*. Anne said, "Only Georgia would make *me* watch the scary parts and tell her about them." Both Anne and Mike recalled that Georgia was very smart and did well in school when she was interested in the subject, but she struggled in math.

When Mike left home for college, he chose to go to school in New York, and after college he went directly into the Army. Whenever he came home on leave, he would pick up right where he left off with Georgia and Anne, always having fun, while also helping their mother around the house.

In her junior year of high school, Georgia was diagnosed with what doctors thought was breast cancer. Luckily, when the tumor was removed, it turned out to be benign. However, the next year Georgia developed another tumor and her mother decided to send her to their family doctor in New York because she wanted to make sure Georgia was getting the best care.

Cancer was a scary diagnosis in those days—as it is today—but the incidence of death from the disease was much higher then. While Georgia was in the hospital, she received such outstanding care from the nurses at both hospitals that it left a strong impression on her. She decided that one day she would become a nurse and help others as the nurses had helped her.

However, her dream was not so easy to fulfill. Georgia's mother, a teacher, couldn't afford to put her children through college, so Georgia decided to find work as a medical assistant, not only to get enough money to one day afford to go to nursing school, but also to find out if being a nurse was truly what she was meant to do.

Georgia loved working as a medical assistant. Over time she saved up enough money to go to nursing school. After completing her courses, Georgia received her degree and immediately began to look for a job. It didn't take long before she landed one at Centinela Hospital in nearby Inglewood in the orthopedic unit. As soon as a cardiac unit opened, Georgia was selected to work there.

As a cardiac-care nurse, Georgia not only helped the patients with their physical needs but also talked to them about their psychological problems. She came to understand that many of the patients weren't able to tell their families about what they were going through, so she served as a sounding board for their hopes and fears. Understanding, kind, and sympathetic—those were some of Georgia's many fine qualities. Open, gregarious, witty, and inquisitive—those were others. "She had no enemies and was universally liked," Anne said.

By 1977, Georgia was twenty-seven years old and everything was going her way. She was making good money. She was working at a job she enjoyed. She continued to be an open, gregarious person with a sharp wit and an inquisitive mind. She didn't have an enemy in the world. She was enjoying new experiences and wanted to become more independent and move into a place of her own.

Georgia felt that being on her own was an important step to take. To that end, she moved into a lovely ground-floor apartment in the Malibu Surf apartment complex. From her front windows she looked onto a lovely patio. The distinct smell of ocean spray was everywhere.

Georgia Wixted had simple dreams: She wanted to be a

nurse. She wanted to live on the beach. She got both—for a very short time.

Georgia's co-worker, Barbara Gale, worked the same shift as Wixted, from 3:00 p.m. to 11:30 p.m. in the postcardiac "step-down" unit at Centinela Hospital. Gale was a ward clerk, carrying out the orders of doctors and nurses and transmitting information between departments. Georgia was the charge nurse for the shift.

After work on December 15, Wixted accompanied Gale to celebrate Gale's friend's birthday at Brennan's Pub. Georgia didn't know anyone else at the party except her friend Gale. Afterward, Georgia dropped off Gale at her home in Santa Monica. Gale was in bed by 2:15 a.m.

The two had arranged that later that day Wixted would pick up Gale for their three o'clock shift as usual, since Gale's little Honda 50 motorcycle had broken down several weeks before.

However, when 2:30 p.m. came and went and Wixted still hadn't shown up, Gale called her apartment. Maybe her friend was sleeping in.

No one answered the call. At 2:55 p.m., Gale decided to call her own mother and ask her if she would mind swinging by and taking her to work. She told her that Wixted had not stopped by to pick her up, as the two young women had arranged.

When Gale arrived at the hospital, Wixted was not there, nor had she called in sick. Gale tried to reach her several more times but to no avail. Gale's mother urged her to call the police.

Chapter Twenty-five

Georgia's sister Anne was twenty-two years old and a college student when the LAPD called her and notified her of her sister's death. Their brother Mike was in the Army when he learned the news.

The first thing Mike did when he arrived home was to take down the Christmas tree in their family home and put away all the presents. The next thing he did was go to Georgia's apartment. Someone had to clean it out.

After he opened the door and took a quick look inside, he turned around, went outside, fell to his knees, and vomited. When he was able to gather himself together, he went back in.

There were bloodstains on the bed; blood smears on the side of the bed; blood on the clothes; blood on the floor; blood all over. He kept hearing the words that soldiers in the Army often say, "Suck it up and tough it out," so that was what he tried to do. He cleaned up as much of the apartment as he could, collecting anything that had no blood in it, and got out of there as soon as possible.

Once Georgia's mother and father heard the news, they were inconsolable. Mrs. Wixted took a leave of absence for the rest of that school year. She tried to go back to work, but she just couldn't. Right after Christmas, she went into a mental institution to seek help. She couldn't accept what had happened to her beloved daughter.

It was up to Anne now to make all the decisions. She arranged for the funeral as she tried to comfort her mother. Anne herself found that she couldn't focus on anything. She had been a great student, but now she couldn't hold a thought. Soon she quit school.

Neither Mike nor Anne viewed Georgia's body. The funeral director advised them not to because "we can't put her back together."

Who could have done this to our beautiful Georgia?

While the Wixted family was dealing with their overwhelming grief, Alcala was living at his mother's house, working daily at the *Los Angeles Times*, taking photographs on weekends, and partying at clubs and bars in the evening.

Chapter Twenty-six

According to the *Psychodynamic Diagnostic Manual*, sadistic personality disorder "is organized around the theme of domination." The sadistic person might be "dead" inside, and this lack of feeling is "relieved by inflicting pain and humiliation, in fantasy and often in reality."

PDM reports that the overriding motivation of sadistic people "involves controlling, subjugating, and forcing pain and humiliation on others." The sadistic person needs to be in total control over another, comparatively powerless person—"turning impotence to omnipotence." He or she has no emotional attachment or guilt feelings when assuming domination and control, as the person dehumanizes the object of sadism.

PDM states the following as beliefs held by sadistic persons:

"Others exist as objects for my domination."
"I am entitled to hurt and humiliate others."

PART
IV

PART

IV

Chapter Twenty-seven

A spate of grisly homicides sent shivers down the spines of the residents of the state of California during the 1970s. Practically every day, local newspapers offered up lurid details about yet another victim that had been savagely beaten, cruelly tortured, viciously raped—then discarded nonchalantly on the side of a freeway, buried in a shallow grave, or left in the wild for animals to feast on.

At first it seemed that each murder was a solitary event—an evil individual seeking vengeance on a specific victim. Soon, however, the police realized that clusters of murders were linked by a similar modus operandi, and they began to suspect that they were dealing with more than a string of isolated incidents. They believed they had a number of different serial murderers on their hands, each with his own signature and MO.

For whatever reason—it's still not understood by criminologists—California in the 1970s was ground zero for serial killers. Among the most heinous were:

William George Bonin, nicknamed the "Freeway Killer," who tortured, raped, and beat at least twenty-one boys and young men and left their bodies on the sides of freeways.

Juan Corona, known as the "Machete Murderer," who raped and stabbed to death twenty-five or more itinerant laborers, discarding their machete-slashed bodies in shallow graves.

Richard Trenton Chase, dubbed the "Vampire of Sacramento," who murdered six people, drank their blood, engaged in sex with their corpses, and then cannibalized their remains.

Patrick Wayne Kearney, sometimes *also* referred to as the "Freeway Killer," who picked up at least twenty-one young men, shot them, had sex with their dead bodies, then dismembered and mutilated their corpses before wrapping them in garbage bags and dumping them along freeways.

Randy Steven Kraft, known as the "Southern California Strangler," who drugged, tortured, mutilated, and strangled at least sixteen young men and was strongly suspected of committing at least fifty-one other murders. He often left his victims on roadsides after shoving them out of a fast-moving car.

Gerald Parker, known as the "Bedroom Basher," who raped and murdered five women and killed the unborn child of a sixth.

Chapter Twenty-eight

Soon after the body of Jill Barcomb was found on the dirt road off Franklin Canyon Drive in Los Angeles on November 10, 1977, police suspected that she was the victim of an as-yet-unidentified killer, dubbed the "Hillside Strangler." The name was spawned because so many dead women's bodies—Barcomb's included—were found discarded on hillsides around LA. Plus, Barcomb's remains were strikingly similar to the other dead women's: nude, strangled, sexually molested, tortured, beaten, bound or handcuffed, and posed.

A thirty-person police task force was set up to find the killer or killers. Newspapers and TV and radio shows reported round the clock on the gruesome details. The public was in a panic. Parents warned their children to come directly home after school and not to speak to anyone along the way. Some residents started carrying guns. Others took self-defense classes. Many ordered new locks for their doors. Some even bought guard dogs.

In spite of these precautions, at least eleven women and girls were abducted and killed in the fall of 1977. As the killing continued, the carnage and brutality only seemed to grow worse. The Hillside Strangler was growing more brazen.

On October 18, 1977, the body of Yolanda Washington had been discovered dumped near the entrance to Forest Lawn Cemetery in Glendale. She was a known prostitute.

Washington had been beaten, raped, and tortured.

Her legs were splayed.

A cloth that was used to strangle her was wrapped around her neck.

She was believed to be the Hillside Strangler's first victim.

On October 31, 1977, the nude body of runaway fifteen-year-old Judith Lynn Miller had been discovered in a garden in La Crescenta, a suburb near Glendale.

Miller had been raped, sodomized, and strangled.

Her body had been placed on an anthill.

"Five-point" ligature marks were found. The five points were her neck, both wrists, and both ankles.

Her legs had been positioned knees out, creating a diamond shape.

On November 6, 1977, the nude body of Lissa Teresa Kastin, a twenty-one-year-old waitress and serious ballet student with dreams of becoming a professional dancer, had been discovered in Glendale, near the Chevy Chase Country Club.

Kastin had the same five-point ligature marks.

She had been raped.

On November 10, the nude body of eighteen-year-old Jill Barcomb, was discovered in Franklin Canyon, north of Beverly Hills, showing the same characteristics as the previous three victims.

On November 18, the body of seventeen-year-old high school student Kathleen Robinson was found near Pico Boulevard in the Wilshire area of LA.

Robinson had the same five-point ligature marks.

On November 20, the body of Kristina Weckler, a quiet twenty-year-old honors student at the Pasadena Art Center of Design, was discovered by the LAPD in a secluded spot near Glendale.

Weckler was nude.

Ants covered her body.

She had the same five-point ligature marks.

Blood surrounded her rectum.

There were bruises on her breasts.

Two puncture marks pierced the skin on her arms, but they were not track marks like those found on intravenous drug users. (An autopsy revealed that she had been injected with cleaning fluid.)

A few hours later, on November 20, two more bodies were discovered on the other side of the hillside from where Weckler had been found. Dolores Cepeda was twelve years old.

Sonja Johnson was fourteen years old.

Cepeda's and Johnson's nude bodies were overrun with maggots.

On November 23, the badly decomposed body of Jane King, twenty-eight, actress and Church of Scientology student, was found near the Los Feliz exit ramp of the Golden State Freeway.

King had been strangled with her own stockings.

Her body showed signs of severe bruising.

On November 29, the nude body of eighteen-year-old Lauren Wagner, a student who lived with her family in the San Fernando Valley, was found in the hills around the Glendale–Mount Washington area.

Wagner had the same five-point ligature marks.

Her palms were burned.

Puncture marks pierced the skin on her arms.

A shiny path of sticky liquid—secretions from the ants that covered her—oozed over her body.

On December 13, 1977, Kimberly Diane Martin, seventeen, a prostitute, was found dead in a vacant lot on a steep hillside in Echo Lake.

Martin's body had been posed.

* * *

After Martin's body was found, things quieted down for a while. Residents of the area allowed themselves a sigh of relief. No more female bodies were found strewn on the hillsides in the Glendale–Highland Park area for the rest of 1977. Christmas, New Year's, and the month of January passed without any recurrence.

Could it be that the Hillside Strangler had finally gotten tired of killing—or maybe even was dead?

Chapter Twenty-nine

Disagreement exists as to exactly when the term *serial killer* entered the English lexicon.

Some cite the 1886 textbook *Psychopathia Sexualis* by Dr. Richard von Krafft-Ebing, in which the doctor chronicled numerous examples of serial murders.

The *Oxford English Dictionary* states that the expression first became recognized at the end of the 1800s when "Jack the Ripper" went on a murderous rampage in London.

Other sources report that the concept was coined by the director of the Berlin criminal police, Ernst Gennat, in 1930 while working on the cases of Friedrich "Fritz" Haarmann and Peter Kürten. Haarmann, known as the "Vampire of Hanover," was believed to have been responsible for the murder of twenty-seven boys and young men between 1918 and 1924. Kürten, dubbed the "Vampire of Düsseldorf," committed his sex crimes, assaults, and murders against adults and children, mostly in 1929.

Still others attribute coinage of the term "serial killer" to FBI special agent Robert Ressler, who in the 1970s, while working in the FBI's Behavioral Science Unit, came up with the term after studying the repeated nature (series) of the crimes committed by offenders who selected victims at random. (Ressler later helped establish ViCAP—the Violent Criminal Apprehension Program—a comprehensive case listing of violent crimes, used by law enforcement for purposes of comparison, established by the Department of Justice in 1985.)

Anne Rule suggested in her book *Kiss Me, Kill Me*, published in 2004, that the English-language credit for *serial killer* should go to LAPD captain Pierce Brooks, who was considered the brains behind the ViCAP system.

Regardless of when the term first became part of the English language, serial killers have been committing their heinous deeds for centuries.

According to criminologists, not all serial murderers can be lumped into the same batch of humanity—or inhumanity—but instead belong to four distinct categories, based on motive:

1. **Visionary serial killers** hear voices in their heads that tell them to kill. These killers usually get their "calling" to kill from either God or a demon. "The devil made me do it!" is often heard from these perpetrators. This type of serial killer exhibits psychotic breaks from reality.

   David Berkowitz, aka the "Son of Sam," who terrorized the New York City area in the late 1970s, was a demon-mandated killer.

2. **Mission-oriented serial killers** justify their acts as "ridding the world" of certain types of people—homosexuals, prostitutes, people of a certain religion, etc. Generally, mission-oriented serial killers are not psychotic: Reality is *not* lost or greatly distorted during their killings.

   Ted Kaczynski, the "Unabomber," attempted to rid the world of modern technology, believing that it was a threat to the future of humanity. He is considered a mission-oriented serial killer.

3. **Hedonistic serial killers** find pleasure in killing. They believe people are expendable. Forensic psychologists divide hedonistic serial killers into three subgroups:

(a) *Lust killers'* primary motive is sex, and their sexual gratification is in direct proportion to the intensity of torture and mutilation they inflict.

Jeffrey Dahmer—who not only tortured and killed young men but also dismembered them and ate their body parts—was a lust killer.

(b) *Thrill killers'* primary motive is to induce pain or create terror. Their adrenaline rush comes from the hunt and the kill. Usually there is no sexual aspect involved, and most often, the victims are strangers.

Lee Boyd Malvo and John Allen Muhammad, the Beltway snipers, who randomly picked off residents of the Washington, D.C., metropolitan area with a semiautomatic assault rifle over a three-week period in 2002, were thrill killers.

(c) *Comfort (material gain) killers* usually choose victims from their own family or close friends. They often use poison, such as arsenic. Female serial killers are often comfort killers.

Dorothea Puente, who took elderly boarders into her home and then killed them for their money, was considered a comfort killer.

(4) Power/control serial killers get a rush from having power over their victims and raping them as a way to show domination.

Ted Bundy, who killed more than thirty women, is perhaps the most notorious power/control serial killer.

Serial murderers are distinct from mass murderers, for example, in that the latter commit multiple murders at one time; and from spree killers, who kill in two or more distinct locations with virtually no cooling-off period in between.

* * *

Despite all that's now known about serial killers and their motivations, there is no easy way to identify a serial killer, based on his or her everyday interactions.

"Unfortunately," reported Jacqueline Helfgott, associate professor of criminal justice at Seattle University in Washington, "you can't tell if the person sitting next to you in the pew at church is a serial killer or not."

When asked to provide a composite of a serial killer, Vernon Geberth didn't hesitate. Former commander of the Bronx Homicide Task Force of the New York Police Department, homicide and forensic consultant, and author of the bible on death investigations, *Practical Homicide Investigation: Tactics, Procedures, and Forensic Techniques*, as well as *Sex-Related Homicide and Death Investigation: Practical and Clinical Perspectives*, Geberth knows more about serial murderers than practically anyone else.

Geberth noted that most serial killers are streetwise rather than IQ smart. "They often know of police procedure from watching TV or even by reading about other serial murderers. However," he added, "Ted Bundy, with an IQ of 124, and Edmund Kemper, known as the 'CoEd Killer,' with an IQ of 136, are exceptions."

Many serial killers, Geberth reported, develop a ruse to be able to help lure their victims away from a safe area to a location where they can control them. These types of offenders are able to engage their victims in conversation. "They are seemingly charming, charismatic, and easy to trust. They select vulnerable types who are easy to control, often young women, whom they can impress and dominate."

Mark Safarik, one of the most senior and respected members of the Federal Bureau of Investigation's elite Behavioral Analysis Unit—the famed profiling unit showcased in the movie *The Silence of the Lambs* and on the television series *Criminal Minds*—and an internationally recognized expert in the analysis and interpretation of violent criminal behavior, also weighed in on serial killers.

He stated, "Serial killers vary in many ways. They are motivated differently. They target different types of victims, who vary in gender, race, age, as well as physical characteristics. They kill in different ways and for different reasons. Some kill in order to interact with a dead body, while others have no interest in such aspects. They come from all racial, ethnic, and socioeconomic backgrounds. Many were abused, but some were not. Some come from broken families with absent fathers, mothers, or both, but some come from intact families."

However, he pointed out, "Serial killers usually have a particular MO, which is similar in each of their killings, and they frequently have a victim preference, such as a certain sex, appearance, age group, race, or occupation."

Serial killers have a variety of attributes that make them successful "killing machines." They use "their ability to be superficial, engaging, and glib to get what they want—to be alone with a soon-to-be victim."

A cautionary tale appears in both the Christian Bible and Aesop's fables: "Beware of a wolf in sheep's clothing." The saying seems to apply to serial killers, but the question remains: How does one recognize the disguise before it's too late?

PART
V

PART

V

Chapter Thirty

In California in 1978, Johnny Rotten quit the Sex Pistols after the final show of their American tour at the Winterland Ballroom in San Francisco.

Roman Polanski skipped bail in Los Angeles and fled to France after pleading guilty to having sex with a thirteen-year-old girl.

Pacific Southwest Airlines flight 182, a Boeing 727, crashed midair into a Cessna 172, killing 144 people.

On the hills above LA, an overhauled "Hollywood" sign was revealed, replacing the original one, built in 1923.

San Francisco Mayor George Moscone and openly gay city supervisor Harvey Milk were assassinated by former supervisor Dan White.

At the fiftieth Academy Awards, *Annie Hall* received the Oscar for Best Picture.

In the sixth game of the World Series, the LA Dodgers lost to the New York Yankees, 7 to 2.

In Santa Monica, Charlotte Lamb, thirty-two, was viciously murdered.

Chapter Thirty-one

Just as the LAPD was letting out a cautious sigh of relief that perhaps the Hillside Strangler had finally concluded his murderous rampage, the body of twenty-year-old clerk Cindy Hudspeth was found in the trunk of her Datsun on February 17, 1978. The car had been pushed off a cliff on Angeles Crest, but otherwise the murder shared certain similarities with killings attributed to the Hillside Strangler:

Hudspeth had been strangled and raped. Signature five-point ligature marks were on her neck, wrists, and ankles.

The members of the Hillside Strangler Task Force now had another body on their hands. They had already begun questioning all registered sex offenders in the area, hoping that these meetings might lead them in the direction of the perpetrator. And they continued these interviews with greater urgency after Hudspeth's body was discovered.

One person of special interest to them was Rodney Alcala, a known sex offender, who was living at his mother's home in Monterey Park.

In March 1978, members of the task force knocked on Alcala's front door. They interviewed him and found him surprisingly articulate. He had an explanation as to where he had been on each and every day the "Hillside" crimes had been committed. After a long interview the officers felt he was clean. However, they did see some marijuana and decided to take him down to the station house and book him for drug possession.

Alcala spent a short time in jail but was soon released on parole. This was just a tiny blip in the trajectory of his life.

Chapter Thirty-two

Zaffar Shah lived at 617 Illinois Court, an apartment complex, in the city of El Segundo. In the early morning hours of June 24, 1978, he trudged down to the laundry room at his complex, where the washers and dryers were located. He had several loads to deal with.

When he got there, he immediately dropped the bags. In front of him on the concrete floor lay a naked and bloodied woman. She was faceup and posed grotesquely. He thought she looked dead.

After several seconds, when he was finally able to move, he ran to the apartment manager's office. The manager and his wife, a nurse, rushed to the laundry room. As soon as they saw the woman on the floor, they knew there was no reviving her. They called the police.

William Gaynor of the Homicide Bureau of the Los Angeles County Sheriff's Department took the call. As a deputy sheriff investigator, he handled homicide scenes and other suspicious deaths. At approximately 11:45 a.m. he arrived at 617 Illinois Court, located at the end of a cul-de-sac.

He was met by the manager and his wife. They led Gaynor to the laundry room, where he noted the following:

A nude female was lying on her back.

Blood surrounded her body.

A long shoelace was wound tightly around her neck and attached to a sandal, which hung to the side of her head.

Her arms were bent under her back, propping up her breasts.

Blood splatter dotted a piece of wood on the floor near the body.

Her legs were spread wide, with her genital area facing the open doorway of the laundry room.

After backup was called and the scene was photographed and taped off, the as-yet-unidentified Jane Doe was bagged and taken to be autopsied. That afternoon medical examiner Joseph Lawrence Cogan recorded these observations about the condition of the victim:

There was massive trauma to her head and face.

The ligature was so forcefully tightened that the cartilage around her voice box and thyroid was fractured and the blood vessels in her eyes were ruptured.

There were bite marks on the right side of the nape of her neck.

There were abrasions above her left breast and on her right shoulder.

There were lacerations over her entire genital area, and a contusion over the right labia.

There was hemhorraging around the anal rim, consistent with blunt-force trauma caused by the penetration of a penis or another object.

In his conclusions in the autopsy report, Dr. Cogan noted:

Most of the injuries were inflicted while the person was alive and blood was pumping through her body.

More than one kind of strangulation was used. A choke-hold may also have been applied.

Bloodstains showed that she was facedown then moved from that position to how she was found, faceup.

Cause of death: Strangulation.

Swabs of fluid were taken from her vaginal area.

Sperm was discovered there.

Technology was not yet available to match DNA.

* * *

After interviewing the manager and nearly all the residents of the complex, the officials determined that the dead woman did not live at Illinois Court. They had never seen her before.

Who, then, was this Jane Doe?

Chapter Thirty-three

On Friday night, June 23, 1978, at around eight p.m., Charlotte Lamb, thirty-two, called her close friend James Fraracci and asked if he and his girlfriend wanted to check out a new club in Santa Monica, called Moody's. At the time, both she and Fraracci were attending Santa Monica College and they often spoke on the phone, recommending teachers to one another and sharing class notes as well as going out to clubs, where they both enjoyed dancing, although neither partook in drinking. According to Fraracci, wherever Charlotte went, she attracted nearly every man's attention, with her long blond hair and gorgeous figure. A natural blonde, she had the alluring, sultry look of a young Lauren Bacall.

Fraracci told Lamb that that evening he and his girlfriend wanted to have a cozy night at home, so he begged off. Lamb said she thought she'd go to the club anyway. "Why not?" she said. "You're only young once!"

"Tell me all about it in the morning!" said Fraracci.

On June 24 and again on June 26, 1978, patrol officers in Santa Monica gave a Datsun a citation for being illegally parked overnight in a parking structure on Fourth Street in Santa Monica, less than a block from Moody's.

On Monday, June 26, Lamb's sister Celia called her baby sister to wish her a happy birthday, as she did every year. Lamb did not pick up the phone. Celia called on and off all that day, that night, the next day, and the next night, but Lamb still didn't answer. Celia was surprised, because not only had Charlotte failed to acknowledge the birthday card that Celia always sent her several days before her actual birthday, but also because it was totally out of the ordinary for Charlotte not to be at home for several days.

What was her baby sister up to?

Because the Datsun, three-quarters of a block from Moody's, still hadn't been moved by the twenty-ninth, the cops removed and impounded it.

In 1978, Richard Plasse was a police officer in homicide in the City of Santa Monica. On June 28, he responded to a call to investigate a missing person—Charlotte Lamb—at 2434 Fifth Street, apartment 203. She hadn't shown up at work for several days and no one in her family or at her office had been able to reach or locate her.

When the police arrived, they knocked on the locked door, but they got no answer. They asked the manager if he would let them in.

Once inside, they walked through the place. The apartment was neat and clean. Everything appeared to be in its place. A *TV Guide* was open to June 23.

The detectives needed to find more about this young, seemingly missing woman, Charlotte Lamb. They called her family and friends and put together a profile.

Charlotte Lee Lamb was born on June 26, 1945, in Lexington, Kentucky, the fourth child of a growing family that would eventually number eight kids—six girls, two boys—and a mom and dad. Starting with the oldest, their names were Carolyn, Claudia, Larry, Charlotte, Celia, Colleen, Janie, and Lex. Charlotte was born on her Dad's birthday, and because she was such a sweet-tempered baby, he nicknamed her "Shug," saying she was "sweet as sugar."

Shug's father was a tenant farmer, a job that included working on a farm for a small wage, a house (sometimes without electricity or running water), a cow to supply milk for the family, and ample space for a garden and chickens. The family didn't live too long at one location with a few exceptions, due to the wanderlust of Mr. Lamb or his dissatisfaction with his jobs. Shug's mother was a stay-at-home mom and tried to make life tolerable with what little she had. She was a superb cook, baking biscuits every day. She knew every wild edible plant that would provide a big pot of "greens" for the family. In the winter she made "snow cream," since they had no refrigerator. Snow cream "sea foam" was made by mixing fresh milk, sugar, and vanilla into a huge bowl of snow. "Mama wouldn't use snow from the first snowfall," said Celia. "She felt there were too many impurities in the air. She felt the second snowfall was much cleaner." Mrs. Lamb also often made her specialty, "sea foam candy," by beating hot sugar syrup into a bowl of freshly beaten egg whites until the mixture became stiff, then spooning it out into individual pieces and allowing it to cool. "Needless to say," remarked Celia, "we could hardly wait until this delectable sweet treat cooled!"

When Charlotte was three years old, the family moved from Kentucky to Ohio and lived on several farms before finally moving to Troy, Ohio, where they settled for several years. They were poor growing up in Troy, and never had many extras. Halloween was their favorite time of year because on that day they always got plenty of candy, which they would all share with one another.

Farm life provided wonderful opportunities to play outdoors and to have pets. Shug loved animals, especially cats and Pal, a beautiful Collie and the family's watchdog and playmate for the children. Shug was a gentle, compliant child, with a sunny disposition.

Shug enjoyed school and was a good student, although she wasn't particularly athletic. She was rather shy and had an endearing little laugh. She was also kind and compassionate and would give you the blouse off her back, if you asked. One time in LA, an elderly man took his wallet out of his pocket and all his bills flew about. No one moved to help the man except Lamb, who ran this way and that to make sure he got all his money back.

As Charlotte grew older, she regularly visited an elderly neighbor who had moved into a nursing home, making sure to always bring a gift and some good cheer. At school, she was consistently on the honor roll, excelling most in shorthand and spelling.

In the eleventh grade, Charlotte took a job in the local dime store to help pay for expenses. In her senior year she worked as a part-time secretary at the law firm of Miller & Bazler. She enjoyed working for lawyers because she could use her shorthand and typing skills. She was also a skilled seamstress and in her spare time would sew dresses and shirts. She liked to paint and sang beautifully.

Despite the crushing poverty and the binge drinking of the father, there was always music in the home. Shug's dad was a masterful harmonica player and had perfect pitch. Her mother was always singing hymns that she'd learned as a child at church, and it wasn't long until Shug learned to harmonize with her sisters. She had a lovely alto voice, and later sang with her older sisters in a trio at church.

After high school, when Charlotte had just turned eighteen, she left Ohio with her boyfriend and headed out for California to live in a more exciting place than the Midwest. It was an adventurous move, and the couple thrived for some time. In time, however, the romance faded and they both went their separate ways.

Over the years, Charlotte had gone home whenever she had vacation time. All her siblings would beg her to move back home, but she'd laugh her cute little laugh and say, "Oh, I'd be bored stiff." Even so, her siblings felt that she had many lonely times in California and missed them all, especially around the holidays. Shug called at least one of the siblings weekly and they'd share their chats with the other family members.

The entire Lamb family loved seeing Shug and listening to her stories of life in LA, where she worked as a legal secretary, a job she loved. It seemed that her visits were always too short, but Charlotte was eager to get back to her home on the coast, where she soaked up the sunshine and the laid-back lifestyle, but also enjoyed her job, her friends, and her studies.

Charlotte's apartment was just five blocks from the beach and the bikeway that led to Venice, where people roller-skated in their bathing suits and outdoor vendors sold funky jewelry and crafts. If location is everything, Charlotte Lamb's life was idyllic.

But where was she, Lamb's family, friends, and the police wondered. *Had she met someone? What could have prevented her from returning home that night after she went to Moody's?*

Before long, investigators connected Lamb's disappearance to the bloody murder in El Segundo, thirteen miles south of Lamb's home. Late on the night she went to Moody's, someone had lured her or forced her to go with him, instead of returning to her car.

That same evening, while Lamb was enjoying herself at Moody's, Rodney Alcala was driving around the neighborhood and decided to stop off at the same bar, a place he often frequented, just to see what the night might have to offer there.

In the same month that Charlotte Lamb was murdered, police in New York City located the body of Ellen Hover—or what was left of it. Eleven months after Hover mysteriously disappeared from her Manhattan apartment, her skeletal remains were discovered in a shallow grave in North Tarrytown, on the vast Rockefeller estate in Westchester County. The remains were confirmed to be Hover's by dental records and the identification of two rings, an ankle bracelet, and a barrette. This discovery was no accident. After the FBI interviewed Rodney Alcala in December 1977 and he admitted to seeing Hover the day of her disappearance, the NYPD Missing Persons Squad began interviewing people who had known Alcala in New York. They received a tip that Alcala liked to watch the sunset from cliffs above the Hudson River, just north of the city. Detective Donald Tasik of the Missing Persons Squad honed in on a six-hundred-acre tract of dense woodland as the most likely spot, and doggedly combed the woods in search of evidence. Although he was out of the NYPD's jurisdiction, Tasik visited the woodland site twenty-four times before finding a pair of women's underwear and a bra that he presumed had belonged to Hover. Days later, while searching the nearby area with a garden hoe, he uncovered bones.

After the news broke, a young, attractive, single woman called the New York City detectives. She stated that she had posed for a photo session with a photographer named Rodney Alcala on the Rockefeller estate, almost exactly where they were saying the remains of Hover were found.

Could this be the break the authorities were looking for?

Chapter Thirty-four

According to homicide and forensic expert Vernon Geberth, a particularly heinous subgroup of serial killer is labeled a "psychopathic sexual sadist." "Psychopathic sexual sadism," he said, best describes offenders who "obtain intense sexual arousal while sexually violating their victims. To achieve sexual gratification, they engage in sexually sadistic activities such as biting, torture, mutilation, and/or killing."

According to the *DSM-IV*, "sexual sadism" is defined as: "over a period of at least six months, recurrent intense sexually arousing fantasies, sexual urges, or behaviors involving acts (real, not simulated) in which the psychological or physical suffering (including humiliation) of the victim is sexually exciting to the person."

Psychopathic sexual sadists enjoy torturing and inflicting pain on their victims, said Geberth. They have no empathy for their victims as human beings. For them, "their victims are simply objects to be used to satisfy their cravings. The victim's pleading and begging for mercy only further stimulates the sexual sadist in inflicting pain and torture. Psychopaths do not value human life nor can they relate to a victim's suffering because they are unable mentally to create a human facsimile of another being. They are totally into themselves with an overwhelming need for power and control. They have no remorse and justify their actions by minimizing and degrading their victims as they satisfy a perverse sexual lust.

When they are done with them, they are simply disposable trash."

A classic example of the sexual sadist, said Geberth, is one who "tortures victims by strangling them, then letting them breathe, and then strangling them again. This type of offender is *extremely* sadistic."

Sexual sadists are "collectors," said Geberth. "There is an element of compulsivity as well as an obsession on the part of the sadist to keep trophies of the successful 'hunt,' as a reminder of the event (providing the killer with a psychosexual memento) as well as to record the events." Earrings, necklaces, rings, photographs, clothing, shoes, and other "trophies" serve as "engrams, or mind pictures, which sexual sadists conjure up in their imagination or fantasy."

Sexual sadists rely heavily on fantasy and ritual to obtain sexual satisfaction, continued Geberth. To satisfy a perverse sexual fantasy, some sexual sadists manipulate the victim's body by posing it or propping it up, or by performing sexual mutilation or evisceration. These activities are done out of anger or revenge to further degrade the victim.

Psychopathic sexual sadists are experts at compartmentalizing, said Geberth, allowing them to feel insulated from the suffering of their victims. In psychology and in criminal profiling, Geberth stated, "compartmentalization" is defined as "the ability to split parts of our psyche, inhibiting them from mixing together. It provides the offender with insulation from the reality of the horror they are capable of by isolating events into compartments."

Mark Safarik of the FBI noted that sexual sadists tend to be above average in intelligence. "They plan and organize their crimes; they are hard to catch; they are often more evidence-conscious than other killers." Their downfall, stated Safarik, comes from their narcissistic view of themselves: They believe they are simply smarter than the cops and will not get caught. "With this view, these killers keep items from their victims as trophies or souvenirs because, after all, the cops won't be smart enough to figure out who the killer is. To them, there is no need to dispose of very incriminating evidence."

Many sexual sadists "pose" or "display" their victims, added Safarik. He was quick to point out that "posing" and "displaying" are sometimes mistakenly labeled "staging," which, according to forensic psychologists, is defined as "the intentional and purposeful manipulation of the behavior and/or forensic evidence found at the original crime scene."

According to Safarik, staging at a crime scene is "an effort by the offender to create a 'new' or different scene and a 'new' motive for the purpose of misdirecting the investigation *away* from himself. The offender attempts to overwhelm what would otherwise be a law enforcement investigator's logical inference regarding what occurred."

Most commonly, sexual sadists *pose* the dead bodies of their victims to further fulfill a sadistic fantasy or for the purpose of degrading the victim.

Sexual sadists lack empathy and remorse, which allows them to go on after a murder as if nothing happened, said Safarik: "[They] have none of the usual indicators that would create great turmoil within us, eventually manifesting itself in some recognizable problematic behavior."

After killing, they just go back to being their regular, charming selves.

Chapter Thirty-five

"It's *The Dating Game*!" boomed the voice of Jim Lange on September 13, 1978, as he welcomed the audience to the wildly popular weekly TV show. "It's time to meet our three eligible bachelors . . . and heeeeerrrrrrrrrre they are!"

The camera cut to a shot of three bachelors in silhouette sitting on stools, waiting to be introduced.

"Bachelor Number One is a successful photographer who got his start when his father found him in the darkroom at the age of thirteen, *fully developed*. [laughter] . . . Please welcome Rodney Alcala."

The audience applauded as the camera alighted on the handsome, smiling face of Alcala, poised on the stool farthest to the left, wearing a wide-lapeled brown leisure suit, a gold chain, and a white shirt with the top buttons undone. His hair was dark and curly and cascaded down to his shoulders. He appeared confident and relaxed. He was ready to have fun.

After introducing the other two bachelors, Lange brought out the bachelorette. "Here's a young lady [who] . . . once earned a living massaging feet, but she quit when her boss suggested that she work her way up." [laughter] Lange said that the attractive school teacher from Phoenix would "educate our three bachelors in the art of *amour*. Welcome . . . sensational Cheryl Bradshaw."

Bradshaw walked on stage. A brown-haired, brown-eyed, wide-smiling young woman, she wore a colorful dress that came down almost to her ankles, with a dramatically plunging neckline. As she took her seat, she showed plenty of leg.

Lange explained the rules. Bradshaw could ask the bachelors anything except their names, professions, ages, or what they earned. He then invited each bachelor to say hello.

"We're going to have a great time together, Cheryl," said Bachelor Number One.

Bachelors Number Two and Three gave Bradshaw big hellos.

Bradshaw then began her questions. In a slow, drawn-out voice, with emphasis on any word that might have a sexual implication, she proceeded to question and banter with her would-be dates:

She asked Bachelor Number One what his *best* time was.

"The best time is . . . nighttime."

"Why . . . ?" Bradshaw asked.

"Because that's the only time there is," responded Alcala in a smooth, flirty voice.

". . . What's wrong with morning, afternoon?"

"Well they're okay, but nighttime is when it really gets good. Then you're really ready."

The audience loved it. They applauded wildly.

After asking the other two bachelors some questions, the young drama teacher announced that she wanted to "audition each of you for my *private* class. Bachelor Number One: You're a dirty old man," she said in a phony dirty-old-man voice. "Take it."

Alcala immediately made a guttural-sounding growl, and then responded with a smirk, "Come on over here. Grrrrr. Grrrr. Take it." He didn't sound much like an old man, but it was plenty dirty.

Bradshaw laughed hysterically. Apparently, she loved the answer.

"I am serving you for dinner," she later told Bachelor Number One.

"What are you called, and what do you look like?"

Without a second's pause, Alcala said, "I am called the banana and I look really good."

Bradshaw seductively asked him to be "more descriptive."

"Peel me!" responded Alcala. The audience went wild.

After a short commercial break, Lange asked Bradshaw who she was going to choose for her date.

There was a moment's suspense before Bradshaw answered.

"Well, I like bananas, so I'll take number one."

The audience seemed delighted with Bradshaw's choice, as they applauded heartily.

The camera panned to Alcala, who smiled his broadest smile yet. He had perfect camera-friendly white teeth.

Bradshaw held her hands in prayer, hoping the man she had chosen but not yet laid eyes on, would be the man of her dreams.

Lange then told Bradshaw that the man she chose liked to skydive and ride motorcycles and obviously has "a lot of nerve." Plus, Lange reminded her, he's a talented photographer. "Say hello to Rodney Alcala!"

Alcala walked confidently over to the bachelorette—in his fashionable, tight-fitting leisure suit. He gave her a peck on the cheek and put his arm lightly around her shoulder. The two looked at each other for a long moment, both seemingly happy with the choice that Bradshaw made.

After Lange told the couple that their date would include tennis lessons and a roller coaster ride at Magic Mountain, the show then cut to a commercial. Left in the audience's mind was that the two would go on their date and with any luck, live happily ever after together.

PART VI

PART

IV

Chapter Thirty-six

In 1979, Margaret Thatcher was elected prime minister of the UK.

John Wayne died.

Sixty-three Americans were taken hostage in the American Embassy in Tehran, Iran.

China instituted the one-child-per-family rule to help control its exploding population.

Trivial Pursuit was launched.

The Deer Hunter won the Academy Award for Best Picture.

Billy Joel won the Grammy for Best Album of the Year for *52nd Street*.

Fifteen-year-old Monique Hoyt was brutally raped on February 14.

Jill Parenteau, twenty-one, was viciously murdered on June 14.

Twelve-year-old Robin Samsoe went missing on June 20. Her skeletal remains were found on July 2.

Chapter Thirty-seven

On January 12, 1979, Karen Mandic, twenty-two, and Diane Wilder, twenty-seven, students at Western Washington University, went missing. Wilder was majoring in dance; Mandic, in business administration. Their bodies—strangled, mutilated, and raped—were found eighteen hours after the young women were last seen, not in the hillsides around the LA area, but in Bellingham, Washington. However, because the two women's murders were eerily similar to those attributed to the Hillside Strangler, the police felt it was possible that the Strangler had expanded his "territory."

But in addition to the disparate locations, another factor was startlingly different: Whoever did the Bellingham killings was incredibly sloppy. He left many clues behind.

Luckily for the authorities, all the clues led directly to one man.

Kenneth Bianchi was born in Rochester, New York, in 1951, to an alcoholic prostitute, who gave him up for adoption when he was two weeks old. When he was three months old, Kenny was adopted by Frances Scioliono and her husband, Nicholas Bianchi. Early on, said Scioliono, Bianchi showed signs of mental illness. He was a compulsive liar, had long trancelike daydreams, had a quick temper, and was an underachiever, even though he was of above-average intelligence. At five years of age he was diagnosed with petit mal seizures. (A petit mal seizure is a kind of seizure that lasts an average of ten to twenty seconds, during which the person abruptly stops his or her activities and stares blankly or loses consciousness). At ten, he was diagnosed with passive-aggressive personality disorder (according to the *DSM-IV*: "a pervasive pattern of negativistic attitudes and passive resistance to demands for adequate performance").

After graduating from high school, he married his high school sweetheart, but the marriage was annulled after only eight months. Neither was mature enough to make the marriage work.

Bianchi tried attending college but dropped out after one semester. He soon landed a job as a security guard at a jewelry store. As it turned out, this offered him a great opportunity to engage in petty thievery.

In 1977, at age twenty-six, Bianchi decided to move to LA to spend time with his older cousin by seventeen years, Angelo Buono, also born in Rochester. By the time the two got together, Buono, a self-described ladies' man, already had a long rap sheet that included failure to pay child support, grand theft auto, assault, and rape.

The two cousins set up a flourishing business in LA. They worked as pimps, sharing the belief that women should be put in their place. One way to do this, they believed, was to murder them. They posed as undercover cops to trick prostitutes into getting into their car, and with other victims they used ruses, such as asking for directions, to lure them close enough to grab them and then shove them into their vehicle. However, before strangling a woman to death, the two would sexually abuse and torture her, sometimes giving her lethal injections and electric shocks.

In May 1978, after a violent argument between the cousins, Bianchi decided to leave Buono and head to Bellingham, Washington, where his girlfriend and their infant son lived. At first Bianchi seemed to adjust well to the more "normal" lifestyle in the Pacific Northwest, but he soon became dissatisfied with the love and attention of an adoring girlfriend. He began to look elsewhere for kicks.

On January 11, 1979, Bianchi went on the hunt. He hit the

jackpot with two students from Western Washington University, Karen Mandic and Diane Wilder, whom he duped into thinking they were applying for a house-sitting job. However, without the cunning of his cousin Buono, the "brains" behind the previous murders, Bianchi left behind clues at the crime scene—including a piece of paper with his name on it in Mandic's car.

On January 14, after Bellingham investigators had spoken with LA detectives about the similarities between Mandic's and Wilder's deaths and the many Hillside Strangler murders, LA detectives headed up north and, together with Bellingham police, paid a visit to Bianchi's home to have a chat. When they arrived with a search warrant, they saw a large turquoise ring and a gold ram's-horn necklace, both of which matched the descriptions of jewelry worn by Hillside Strangler victims Kimberly Martin and Yolanda Washington.

Bianchi was immediately arrested.

On January 26, 1979, the police charged Bianchi with two counts of first-degree murder for the killings of Mandic and Wilder.

To save himself from the death penalty, Bianchi cut a deal to get a life sentence instead. In return, he agreed not only to plead guilty to the two murders in Bellingham but also to provide information about the serial killings of at least ten women in Los Angeles *and* to give details about and testify against Buono, his "Hillside Strangler" accomplice.

Finally, the Hillside Strangler—strangler*s*, it turned out—had been caught.

On October 31, 1983, Angelo Buono was convicted of nine Hillside Strangler murders and received nine concurrent life sentences without the possibility of parole. Kenneth Bianchi was convicted of five Hillside Strangler murders he had pleaded guilty to. He was sentenced to 118 years in prison.

When Bianchi's girlfriend, Kelli, was told that her boyfriend was implicated in a series of murders, she was shocked. She couldn't believe that someone "as kind and gentle as

Kenny could be a suspect in a murder case." That sentiment was echoed by Bianchi's employer, who proclaimed that Ken was a valuable member of his business.

No matter how many times the cousins were interviewed that year and the following years, Bianchi and Buono continued to deny having had anything to do with the murder of one young woman whose corpse had been found near Mulholland Drive in 1977.

Jill Barcomb's death was thought to have been their handiwork. She had been strangled, sadistically beaten, and horrifically posed—just like many of Bianchi and Buono's victims. The two Hillside Stranglers declared, however, over and over again that Jill Barcomb had *not* been among their prey.

It is an old saying that the best place to hide a tree is in a forest. It appeared that a homicidal maniac could hide surprisingly easily in California in the 1970s—in a "forest" filled with other predators.

Chapter Thirty-eight

Pasadena is an energetic and diverse city in Los Angeles County, host to the annual Rose Bowl football game and the Tournament of Roses Parade, a lively festival of flower-covered floats with more than one hundred thousand blossoms on each. A thriving and magnetic place with orange trees and an overdose of natural beauty, Pasadena is bordered by the San Rafael Hills and the San Gabriel Mountains, and is located ten miles east of the downtown LA area.

It was there, on one of its downtown streets, on February 13, 1979, that Monique Hoyt, age fifteen, was hitchhiking when a "charming, nice, mild man" pulled up in his car next to her.

"Hey," he called out. "Wanna pose for some photographs? It's a contest. We could be winners!" Flattered that the man thought she was pretty enough for a contest photo, Hoyt hopped in the car. At that time in her life, she was a runaway, game for practically anything, and this sounded like fun.

The man was chatty and had tons of photography equipment in the car. To Hoyt, he looked like the real deal. The man said his name was Rodney Alcala. She introduced herself. "I'm Monique Hoyt."

They first drove to Alcala's mother's house, where Alcala was living. Alcala told Hoyt that he needed to pick up more photography equipment. By now, however, the sun was going down and it was too late for taking pictures, so the two spent the night in Alcala's home.

COS J2ANBR2

NO POSTAGE
NECESSARY
IF MAILED
IN THE
UNITED STATES

BUSINESS REPLY MAIL
FIRST-CLASS MAIL   PERMIT NO. 349   HARLAN IA

POSTAGE WILL BE PAID BY ADDRESSEE

COSMOPOLITAN®

PO BOX 6059
HARLAN IA 51593-3559

COSMOPOLITAN ®

Best Deal!

☐ 1 year just $15
Or text 12COS to 467467

☐ 2 years only $28
Or text 24COS to 467467

NAME _____ (PLEASE PRINT)

ADDRESS _____ APT _____

CITY/STATE/ZIP _____

EMAIL _____

☐ **Payment enclosed**   ☐ **Bill me later**

Continuous Service Guarantee: Your subscription will continue unless you ask us to stop.
Each year you'll receive a reminder notice followed by an invoice for the low renewal rate
then in effect. You can cancel at any time and receive a refund on all unmailed issues.

For faster service order online at order.cosmopolitan.com

The next morning Alcala and Hoyt drove to a deserted area in the mountains outside of Banning, in Riverside County, around eighty miles east of downtown LA, where Alcala said he wanted to take some photographs. They parked the car and began walking. After fifteen minutes or so, and now deep in the woods, Alcala finally came to the location he was looking for.

With camera poised, he began taking shots of Hoyt. Then he asked Hoyt if she would object to his taking some nude photographs. Alcala then took many shots of the young girl naked.

Finally Alcala asked Hoyt if he could shoot some silly pictures of her.

"Let's see," he said. "Pull your shirt up over your face."

Hoyt did as she was asked. Just as she got her T-shirt over her eyes, she felt a whack to her face and immediately slumped to the ground. She could see that Alcala had bashed her head with a tree branch, but then she blacked out.

Sometime later, Hoyt slowly came to. Being a streetwise kid, instead of panicking, her instincts told her not to move or open her eyes but to pretend to be asleep. She began thinking about what had happened and what she could do to save herself. Her first thought was that she should get up and make a run for it. But then the rape began.

First, the man began to bite her genital area and her breasts. She tried as hard as she could not to wince. Instinctively she knew crying out would be a bad move. Then he penetrated her vagina. Then he sodomized her. Unable to remain quiet any longer, she began screaming. Enraged, the man stuffed her T-shirt into her mouth. "Shut up!" he yelled. "Shut up!"

Finally he choked her with his hands until she lost consciousness again.

Sometime later, once again, Hoyt regained consciousness. She wiggled her hands and feet, just to see if she could move them. At once she realized that her wrists and ankles were tied with ropes. She couldn't move.

Opening one eye slightly, she saw that the man was lying

on the ground next to her and she thought she heard sobs. Yes, he was crying. Thinking quickly, she came up with a plan. She decided to act as friendly as she could, hoping that by acting concerned, maybe he would trust her and somehow, some way, she would be able to escape alive.

First, Hoyt told him that she wanted to spend more time with him. She then rolled over on the ropes and touched Alcala on his arm. She asked *him* if he was okay. No answer. "Don't tell anyone what just happened," she pleaded. "Please don't say a word." Again no answer. "Could I stay at your house? Could we go there together?"

Her "reverse psychology" seemed to work. After a few minutes Alcala untied her hands. Hoyt stood up shakily and got dressed, and the two walked back to the car in silence. Although Hoyt's heart felt like a jackhammer in her chest, she tried to hold herself together. It was her only chance.

As the two began to drive back down the mountain, Hoyt remained silent, afraid that anything she might say would touch him off. At some point Alcala stopped the car at an "in-and-out thing" and bought a soda. He then told Hoyt that he had to use the men's room and would be right back. Hoyt said she'd wait for him.

The second he shut the bathroom door, Hoyt made a run for it. She raced to the motel that was next door and frantically began screaming. People heard her and came running. "Call the police. Call the police!" she screamed. "A man kidnapped me. He raped me. Help!"

A motel guest called 911. Meanwhile, others staying at the motel hurried the badly injured girl into a room to wait for the police. Within minutes the cops arrived, but by then the man who had nearly killed Hoyt had sped off.

The police took a horribly frightened, beaten, and hysterical young girl to the station house, where she told the officers what had taken place. They asked her to describe the man. After hearing the description, they offered up a six-pack of photos, all of which had features that resembled the man she was describing. They asked her if any of them looked like the person who had victimized her.

It took only a second for Hoyt to point to one: "That's him! That's the man."

Hoyt had identified Rodney Alcala.

Hoyt was taken to the hospital, where she was treated for bite marks, rope burns, and chest injuries.

Once the detectives knew who they were looking for, they drove to Alcala's mother's home, where they found Alcala lounging in the living room, calm and cool. When asked about his recent past, he told the cops that he had been discharged from parole eight months earlier, after a short stint in jail for marijuana possession. When asked what he had been doing that day, he hemmed and hawed, unable to come up with a plausible alibi. The officers were convinced that they had their man, so they advised him of his rights and placed him under arrest for rape. Alcala put up no resistance. It was February 14, Valentine's Day.

After being taken to the station, Alcala was jailed. According to a book *Perfect Justice* by Don Lasseter, which offered many details about the Hoyt incident, Alcala agreed to a taped interview with the police concerning his version of events. He stated that Hoyt had agreed to be photographed and to "simulate" sex acts with him, and that she had agreed to be tied up as part of the photographic session. Alcala admitted that after a while, when Hoyt began to struggle against the restraints, her consent stopped. Alcala said he then choked her until she became unconscious. He admitted to stuffing her shirt in her mouth so she would stop yelling.

When asked why he had done what he had, he said, "You're in an unreasoning situation. Your brain and you just don't know what to do. . . . You're not reasoning. . . . You're not thinking. . . . I raped her."

Days later, when he appeared before a judge, the prosecutors requested a $50,000 bail. It didn't seem like such a large request for a recidivist convicted child molester and newly admitted rapist. But the judge set Alcala's bail at just $10,000.

Alcala's mother didn't hesitate to come to the aid of her son, believing that there must have been some dreadful mistake. She posted bail and Alcala was let out of jail on March 16.

A trial date was set for September.

Alcala was once again a free man, able to live the kind of life he desired.

At the end of April 1979, Alcala gave two weeks notice to the *Los Angeles Times* that he would be leaving his position there as part-time typesetter in the composing room on May 12. He told his supervisors that he wanted to open up his own photography business and perhaps move to northern California. More likely, he was preparing for his upcoming trial.

And as for the Ellen Hover case, one year after Hover's bones were discovered in Westchester, New York, New York City detectives were still trying to connect Alcala to her death, but they were unable to find any hard evidence to link him. No clues had been left at the scene, and DNA testing was still years in the future.

Chapter Thirty-nine

Jerry Parenteau was sixteen and his sister Deidreann, called Dedee, was nine when they were sitting at the kitchen table one morning in their home in Glendale, California.

"I'm going to have a baby," said their mother casually as she placed freshly squeezed orange juice on the table in front of them. Mrs. Parenteau was nervous about having a child at this time in her life, when other mothers were experiencing midlife crises, but she was nevertheless excited.

Dedee's mouth dropped open. She was over the moon. "Oh, Mommy, really? When? I can't wait! Will it be a girl?"

Totally deadpan, teenage Jerry had an altogether different reaction. "I'd rather have a '36 Ford."

When baby Jill came home, even Jerry was won over. A perfect little girl, Jill became everyone's dream come true, although at first Dedee wished the sweet bundle would do something other than just sleep all day. Dedee loved her little sister and had so much fun dressing her and taking her with her wherever she went. And Jerry, too, adored the baby, in spite of his teenage swagger that sometimes suggested otherwise.

Theirs was a close-knit, middle-class family. Mrs. Parenteau was a perfect homemaker who took great pride in ironing her curtains and rearranging her furniture whenever the mood struck. She prepared fresh-squeezed orange juice for breakfast every morning, a home-cooked dinner at exactly 5:30 p.m., and a special dessert of her own creation each

night. She loved to sew and enjoyed making her daughters'
clothing. When the girls were old enough, Mrs. Parenteau
taught them to sew and knit, and in time, they became almost as expert as she was.

Mrs. Parenteau worked as a part-time hairdresser at Thel-
ma's Beauty Shop in Glendale. On Saturdays, Dedee was put
in charge of taking care of Jill, a "chore" Dedee loved. When
Jill was young, the girls would play together in the sandbox
that their father had built in their backyard. As Jill got older,
the sisters would turn on the radio and dance in front of the
mirror to the latest tunes.

Mr. Parenteau worked as a supervisor in the paint shop of
the Lockheed Corporation, and he never missed a day. A
loving and affectionate man, he would often dance with one
of his girls to a record from "his era," such as the jazz hit
"When My Baby Smiles at Me."

Family vacations were often taken in Minnesota, where
Mr. and Mrs. Parenteau grew up. With a huge extended family, all the aunts, uncles, and cousins had plenty to talk about
and loads of things to do. At Christmas the entire clan would
go caroling after dinner.

When Dedee moved out on her own at age twenty-one,
Jill was only twelve. Jill looked up to her big sister as a role
model and used to visit Dedee as often as she could at Dedee's
cozy apartment, with its slanted ceilings. Jill dreamed of
one day getting a place of her own just like Dedee's—and
just like Mary Tyler Moore's on *The Mary Tyler Moore Show*.

Jill had many friends growing up, but two of her closest
from the time she was in first grade until after she moved
out on her own were Nancy Casserly and Kathy Bowman.
Caserly said, "We were inseparable all through high school.
Jill went on all our family vacations with us and we pretty
much spent alternating weekends at each other's homes. I
had two families growing up, and I felt like the luckiest girl
in the world."

According to Bowman, she and Jill were best friends
throughout junior high school, high school, and even after
Jill moved into her own place. They attended the same Cath-

olic elementary school and church, St. Dominic's. In high school, they both lived in the Eagle Rock section of LA, around eight miles northeast of downtown, where "everyone knew everyone else." Looking back on it today, said Franco (Bowman's married name), "It seems so small-town and old-fashioned but we had so much fun, and I'm so glad we grew up there."

One year the father of a friend of Jill's offered his son tickets to the Academy Awards, and he asked Jill to go with him as his date. Jill was thrilled. She had the perfect dress and the perfect shoes, but she didn't have a "wrap."

"My mother had a beautiful lace tablecloth that my grandmother had crocheted," said her older sister Dedee later, "and Jill folded it and flung it over her shoulders. 'Don't worry, Mom,'" Jill said as she sashayed out the door, "if it gets too late, I'll just say I have to get home and get this tablecloth back on the dinner table."

As Jill grew up, she had transformed from a skinny girl with braces to a knockout, a "fox" who could have any boyfriend she wanted. But, according to Casserly, "Jill never knew the power she could have had." Jill was five feet, six inches tall, neither heavy nor thin, and strikingly beautiful. But not only that, she was gentle, kind, and the most loyal friend a person could have.

Once Jill graduated high school, she started working at Technibilt, Ltd., in Burbank, in the data entry department. She was also attending Pasadena City College, taking business classes. In practically no time, Jill was promoted to supervisor. Although young, she was smart and quick to catch on.

During that time, many of Jill's friends from Eagle Rock hung out a few times a week at the Handlebar Saloon in Pasadena, where bands would play and patrons would kick up their heels. The place was full of locals who all knew the bartenders, bouncers, owners, waitresses, and musicians in the bands. Whenever Jill went to the Handlebar—or anywhere else, for that matter—plenty of men asked her to dance.

With her promotion to supervisor, Jill felt she was now financially able to move into her own apartment. Although her father didn't want to let her go, he knew she needed to spread her wings. Jill, the baby, was the apple of Mr. Parenteau's eye. No matter what adverse situation Jill found herself in, he would always come to her rescue. Once, when Jill was living on her own and there were long gas lines during one of the many gasoline shortages in the 1970s, Mr. Parenteau went to Jill's workplace, picked up her car, drove it to the gas station, and waited in line to fill up her tank so she wouldn't have to do it after work.

Jill first moved into an apartment on the ground floor in Burbank, but at the time she asked the manager if she could move to a second-floor apartment if one became available. She said she'd prefer to live on the second floor because she would feel safer there. Also, the second-floor apartments had the same slanted ceilings as Dedee's apartment did years before—and Jill wanted to be just like Dedee.

Jill did move to a second-floor apartment and, just like her mother, took great pride in her homemaking skills: ironing curtains, puffing pillows, and preparing fresh orange juice every morning.

On June 13, 1979, Dedee called her sister. Jill mentioned that she was going to a Dodgers game that evening with Dan Brady, whom many believed had harbored a crush on Jill since high school. It was Jill and Brady's first and only "date." Dedee was thrilled for Jill. Maybe, just maybe, Jill would see what a great guy he was and . . . No, she couldn't let herself think of that. When it was time for Jill to fall in love, she would certainly know who to fall in love with.

Dedee wished Jill a great time and said she'd speak to her again in a few days.

That night at Dodger Stadium, the game was a cliffhanger, but the Dodgers finally eked it out, 9 to 8, against the St. Louis Cardinals. When Jill got home, she was exhausted but happy. Her team had won.

The next morning Kathy Bowman waited to hear from

Jill. It was a ritual. They would chat before work every day. After not getting her customary call, Bowman decided to phone Jill. Maybe her friend had overslept. When no one answered the phone, Bowman thought that perhaps Jill had gone into work early that morning.

A little while later Bowman left for work. Once there, she called Jill at her office. No one answered. Bowman decided to phone Jill's boss, Sandy, whom she also knew. Sandy said she, too, was surprised that she hadn't heard from Jill, but she assumed that Jill would show up sometime soon.

As the day wore on, Bowman found herself unable to concentrate. Something wasn't right, she just knew it. Bowman and her boss, Richard, who also knew Jill, decided to phone Jill's brother and sister—not Mrs. Parenteau, whom they didn't want to alarm in case it turned out to be nothing at all. But neither Dedee nor Jerry picked up the phone. Finally, Bowman called Jill's office again and asked if Sandy would send a co-worker to Jill's apartment. "Something just isn't right," she said. Jill's co-worker Janet Jordan volunteered to go.

At the same time that Jordan was driving to Jill's, Dedee and her husband Don were driving to work. For some reason Dedee was thinking about Jill and said to Don, "I hope Jill will meet someone and live happily ever after. She deserves that." Dedee then told Don that she felt Jill would make a wonderful mother and wife. "I think that is what she really wants."

Chapter Forty

Gordon Bowers worked as an investigator in the crimes-against-persons unit in the relatively small 150-officer Burbank Police Department, located in Los Angeles County. After taking a call on June 14, 1979, it fell on his shoulders to investigate a dead body at 1921 Peyton Avenue, second floor, apartment M.

Bowers and his team immediately headed out to the location. When they arrived, they found a hysterical Janet Jordan saying that she had gone inside the apartment already and— She couldn't complete the sentence.

The authorities cased the area. Right away they noticed that a louvered window with seven glass panes had been removed and that the screen had been cut vertically and horizontally to make a flap large enough for a person to crawl through. They also noticed that a lightbulb in the stairwell outside the apartment had been unscrewed.

After gaining access to the apartment, the detectives found themselves in a narrow space that led straight to the back of the building. Inside the front door, to the left, was a kitchen and eating area. On the kitchen table lay a Dodgers baseball program along with a purse. Inside it they saw a Dodgers game receipt for the previous night, June 13 at 7:30 p.m. The receipt was torn, indicating that it had been used.

To the right of the kitchen area was the living room. All the furniture looked to be in place. A bicycle was propped against the wall.

The investigators walked farther into the apartment. Toward the back were a bathroom on the left and closets. Nothing out of place there, either.

However, when they looked into the room on the right, the bedroom, they saw what Jordan hadn't been able to talk about.

There lay a nude female, faceup on the floor next to the bed.

Her legs were spread wide directly facing the entrance.

Her shoulders and upper back were propped up by pillows, as if posed.

She had suffered severe trauma to her nose, cheeks, teeth, and head.

Ligature marks rimmed her neck.

Torn and knotted nylon stockings lay by the side of the bed.

Blood-covered blankets, sheets, robe, shoes, and socks were strewn about at the foot of the bed.

A lamp in the pile of clothing was pointing toward her body, the cord running under her body toward her neck.

A long cord from an electric blanket wound under her body up to her neck and then was wrapped around her neck.

A jewelry box lay open on the dresser.

Beautiful, vivacious Jill Parenteau had been slaughtered in her own bedroom.

After crime tape was set up, the officers called for backup.

The scene was photographed and the coroner arrived to remove the body for autopsy.

The coroner recorded these findings about the violence inflicted on Jill Parenteau:

Extensive scalp hemorrhage six inches from side to side, with trauma so severe that she bled into the undersurface of her scalp.

Significant pulling or striking blunt traumas to the head by an object broader than a hammer, or the head slammed against a flatter object, or a human fist used against head.

Knots tied in nylons that created ligature marks on neck;

severe hemorrhaging thorough the area of her thyroid, voice box, and epiglottis. The victim had been strangled so severely that the small blood vessels in her eyes had ruptured.

Bruises to the tip of tongue; bleeding inside mouth; and injuries to the corners of the mouth, consistent with forcible oral copulation.

Deep scratches around both breasts; tooth marks and puncture-type wounds around right breast; puncture wounds below the left nipple and cuts on the left side of the left breast.

Deep wounds to the vaginal and rectal areas.

The coroner concluded that most of the injuries were suffered while Jill was still alive.

Cause of death: Strangulation.

Blood samples were taken from the robe found in the bedroom.

Sperm was found inside the oral cavity.

Semen was found on the vaginal smears.

Inconclusive findings appeared on the anal smear.

In 1979, DNA testing was not yet available to match these findings with a specific person.

When Deedee was called and told about her sister, she broke down in tears. She knew life would never, ever be the same—and it wasn't. Her mother met her at the apartment manager's office and sobbed uncontrollably. Her father was unable to speak. It was simply inconceivable that their precious sister and daughter was dead and that she had died in such a heinous way.

Meanwhile, Rodney Alcala was enjoying life, photographing girls and women at the beach, no longer working nine to five, and giving some thoughts now and then to his upcoming trial in September for the Hoyt "incident."

Chapter Forty-one

On June 17, just days after the discovery of Jill Parenteau's body, an investigation began into vicious attacks that had been perpetrated against three young people in Oxnard, located in Ventura County, to the west of Los Angeles County.

A ten-year-old girl, Robyn Billingsley, had been kidnapped while she was on her way to the beach. A day later she was found beaten and raped but alive in a ravine between Oxnard and Malibu.

Two boys' bodies were dumped in remote areas. Both had been sexually molested.

The residents of Oxnard and the surrounding areas were on high alert that there was a possible serial murderer, a pedophile, roaming the streets of their neighborhood.

Chapter Forty-two

On June 19, 1979, Toni Esparza, fifteen, and Joanne Murch-land, fourteen, were spending the day at Orange County's Huntington Beach, known as the West Coast's longest stretch of clean, uninterrupted beach and the place where epic waves drew in some of the best surfers in the world. As the two roller-skated along after lunch, a man pulled up alongside them. "Hey," he called out, "I'm a photography student. Mind if I take your pictures?"

The girls looked at each other and giggled. No one had ever asked them before if he could take their pictures. "There's a prize for whoever takes the best photo and another one for whoever's in the picture," he continued.

The girls noted an impressive-looking camera held by a wide, colorful strap around the man's neck. Toni whispered to Joanne: "He must be a photographer. Look at that stuff!"

Joanne said, "I guess it could be kind of neat."

"Yeah, why not?" said Toni.

Flattered, the girls decided to let the man take their pictures. What harm could there be? Besides, they might win a prize.

The man got out of his car and told the girls how he'd like them to move in order for him to get the best shots. He asked them to skate toward him, away from him, stand still, move this way, turn their heads that way. For one shot he asked the girls to stand back-to-back with their heads toward each other. Then he asked them to put their heads up, back, next to each other. And then he asked them to face each other, put their hands on their hips, and pose.

They were having fun.

Then the man took a series of seven or eight shots with only Joanne while Toni stood watching.

Having gotten all the shots he needed, he said to the girls, "Can I have your phone numbers in case you win?"

Toni immediately blurted out, "No."

Joanne hesitated.

"No, Joanne," said Toni softly. "I don't think that's a good idea."

"Well," asked the man taking a different tack, "give me your addresses and I'll contact you that way."

Once again Toni said no.

Discouraged but not dejected, the man got back into his car, started it up, and asked the girls, "You wanna go and get loaded?"

Now even Joanne knew this was trouble.

The two skated away as quickly as they could.

Chapter Forty-three

The following day, June 20, Lorraine Werts, fifteen, was spending a fun day at Sunset Beach, northwest of Huntington Beach, with her new friend Patty Elmendorf. When it was time to go home, they began roller-skating toward Seal Beach and the bus stop. When they were just about there, Elmendorf realized that she ought to go to the bathroom before getting on the bus. She told Werts to wait for her right there and she'd return in a minute.

No sooner had Elmendorf skated off when a man approached Werts. "Hey," he said, "I'm in a photography class and can win a prize if I get the best picture of a girl roller-skating. Wanna do it?"

Werts had always been interested in modeling and was flattered that the man wanted to take *her* photo. Since she had a few minutes to kill, she figured, *Why not?*

"Sure," she said.

The man had a very impressive-looking camera. He began shooting pictures of her in her blue bikini as she skated toward him, then away from him. Then he started asking her some personal questions: "Where do you live? Do you have a boyfriend? How old are you?"

Werts instinctively knew something was wrong. Luckily, just at that moment, Elmendorf skated out of the bathroom and saw the man talking to her friend.

"Come on, Lori, we've got to get going," she said. "Come on!"

Relieved, Werts waved a quick good-bye to the man and the two girls skated off.

Early in the same afternoon, twelve-year-old best friends Robin Samsoe and Bridget Wilvert decided to head to Huntington Beach. It was a five-minute walk from Bridget's apartment, and with school out, the girls felt they could finally enjoy themselves at the ocean, something they always loved doing together.

Robin was excited for another reason too: Today would be her first day at "work," answering the telephone at the ballet studio where she had been taking lessons for years but then abruptly had to quit. Her mother, Marianne Frazier, had been in a car accident in April and could no longer afford the ballet lessons that her daughter lived for. It broke Mrs. Frazier's heart, so she worked out a deal with Robin's ballet teacher. Robin was to arrive an hour before her class and answer the phone at the ballet studio in exchange for free lessons.

Robin could hardly wait.

Robin and her mother were extremely close. In fact, Robin idolized her mother and hoped to one day be just like her. But most of all, Robin wanted her mother to be proud of her. One day, Robin promised herself, she would be a ballet star.

In 1979, Robin had just finished the seventh grade at Dwyer Middle School in Huntington Beach, after having moved from Kenosha, Wisconsin, two years before. She presently lived in Huntington Beach with her mother, her two brothers Tim and Robert, and her sister, Taranne. Frazier's sister was also temporarily staying with them after their house in Signal Hill burned down around six months before.

Robin was the baby of the family, the adored golden child, with blond shoulder-length hair and stunning blue eyes. Five feet tall and weighing around eighty pounds, she looked like a poster child for the innocence and health of youth.

Robin arrived at her friend Bridget's apartment at 222 Fourteenth Street in Huntington Beach at around 11:30 a.m.

on June 20, wearing a black bathing suit under white shorts and a red T-shirt that proclaimed: *Here comes trouble.* The irony of the shirt was that the greatest trouble Robin had ever gotten into was when she borrowed her mother's jewelry without asking first.

As usual, the best friends chatted nonstop as they lay out on Bridget's deck until around one o'clock. Then they prepared lunch, ate quickly, and headed off for the two-block walk to the beach.

It was windy as they crossed the Pacific Coast Highway and slid down a ten-foot cliff near the end of Fourteenth Street. Finding a comfy spot, they sat on a small ledge near the service road that paralleled the highway, staring out at the ocean, watching birds, and talking about what they loved to talk about most: gymnastics and ballet. Bridget was a promising gymnast.

As the two were about to jump up and turn cartwheels on the sand, a man with dark, curly shoulder-length hair came up to them, a huge camera dangling from his neck. They laughed at the sight of him. Wearing a plaid shirt and slacks, he didn't look like he belonged at the beach.

Walking over to the girls, the man asked, "Can I take your pictures? It's for a photo class. You two are real pretty!"

Looking at each other, the girls giggled again, then nodded. "Sure. Why not?"

After taking a few shots of both girls, he then leaned in and put his hand on Robin's knee, posing her. He took one photo of her and then began positioning her for another.

Meanwhile, down the beach a short distance away, Jackye Young was lounging on the sand. From afar, she saw that two young girls had been approached by a "very weirdly dressed" man. One of the little girls looked exactly like her niece. Young watched the man as he took some photos, but something didn't look quite right to her. *Why was a grown man taking pictures of young girls?* She decided to investigate.

Crossing the sand and climbing up the cliff, she walked right up to the trio. The man had his back to her and was kneeling, preparing to take another shot. The blond-haired girl, Young realized, wasn't her niece after all, but the other girl, it turned out, was her neighbor Bridget Wilvert.

"And what are you young ladies doing today?" she asked with a decided edge to her voice.

The man was startled. Without turning to look at who was speaking, he immediately stopped setting up for the shot, stood up, and abruptly walked away without saying a word to anyone. To Young, the man seemed nervous as he went off, looking back over his shoulder from time to time.

"The man just wanted to take our pictures," said Bridget innocently.

"Hmm," replied Young. "I'm not so sure that's a good idea."

After giving the girls a slight reprimand for speaking to a stranger and for allowing him take their photographs, the three walked back to Bridget's apartment, and then Young walked kitty-corner to her house.

It was now around 3:10 p.m. and Robin realized it was later than she thought. She absolutely could not be late for her first day answering phones at the ballet studio *and* for her first ballet class in over two months. She asked Bridget if she could borrow her bike so she could get home quickly to change and then ride off to the studio.

"Of course," said Bridget as the two began heading downstairs to the laundry room where Wilvert kept her prized yellow twenty-four-inch boy's Schwinn ten-speed bicycle. But just as they were leaving the apartment, the phone rang. It was Bridget's mother and she needed to talk with her daughter.

"Go on, take the bike," Bridget said as Robin continued walking toward the basement room. "Bring it up to Dwyer tomorrow."

"Sure thing!" responded Robin. The girls planned to meet up at their school the next day.

"Thanks!" yelled Robin. "See you then!"

Robin hurried down to the laundry room, got the bike, and in no time began pedaling home, around a mile and a half away, where she planned to quickly grab her leotard before heading off to Stepping Stones ballet studio in Seacliff Village, on Main and Yorktown. All in all, the bike ride should take around fifteen minutes and Robin would arrive in plenty of time at the ballet studio.

Between 1:00 p.m. and 3:30 p.m. that same afternoon in the same area of Huntington Beach where Robin and Bridget had been hanging out, city surveyor Richard Sillett was meeting with an engineer to discuss plans for creating a bike path on the ocean side of the Pacific Coast Highway at around Tenth Street. While working out some of the details, Sillett noticed a photographer about ten feet away, walking down an incline from the highway to the beach. Since Sillett was himself an amateur photographer, he took special note of the cameras that other people owned.

Sillett was impressed. The man had a 35mm camera with a nine-inch-long—longer-than-average—telephoto zoom lens. *Wow! One day,* he thought, *maybe I'll graduate to such a precision piece of equipment.*

At around five o'clock that afternoon, Robin's ballet teacher, Beverly Fleming, became concerned. Robin hadn't shown up to answer the phone, as she had agreed to do ahead of time, nor had she appeared for class, which was just about to begin. Knowing how much Robin was looking forward to this first day of work and class, Fleming called Robin's home, just to check up.

Robin's aunt answered the phone. She told Fleming that she couldn't understand why Robin hadn't shown up—Robin was *so* looking forward to it—but said she would call Robin's mother, who was at one of the three part-time jobs she held at that time.

Marianne immediately called Bridget's house and spoke to the young girl. Bridget reported that Robin had left her apartment at around 3:10 p.m. on her yellow Schwinn bike. Robin's plan, said Bridget, was to go home, pick up her bag of ballet clothes, and then head off to the ballet studio. She was sure Robin would show up any second.

From Bridget, Marianne got the phone numbers of several of Robin's friends. She decided to make some calls to see if Robin was at any of their houses.

One after another they reported that they had not seen Robin that day.

When Marianne told Robin's brothers Robert and Tim and sister Taranne, they were perplexed. Robin always called ahead of time to say if she was going to be late. Robert suggested that they drive along the route Robin would have taken from Bridget's house and maybe they would see his sister along the way, chatting with a friend. Tim and Taranne combed the neighborhood.

Marianne and her son drove to Wilvert's house and back again—north on fourteenth to Loma, across to Lake, north to Adams, and finally back home to Alabama Avenue.

There was no sign of Robin anywhere along the way.

That afternoon, around fifty minutes away by car from Huntington Beach, Dana Crappa, twenty, a U.S. Forestry Service seasonal firefighter, was reporting to work to begin a five-day shift. To get to her job site, Crappa had to drive up Santa Anita Canyon Road to the forestry fire base, located at Chantry Flats in a remote section of the hills in the San Gabriel Mountains, within the Angeles National Forest. In 1958 the U.S. Forestry Service had built a firehouse with barracks, an information center, and two three-bedroom houses at Chantry Flats to house employees. Crappa was proud to be a U.S. Forestry Service firefighter. She had worked hard to become one of its first female firefighters—and the only one at Chantry Flats.

As Crappa was driving up Santa Anita Canyon Road at around five p.m., and just about to pass Road Marker 11, she noticed a 1976 Datsun F-10 station wagon parked on a turnout. It caught her eye because she owned a similar car. As she looked more closely, she saw something that looked a bit unusual. A dark-haired man seemed to be "forcefully steering" a blond-haired girl toward a dry streambed. The man turned and looked "straight through her," and Crappa got the willies.

However, with plenty of other things on her mind, Crappa soon forgot all about the two-second sighting and returned her focus to the winding road ahead.

By evening Robin Samsoe's family was at their wit's end and called the police. Trying to calm down Robin's mother, the Huntington Beach police suggested that perhaps her daughter had lost track of time; maybe she had decided to go to a friend's house and would be arriving home any minute. The authorities asked her if she would provide them with the names of anyone Samsoe might have visited that day. They assured her that they would follow up and get back to her as soon as they had any information.

At approximately 9:45 p.m., uniformed police officer Gary Christianson responded to 1805 Alabama Avenue, apartment A, and met with the Samsoe family.

Robin's mother reported that Robin had left the house that morning at approximately eleven a.m. to visit her friend Bridget Wilvert and that at approximately five p.m. she (Marianne Frazier) was contacted by her sister, who said Robin had not shown up at the ballet studio for her work session or ballet class.

Frazier said that nothing like this had ever happened before. "Robin is very responsible and would always call if she was in trouble. There haven't been any past family problems and no recent family problems," she added.

Frazier was nearly paralyzed with fear.

At approximately 11:05 p.m., a countywide broadcast was dispatched, "placing Robin as a missing person with suspicious circumstances, as it is not known the exact whereabouts of her nor the reason why she is missing."

* * *

Back at the police department, close to midnight, Officer Christianson filled out a City of Huntington Beach "Missing Persons and D.O.J. [Department of Justice] Entry Form" for Robin Christine Samsoe.

At one a.m. detectives were called in. A general broadcast went out to all Orange County agencies and contact was made with the Huntington Beach Police Department and lifeguards at the city and state beaches. Detectives were looking for something—anything—that might be considered out of the ordinary.

It was official now: Robin Christine Samsoe was a missing person.

Chapter Forty-four

On the morning of June 21, the day after Robin vanished, Detective Craig Robison arrived for his usual shift at the Huntington Beach Police Department (HBPD). Assigned to the juvenile division, his job was to investigate crimes involving youths: vandalism, theft, sex crimes, and missing children. The juvenile division consisted of three detectives and a sergeant. The entire HBPD force had around twenty detectives.

Robison started as a police cadet on March 1, 1971, where he worked patrol, mostly graveyard shifts. In the summer of 1972, HBPD hired Robison as a full-time officer. He was twenty-one and sworn in on September 5, 1972. In 1979, Robison was moved to the detective division. He had just finished law school and taken the bar exam when he became a detective on March 1. Tall and strapping at six feet three inches, he was an impressive figure, with brown hair and striking blue eyes.

As soon as he arrived at the office on June 21, he was told about the missing young girl. Getting right on it, Robison first talked to the officers who had taken the initial report. "We started from square one," Robison said later, "covering the same territory that the patrol officers did," trying to learn everything they could about Samsoe the day she went missing, as well as who was in her family; who her friends and relatives were; if there were any custody issues, disputes, or problems at home; and who, if anyone, might want to do her harm.

At 9:35 a.m., Sergeant Ron Jenkins assigned Detective Jim Bogdonof, Robison's partner, to contact Robin's mother.

Jenkins had been with the HBPD over twenty years. Bogdonof came to the HBPD from the El Monte Police Department and had been an HBPD detective for about a year. He was twenty-seven years old.

After reviewing the report from Officer Christianson, Bogdonof drove to 1805 Alabama Avenue and asked Frazier for more information about Robin.

Sergeant Jenkins sent a press release to all the local papers, including the *Daily Pilot*, the *Orange County Register*, and the *Los Angeles Times*. Bulletins appeared on all the local stations. Back then, media coverage was limited to a region; there was no *Nancy Grace* crime show on cable TV to "unleash the lawyers."

That day, Marilyn Droz received a call from the HBPD asking her to come down to the station right away. As a police artist (also called a composite artist or forensic artist), Droz's job was to create drawings of suspects, aided by the crime victims or witnesses, as well as to prepare sketches of unidentified dead persons, Jane and John Does. From time to time she was also asked to update images of known suspects, a task that included age progressions, additions or subtractions of hair, weight changes, mustaches, and beards. She also sometimes helped prepare facial reconstructions (from the skulls of unidentified skeletal remains) for the coroner's office.

Droz was told that she would be meeting with twelve-year-old Bridget Wilvert, who was prepared to offer specific details about the man who had taken pictures of her and Samsoe the previous day at Huntington Beach.

When Droz arrived at the station, she and Wilvert went into one of the interview rooms. Around eight feet by eight feet, with a table and plastic chairs, the room was lit by two sets of fluorescent lights. The walls were covered in soundproofing.

Droz sensed that she had to treat this twelve-year-old like

an adult. It was obvious that Wilvert was taking her "job" extremely seriously, and the last thing Wilvert needed, thought Droz, was to be talked to in an informal and chatty manner, thus minimizing the seriousness of their purpose.

Droz came to be a police artist almost by accident. While working in communications at the Huntington Beach Police Department in 1976, she came across countless suspect drawings that had been created using the traditional Identi-Kit product. Identi-Kit was a large collection of five- by ten-inch clear plastic sheets. Each sheet had one facial feature—say, a nose, lips, eyes, eyebrows, or chin. The "operator" guided the victim or witness through the various selections for each feature in order to build a face.

According to Droz, "The end product was pretty generic and the composites tended to look pretty much alike."

Droz had been an art history major in college and was already an accomplished portrait artist, a job that required not only artistic talent but also endless patience and strong interpersonal skills. *Why not give this a try?* she thought. *Maybe I can learn to use the Identi-Kit and help the police nab suspects.*

Shortly after completing Identi-Kit training, Droz was asked to create her first composite. It was for a murder case. However, before she began drawing, Droz realized that she had to draw this composite freehand, because the woman with whom she was to speak was paralyzed and in a wheelchair and was going to be hypnotized.

Droz did just that—drew the composite freehand—and it turned out to be so precise and detailed that the police were able to ID the suspect in no time.

Droz had found herself a new career. To become even more adept at creating composites, she took composite artist courses; the FBI forensic art course at Quantico, Virginia; and a facial-reconstruction-from-the-skull course. According to Droz, however, her most valuable training came from drawing dozens of suspect composites and unidentified deceased persons.

As it turned out, Droz never once used the Identi-Kit in

her professional life as a police artist, preferring instead to draw suspects' portraits freehand.

At one point during the interview with young Wilvert, Droz was having trouble with her eraser. It was depositing as much lead on the paper as it was taking off. Droz kept moving the eraser around, looking for a clean spot, but to no avail. When Wilvert noticed Droz's dilemma, she took the eraser from her, leaned over, and cleaned off the entire eraser on the industrial carpeting. "After that," said Droz, "the eraser looked great. The rug . . . not so good." Seeing that the trick was successful, Wilvert smiled (finally) and said, "I do that at school all the time." Since then Droz has used "that trick for over thirty years, leaving a trail of smudges on interview room industrial carpets in police departments all over Southern California. I always think of Bridget."

With Bridget sitting right next to Droz, Droz began asking open-ended questions, making sure she didn't lead the witness in any particular direction. "The approach was standard," said Droz. "It's a slow process, beginning by getting an overall description of the suspect, followed by getting the proportions of the face, which includes the distances between the features. Then we start working on defining the features.

"There is a lot of drawing and erasing while we continue to refine the features," Droz added. "The witness is in a position to see the drawing the entire time and can easily make corrections and suggest additions."

At four p.m. HBPD detective Raymond Hattabaugh began going door to door on Fourteenth Street, where Bridget lived, speaking to people in an attempt to find some leads as to the whereabouts of missing Robin.

Late that afternoon, Alcala changed the carpeting in his Datsun. He told the store manager that he had spilled some gasoline on it and wanted to get rid of the smell.

* * *

That evening, at 7:15, p.m., Bogdonof, along with Detective Keith Nale, went to Bridget's home to interview the young girl. During the interview, Bridget's mother was present and gave permission for Bridget to be brought into the station at nine a.m. the next day to be interviewed further, in the hopes that she could offer more details about what had taken place. While speaking with Bridget, the detectives ascertained that the man who had photographed her and Robin was about six feet tall and in his thirties.

Later that evening, as forestry worker Crappa was returning to her barracks at Chantry Flats, she passed the same area she had passed the previous day. Looking out her window, she was surprised to see the same Datsun she had seen the day before, now parked at Rendezvous Turnout, not far from where it had been. Crappa noticed a man there, leaning against a rock. From a distance he appeared to have dirt or stains all down the front of his shirt. He looked just like the man she had seen the day before. The car looked like it had dirt up under the tires.

Again Crappa felt there was something odd about the scene: *What has that man been doing there all night?* Still, nothing was *that* unusual about a man, dirty, in the mountains, standing alone.

Once again Crappa went on her way, dozens of seemingly more important things on her mind.

At 10:08 p.m. that night, Alcala spoke on the telephone with his girlfriend, Elizabeth Kelleher. He had met Kelleher at a bar in April, and since then they had been seeing each other practically every day. They would go to movies, to the beach, and for long rides in Alcala's car. Kelleher was fascinated with Alcala's photography and in awe of his talent. She encouraged him to take photographs everywhere he went.

Chapter Forty-five

The next morning, June 22, Alcala and Kelleher took a long drive, lounged on the beach, and then took photos of each other. On that day Alcala was sporting his usual long, curly brown hair.

At 11:20 a.m., Robin's mother, Marianne Frazier, and aunt, Elsa Christianson, went to the Huntington Beach Detective Bureau to be questioned by Bogdonof regarding their family background. That same day, the *Los Angeles Times* reported the following: "Huntington Beach police are seeking a 12-year-old girl who disappeared Wednesday morning while riding her bicycle about a mile from her home. Robin Christine Samsoe . . . was last seen by a friend near Olive Ave and 14th St. Police Lt. Bruce Young said the girl has no record as a runaway and was described as a 'very dependable child who liked the beach and studied ballet.' Her bicycle also had not been found."

A headline in the *Huntington Beach Daily Pilot* read, "Huntington Girl, 12, Feared Kidnapped." A picture of a smiling, proud-looking little girl, Robin Samsoe, appeared next to the article.

The article stated that the girl might have been kidnapped after she disappeared "without a trace" while riding a bicycle home from a friend's house. A round-the-clock command post with six detectives working full-time has been assigned to the case, the article stated. A phone number was given for anyone with any information to call. The last sentence of the article noted, "The mother is very distraught."

That evening, on the five o'clock news, the composite drawn by Marilyn Droz was shown on a local television station. Other stations showed the composite later that night.

The composite depicted the heart-shaped face of a young man with slightly narrow dark eyes, strong cheekbones, and a mane of long, dark, curly hair.

Chapter Forty-six

On June 23, Droz's sketch of the "mysterious" photographer who had taken pictures of Samsoe and Wilvert appeared in all the local newspapers, as well as on the TV news programs broadcast on Channels 2, 4, 5, 9, and 11. Flyers were distributed all over the Huntington Beach area. A twenty-four-hour hotline was set up to receive information about the case.

That day Alcala "straightened" his hair using a chemical solution. He had been telling his girlfriend for some time that he was tired of his curly-haired look.

That evening, Sergeant Jenkins and Detective Bogdonof drove to Robin Samsoe's apartment to obtain details regarding any marks or scars that Robin might have. Her mother reported that Robin had a three-and-a-half-inch scar on her abdomen, a nickel-size mole on the back of her right thigh, and a three-quarter-inch scar on the side of her right hip.

While there, the men informed Frazier about the recent abduction and rape of a young girl in Oxnard, as well as the child molestations and murders of the two boys there, in order to prepare her in the event that the news media contacted her regarding the similarities between Robin's disappearance and what had taken place in the Oxnard community.

Chapter Forty-seven

The investigation at the Huntington Beach Police Department was now in full swing. Every morning a meeting was held in the conference room to plan the investigative agenda for the day and to update information that had developed during the previous twenty-four hours. Detectives were fanning out and following up on leads all over Huntington and Orange County and, at times, also in Los Angeles and Riverside counties. The search for Robin had become a team effort. Although Robison was the primary detective, there was way too much information coming in for just one or two detectives to work alone.

As much as she tried, forestry firefighter Crappa was not able to shake the image of the man and the Datsun she had seen several days before parked near Marker 11. *Did she really see something out of the ordinary, or was it just a normal sighting and nothing to think twice about?* Curiosity got the best of her, and on the evening of June 25, between 7:00 and 7:30 p.m., she decided to go back to the spot—just to assure herself that nothing untoward had taken place. After driving to the location, she got out of her car and walked to the ravine, flashlight in hand. No Datsun was parked there, nor was anyone hanging around.

So far, so good. Crappa was relieved.

Expecting—or perhaps praying—to find nothing more nefarious than a discarded candy wrapper or beer bottle in the ravine, she suddenly stopped cold in her tracks. She was stunned by what she saw in front of her.

It was a body.

Her hand automatically went to her mouth.

Crappa willed herself to turn around and return to her car. She could barely breathe.

After sitting stone-still for several minutes, Crappa finally started up her car and returned to the barracks, shaking the entire way.

She didn't tell anyone what she had seen.

Chapter Forty-eight

On June 26, Alcala decided he wasn't satisfied with the straight look. His curls were coming back anyway, and his hair was just too darn long. So he cut it short.

That day, in an article in the *Daily Pilot*, Sergeant Ron Jenkins, referring to the composite drawing, stated, "That's the guy we want to talk to." Jenkins said that there had been many calls from people who said they saw a photographer taking pictures of girls in Fountain Valley, Westminster, and Huntington Beach recently.

The authorities tried to check out every call, but there were so many that they had to prioritize. "We go after the most likely tips first and get around to the others as soon as we can. It just takes so much time," said Jenkins.

Four calls seemed particularly promising. Two came from detectives at the LAPD, who had been working on a serial murder case. They felt that one of their suspects looked eerily similar to the composite.

Two other intriguing calls came from state parole officers, who felt that the composite looked like one of their former parolees. One officer, Dennis McNaught, mentioned that from "the description of him and the business with the camera," it sounded a lot like the parolee he had in mind. He said that his parolee had an abnormal sexual interest in young girls—*and*, he continued, his guy had recently been arrested

Chapter Forty-nine

Robison and his team were now laser-focused on Alcala. After completing a background check, Sergeant Jenkins informed the detectives that Alcala had been "arrested by our department in 1974 for 207 PC of a 13 yr old." The reference to "207 PC" referred to the California Penal Code Section 207, which defined kidnapping as "the use of force or fear to take a person and move him or her a substantial distance." The detectives had just rediscovered the case of Julie Johnson. In 1974, Alcala had offered to drive the thirteen-year-old Julie to school and, instead, took her to a remote Huntington cliffside, where he embarked on an attempted rape—only to be interrupted by a park ranger. Although Alcala was ultimately convicted only of a marijuana charge in this disturbing incident, it had put him back in prison for two and a half years.

Considering that he had been arrested for kidnapping a girl in *their* jurisdiction *and* had recently been arrested for rape in Riverside, Alcala was looking more than suspicious.

Authorities put together a photographic lineup of six similar-looking men and showed it to several people who had called in to say they had seen the photographer and the girls on Huntington Beach on June 20.

To a person, each pointed to the photograph of Rodney Alcala as the photographer in question.

When the two teens Joanne Murchland and Toni Esparza

came to the station and were separately shown the composite drawing, they each stated that the drawing did depict the man who photographed them at the beach on June 19. Then each was shown photographs of various individuals to see if they could identify any of them as the photographer. Murchland saw one that looked like the photographer. She pointed to it.

"That's him," she said definitively.

It was a shot of Rodney Alcala.

Chapter Fifty

On June 28, Sergeant Jenkins detailed detectives Michael Biggs and John Prchal to go to 1370 Abajo Drive, Monterey Park, where Rodney Alcala was living and check for "vehicles in the 207 investigation [kidnapping] which is currently underway."

At approximately 8:45 p.m., the detectives observed Alcala enter a blue Datsun station wagon located in the driveway and drive away. Visual contact was lost after Alcala "abruptly" made a U-turn into a parking lot.

"No further attempts were made to locate the suspect on the night of 6-28-79."

Chapter Fifty-one

On June 29, forestry firefighter Crappa was working on a spraying crew with colleague William Poepke in a remote ravine off Santa Anita Canyon Road, near Marker 11.

As Poepke was doing his job, he came across a pile of bones. Thinking they were the remains of a deer, he picked up a bone and tossed it to Crappa. Although they often fooled around this way, this time, Crappa didn't think it was so funny. She freaked out.

That night, once again haunted, Crappa decided to drive back down to where she had been with Poepke. She wanted to check out the area, just to see if she *really* had seen what she thought she had seen previously.

It was dark by the time she got there, and she took out her flashlight to light her way. In no time, she came upon a pile of bones. Having worked in the mountains long enough she knew they were *not* the remains of an animal.

Horrified, Crappa raced back to her car.

Once again, she was so overwrought that she told no one what she had seen.

Chapter Fifty-two

At approximately 3:50 p.m. on July 2, while working in the same area he had worked in three days before with Crappa, Poepke saw something *truly* shocking. It was a skeleton. And it was the skeleton of a human body.

Immediately, Poepke understood why Crappa had been horrified at his joking bone toss a few days earlier: She had known then what he had not.

A few minutes later Poepke notified his dispatcher of a possible dead body. The dispatcher contacted the Sierra Madre Police Department.

In a short time a team of investigators arrived. When they asked Poepke about what he had seen, he told them that the skeleton was lying in a "dirt gully approximately a hundred and ten feet northeast from Marker 11." Then he told them that he had observed remains at the same location on June 29 at approximately 3:30 p.m. but "at that time, the skull was not present and I thought the torso was that of a dead deer."

As the police began to investigate, their first thought was that Poepke had come upon *just* a "body dump." With discarded beer bottles and cigarettes all around, it seemed this was a place where teens, runaways, and maybe alcoholics and other addicts liked to hang out after dark.

After all, all kinds of people chilled out in the isolated areas of these hillsides.

Chapter Fifty-three

On July 5, detectives Nale, Bogdonof, Prchal, and Robison once again returned to Monterey Park to surveil the residence of Rodney Alcala.

After Alcala got into his car, they tailed him, hoping to find out where he was working. They wanted to speak to Alcala's employers to discover if he had been at work on June 20. Ultimately the officers lost sight of Alcala, who, they reported, was driving over the speed limit.

The surveillance crew returned to Alcala's house, and at two p.m., they saw "an older woman (approx. 60 yrs) leave the Abajo address walking a dog." When she returned, Robison telephoned the residence and identified himself as Craig Robison. He told the woman that he was getting married on Saturday and needed a photographer on short notice. He also told her that he had gotten Rodney's name and phone number from a friend at the *Los Angeles Times*.

The woman responded that Rodney was out and she didn't know when he would be back. Robison pressed for Rodney's work telephone number so that he could reach him today. "He's not working right now," she replied.

When Alcala hadn't returned to his residence by four p.m., the surveillance was called off.

Chapter Fifty-four

Because of the July Fourth holiday, the autopsy of the skeletal remains that were found in Chantry Flats on July 2 didn't take place until July 6.

On that day, Dr. Sharon I. Schnittker, a veteran deputy medical examiner of fourteen years, performed an autopsy on the remains of "Doe, Undetermined: 79-8366."

Schnittker noted the following characteristics about the human skeleton:

Portions of the hands and left foot absent.

Disarticulation of the skull and upper three cervical vertebrae from the remains of the cervical vertebrae.

Remnants of soft tissue present in the jaws, pharynx, left temporal muscle, orbits, surrounding the rib age, lumbar and thoracic vertebrae, vertebral column, pelvis, and remnants attached to the bones of the extremities.

Brownish soft tissue, firm, and mummified.

Extensive evidence of animal erosion . . . hands absent bilaterally, apparently due to animalized erosion.

No tool marks, chop marks, or saw marks where separation of the hands would have occurred.

No evidence of antemortem fracture, trauma, gunshot wound, stab wound, chop wound, or tool marks.

Skull consistent with Caucasoid race; estimated height: 57¼ inches;

No front teeth.

* * *

Due to the advanced decay of the corpse, Schnittker could not establish the cause of death, nor could she ascertain whether or not the person had been sexually molested.

That day, after ascertaining that the skeletal remains were most likely those of a young girl, the Sierra Madre police checked the teletypes and found an HBPD missing-person notification for one Robin Samsoe, twelve years old. They believed that the remains could be hers.

After being contacted by the Sierra Madre police, Robison called Samsoe's dentist, Dr. Brandon, and asked him to provide him with Samsoe's dental records.

That evening, through the dental records, the skeletal remains were positively identified as those of Robin Christine Samsoe. It was news that not one of the detectives on the case wanted to hear.

As of that date, HBPD officially took over the case from the smaller Sierra Madre Police Department.

Although Sergeant Jenkins learned that the cause of death could not be established, he told a reporter at the *Los Angeles Times,* "I don't think a healthy 12-year-old girl walked 50 miles to the hills and then just lay down and died."

Chapter Fifty-five

On the afternoon of July 7, an HBPD investigative team under the leadership of Detective Robison met at Santa Anita Canyon Road at the approximate site where the skeleton had been located. The group formed a search line, like the one Robison had once used when he and a group of lifeguards went searching for a missing person in the water, and began moving together up, over, and through the terrain, looking for clues.

The detectives found many cigarette butts and beer bottles. But they also came upon many areas of discolored ground. These areas smelled *awful*. The knew immediately that these were places where a body had lain decomposing.

As the team moved up the hill, they saw a shoe. Near it was a large, dense bush. As detectives Nale and Robison crawled under the bush's branches, they saw there was an open area underneath.

There they came upon a Kane Kut knife.

Then they saw some blond hair.

A large area of soil was saturated with what were decomposing body fluids.

The detectives surmised this was where Robin Samsoe had died.

Lower down the hill, they found a fingertip.

The detectives surmised that animals had dragged the human remains around the area.

Robison's team collected and photographed:

A one-inch-diameter manila rope in a rocky area, approximately an eighth to a quarter of a mile up the ravine.

A gold chain with stars.

A white cigarette lighter.

Two Colt .45 sixteen-ounce beer cans.

One three-inch piece of bone.

One one-inch piece of black material.

One blue-and-yellow left tennis shoe. Written with a ballpoint pen around the white rubber edge of the shoe and on the canvas were the words:

Robin + Ralph

Karen + Jason

Robin + Ralph

Wendy + Allen.

A large amount of blond hair matted with leaves, grass, and twigs.

One twelve-inch wooden-handled kitchen knife; the knife blade and handle displayed blood, hair, and possibly tissue traces. The blade read "Kane," "Stainless," "Japan."

The fingertip of a human hand.

A rock with a possible bloodstain.

Several Michelob bottle caps and beer bottles.

Chapter Fifty-six

On July 8, after spending a full day with his girlfriend Elizabeth Kelleher, Alcala told her that he was thinking of moving to Dallas to pursue a business opportunity and open his own photography shop. He said that he was sick and tired of LA and wanted a change. Kelleher thought it sounded like a good idea, since she knew how frustrated Alcala was about not being able to earn a living through his photography. Alcala assured Kelleher that he would keep in touch, and if things worked out, he would send for her.

Chapter Fifty-seven

At four p.m. on July 11, Sergeant Jenkins, Detective Robison, and ID technician Tom Rayl went to Robin's home at 1805 Alabama and met with her mother, Marianne Frazier. From the house Rayl collected articles that Robin had touched: dolls, records, and papers.

While there, Robison geared himself for what he thought would be one of the most difficult encounters he would ever have. First he showed Frazier a photo of a gold chain with stars that was found at Chantry Flats. He wondered if it belonged to Robin. The chain did not look familiar to Frazier.

Robison then inquired if Robin had a pair of blue-and-yellow tennis shoes.

After a long pause, Frazier said yes, she did.

"We found one blue and yellow tennis shoe with the printing 'Robin & Ralph,' 'Karen & Jason,' and 'Wendy & Allen' on it."

With her head now in her hands, she quietly said, "That's hers."

Robison felt sick.

That same afternoon Alcala walked into a storage facility owned by Cecil Lockrem and her husband and asked if he could rent a unit. Only one unit was still available, said Lockrem, so if you want it, you better take it now. Alcala grabbed it up right away. Lockrem showed him where it was and gave him the key. She told him he could also lock it with his own padlock.

After putting many of his belongings into the unit, Alcala double-locked it with two padlocks. He then began to look for a place to stay overnight. Luck was on his side and he found a motel in no time.

However, neither the motel nor the storage unit were in Dallas—where he told his girlfriend he was going—but in a city far away in an altogether different direction.

Alcala was in Seattle, Washington.

After staying overnight, Alcala drove back to LA the next morning and went to see Kelleher. He told her that he planned to leave for Texas permanently on July 24. He said he liked what he had seen on his reconnaissance trip.

He told another friend, Leslie Schneider, that he would be leaving for Mexico in a few days.

He didn't mention the Seattle trip to anyone.

Chapter Fifty-eight

Based on tips provided by two police officers, two parole officers, Donald Haines, and several witnesses who picked out Alcala in a photo array—*plus* the fact that Alcala matched the composite—Sergeant Jenkins and his team decided to make a move.

On July 24, at "0500 hours," several officers from the HBPD Crime Scene Bureau "met at the police department for necessary equipment and transportation and then proceeded as previously arranged to 1370 Abajo Drive, arriving there shortly after 0700 hours." Several other members of HBPD were already at the scene, including Jenkins and Robison.

Robison came armed with a warrant to "make search of the premises between the hours of 7:00 a.m. and 10:00 p.m." as well as to search a "1976 Datsun F-10, station wagon . . . and the person(s) of Rodney James Alcala, DOB 8-23-43 for the following items, to wit: photo albums, pictures, slides, film, film canisters, photographic negatives, camera containing film, undeveloped or unprocessed film containing pictures of Robin Christine Samsoe." The warrant also allowed for the collection of various spelled-out items of clothing; a yellow twenty-four-inch Schwinn ten-speed bicycle; any blood, hairs, or fibers; and "soil or vegetable samples indigenous to foothill area known as Chantry Flats."

* * *

Several officers took their positions around the perimeter of the residence. When Alcala's mother, now married to Pedro German, answered the door, the officers announced who they were and stated that they had a warrant. Shocked, German directed the officers to Alcala's bedroom, where the "suspect was in bed, naked." It appeared that they had awakened him.

After Alcala was told why they were there, the officers allowed him to get dressed and then handcuffed him. Right away they transported him to the HBPD for an interview. According to Robison, "There wasn't much conversation at the arrest or in the car on the way to the police station."

Between 7:05 a.m. and 12:45 p.m., Sergeant Jenkins and other officers took part in the search of the house and Datsun. Expert at his job, Jenkins scanned the residence, looking for anything that might pique his interest. His eyes alighted on a receipt for a storage locker on which the following details were written: Safeguard Mini Storage #E-24, Seattle, Washington, (206) 542 1227. Jenkins noted that the receipt was dated after Samsoe had disappeared. Since he had no search warrant to collect the receipt, he knew he couldn't pick it up, but he jotted down the address and the number of the unit. He had a hunch.

The list of evidence the authorities collected that day read:

1 pair Japanese-made handcuffs
Boxes of photos
Envelopes containing mail
Pieces of rope (manila and blue nylon)
8 magazines *Young & Naked*
2 black photo binders (refills)
Plastic slide (35mm) tray & slides
1 frizzy black wig
1 leather bullwhip
1 pair pink panties w/black tape on each side
1 short-sleeve plaid men's shirt
1 pair blue NBA running shoes
camera equipment

a briefcase containing a set of keys
around 1,200 photos, negatives, and slides.

A Kane Kut knife set was discovered in the house, but no knife was missing from the set.

In the Datsun, they found binoculars, photography equipment, maps, a 35-millimeter camera with a colorful strap, and recently installed shag carpeting.

Alcala was booked at the Huntington Beach Jail on suspicion of murder. Although he claimed that he had a solid alibi for June 20—he claimed he was at the Knott's Berry Farm amusement park being interviewed for a job photographing a disco contest—the detectives nevertheless felt that they had their man.

This time bail was set at $250,000.

Tali Shapiro was eight years old in 1968 and on her way to school in Hollywood, CA, when she was lured by Rodney Alcala into his car.

Courtesy of Tali Shapiro

Alerted by a Good Samaritan who had witnessed the abduction, the police found Tali raped and brutally beaten. Alcala had escaped. *Courtesy of the Los Angeles Police Department*

The Barcomb family from Oneida, NY, included six girls and five boys. They knew that a playmate was only a holler away.

Courtesy of the Barcomb Family

Jill Barcomb, born in 1958, was the fifth of the eleven children. She excelled at French, sang beautifully, and played the trumpet.

Courtesy of the Barcomb Family

In 1977, when Barcomb was 18, she was found dead on the side of a road—bludgeoned, raped, strangled, and posed.

Courtesy of the
Los Angeles Police Department

Georgia Wixted was one of three children, including sister Anne and brother Mike. Here she is before Mike's wedding in 1972.

Courtesy of the Wixted Family

On December 16, 1977, Wixted was found dead in her Malibu apartment—bludgeoned, raped, strangled, and posed.

Courtesy of the Wixted Family

Charlotte Lamb, one of eight children, is enjoying a day of outdoor activities with several of her siblings. *Courtesy of the Lamb Family*

Here is Lamb and her mother. Lamb worked as a legal secretary in California.

Courtesy of the Lamb Family

Charlotte Lamb was found dead on June 24, 1978—bludgeoned, raped, strangled, and posed.

Courtesy of the Los Angeles Sheriff's Department

On September 13, 1978, Rodney Alcala appeared on the TV show *The Dating Game*. The bachelorette chose him as her date.

In 1979, at age 21, Jill Parenteau moved into her own apartment in Burbank.

Courtesy of the Parenteau Family

Parenteau was one of three children. Here she is with sister Dedee. On June 14, police found Parenteau dead—bludgeoned, raped, strangled, and posed.

Courtesy of the Parenteau Family

Robin Samsoe was a talented gymnast who loved going to Huntington Beach with her best friend Bridget Wilvert.

Courtesy of Marianne Connelly

Alcala, 36, was booked on July 24, 1979, on suspicion of killing Robin Samsoe. In 1980, Alcala was given the death penalty.

Courtesy of the Huntington Beach Police Department

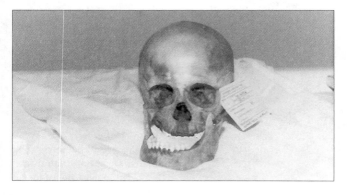

Two weeks after twelve-year-old Samsoe failed to appear at her ballet class, her skeletal remains were found, on June 20, 1979.

Courtesy of Los Angeles County Coroner's Office

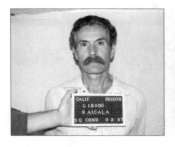

Alcala's second death-penalty trial took place in 1986. He once again received the death penalty. In 1997, he was booked in San Quentin.

Booking photo courtesy of San Quentin

Matt Murphy, Orange County prosecutor, took over the Alcala case in 2003. He credits his successes to help from paralegal Dena Basham (right) and police officer Lisa Hunter.

Photo by DA Investigator Susan Frazier

During Alcala's third death-penalty trial in 2010, DA Matt Murphy showed a composite made in 1979, which helped nab Alcala then.

Michael Goulding, photographer / copyright 2009 The Orange County Register / Reprinted with permission

At Alcala's 2010 trial, Deputy DA Gina Satriano described facial injuries suffered by Alcala's victims. *Michael Goulding, photographer / copyright 2009* The Orange County Register / *Reprinted with permission*

In 2010, Alcala, 66, served as his own defense lawyer against five murder charges. Convicted, Alcala sits on San Quentin's death row. *Michael Goulding, photographer / copyright 2009* The Orange County Register / *Reprinted with permission*

Chapter Fifty-nine

The next morning, Sergeant Louis Ochoa from the Huntington Beach Jail called Sergeant Ed McErlain at HBPD and said that he had listened to a taped conversation between the suspect and his sister, Maria Christine (Krissy) De La Cerda, the previous evening. Ochoa told McErlain that the two had had a conversation about some type of storage shed and he believed he heard that the dimensions were "five foot by five foot by ten foot." Several times during the conversation, said Ochoa, the suspect and his sister would "whisper and switch from English to Spanish."

At eleven a.m. McErlain drove to De La Cerda's home at 602 Brightwood Street in Monterey Park. When asked if she could provide any specific details as to where her brother was on certain dates in June, De La Cerda said she absolutely could. She said that on June 19—the date Alcala was placed at Huntington Beach photographing Toni Esparza and Joanne Murchland—her brother was babysitting for her children starting at eight a.m. "He delivered them between 1 and 1:30 that afternoon to the Auto Auction in Rosemead," where, she said, she had been. She also recalled that on June 20, "when she returned home between 4 and 5 p.m., Rodney pulled into the driveway behind her."

Alcala's mother was at De La Cerda's house that day and she showed the sergeant a telephone bill for the period of June 2 through July 8, 1979. In it, she pointed to a forty-minute call from her residence to the Long Beach home of

Alcala's girlfriend on June 20 at 9:41 p.m. She said her son had placed the call, of course, and that the phone bill provided evidence that he was at home at the time and date indicated on the bill.

That afternoon, at four p.m., William "Bill" McErlain, Robison, and Detective Morris went to Alcala's mother's residence to retrieve the receipt that Jenkins had seen on July 24, the day Alcala was arrested. However, this time, the receipt was not in sight. Alcala's mother stated that she had cleaned out her son's room the previous day, but if they wanted, they "could look through the trash."

The officers did so, but they failed to find the receipt for the Seattle storage locker.

Chapter Sixty

Police were so intrigued by the storage locker receipt that the authorities decided to check it out.

After obtaining a search warrant, Robison and McErlain flew to Seattle on July 26. Then they drove to the storage unit and located the locker in question: E-24. The men noticed that it was secured by two padlocks. The officers pulled out two keys that had been in the briefcase they had confiscated from Alcala's home. The keys opened the locks.

At 5:40 p.m. the men began a thorough search of the locker contents. It took them three hours to complete their job. Among other things, they found:

cold-weather clothing

kitchenware

a red coin purse

several earrings in a jewelry pouch, including a pair of gold rose earrings with a tiny diamond in the middle and a pair of gold ball earrings

boxes containing over 1,700 photographs, negatives, film, and slides, including one marked "Tali VA Rape" and another labeled "Ode to New York by John Berger."

An arraignment was held two days later, on July 26, 1979, in the Municipal Court, West Judicial District, County of Orange, State of California, in *People of the State of California, Plaintiff, v. Rodney James Alcala, Defendant* concerning the criminal complaint filed by "M. Evans, DDA [Deputy

District Attorney]" in Case No. C-42861. The charges against him were kidnapping, lewd or lascivious act upon child under fourteen, murder, and robbery.

Alcala pled innocent to all charges. Judge Engebretsen set a preliminary hearing for August 9 and ordered Alcala held without bail.

Alcala asked the judge for a public defender, which the judge granted after he determined that Alcala's mother had lent him the $2,800 that was on him when he was arrested.

If convicted of murder, Alcala could face the death penalty.

Alcala still faced trial in Riverside County on forcible rape and assault charges with intent to "commit great bodily harm" for the attack on Monique Hoyt that had occurred on February 14.

However, a *Los Angeles Times* article of July 28 stated that authorities "all but cleared" Alcala in the June 17 attack near Oxnard, in Ventura County, of Robyn Billingsley, who was found alive in a ravine, beaten and raped. It was determined that Alcala was not in the Oxnard area on the seventeenth.

Chapter Sixty-one

On August 1, Marianne Frazier went to the HBPD at Robison's request to view the women's jewelry that was recovered from Alcala's storage space in Seattle.

Seeing a particular pair of earrings, Frazier told Robison that she owned a pair of gold ball earrings similar to those, with the same modification on them that she said she had made using nail clippers. She said she would go home and check her jewelry box to see if they were still there. Frazier told Robison that Robin was at an age when she was always getting into her clothes, jewelry, and perfume, and she could have been wearing some of her jewelry without her mother's knowledge.

Later that day Robison "telephoned Mrs. Frazier to see if she located the earrings. She told me that she had looked everywhere she could think of but could not locate the earrings." Mrs. Frazier repeated that "she did have a pair of earrings exactly like [the ones from the Seattle locker], and she could not find them."

Chapter Sixty-two

On August 2, one month after Robin Samsoe's remains were located, the Huntington Beach police asked forestry worker Dana Crappa to come down to the station.

Once there, Crappa was shown several photographs—of Alcala, of Samsoe, and of Alcala's Datsun F-10. After thinking for a moment, she told the officers that she had never seen the man or the girl before. However, she remarked that the Datsun looked familiar. She thought she might have seen it on either June 7 or June 14 between 9:30 and 10:00 p.m. near Mile Marker 11. She felt it had to be on one of those two dates because she nearly collided with the car as she was going back to the fire station the night a firefighter friend of hers had made a special pizza dinner. When asked if the date could have been June 20 or 21, Crappa stated it "definitely could *not* have been."

On August 7, Crappa was once again asked to come down to the station. This time, when she was asked if she could pinpoint the date she had seen the Datsun, she revised the date from the one she had previously given authorities. This time she said it *had* to be June 21 and it was *definitely* between 8:00 and 8:30 p.m. She knew this for sure because she correlated the event to the evening on which she bought groceries and paid for them with a check.

Crappa also claimed to have known nothing about the

crime or the crime scene until the corpse was discovered on July 2.

On Tuesday, August 14, Chris Strople, the deputy public defender assigned to defend Alcala, was taken off the case because he had been told that Alcala had made confessions about Robin Samsoe's abduction and murder to three inmates. Because these informants were also being represented by Strople in another case, a conflict of interest arose and Strople had to step down.

Immediately, John Barnett was appointed to take over as Alcala's public defender. Barnett was a young attorney who had just left the public defender's office and started his own private practice. Barnett said he would seek a new date for Alcala's preliminary hearing because he needed more time to study the case.

Chapter Sixty-three

Preliminary hearings on the Samsoe case began in September 1979.

During one hearing, Crappa told a different version—her third—concerning the day and time of night she saw the Datsun parked on the side of the road. She now reported that it was between 10:00 and 10:30 p.m. on June 21. When asked if she had seen anybody in or near the car, she responded that she had not.

Crappa also informed the police, after the preliminary hearings but before the trial, that she first saw the corpse on June 29—a new bit of information. At that point, Crappa said, the corpse was decomposed and without any flesh.

West Orange County municipal judge John Wyatt ordered Alcala to stand trial on kidnapping and murder charges on October 4.

Alcala was also expected to appear in court in Riverside County that month to face charges of the rape and assault of Monique Hoyt with intent to commit great bodily harm.

However, on the appointed date, Hoyt failed to appear in court. Deputy DA Daniel Bacalski surmised that Hoyt was uneasy about testifying against Alcala after a judge ordered her to have a psychiatric examination.

It seemed as if the sun that had once shone so brightly on Alcala was passing behind many different dark clouds—and that very soon a thunderstorm would erupt.

PART
VII

Chapter Sixty-four

In early 1980, Dana Crappa, no longer a firefighter, was attending community college, hoping to get her life back on track. For the past six months she had been emotionally racked about what she had seen—or thought she had seen—the past June in the mountains near her forestry barracks. In fact, at one point during the fall, she had become so distraught that she suffered a nervous breakdown. She simply couldn't shake the feeling that *perhaps* if she had spoken up sooner, she could have saved the life of the young girl.

In February, Crappa approached one of her college instructors and asked him a question. "What if someone had seen something . . . and didn't say anything about it . . . and . . ." Crappa trailed off. She needed to talk about something awful that had taken place, she said, but she wasn't able to.

After giving the situation some thought, the instructor contacted the Huntington Beach Police Department, and Detective Robison suggested that Crappa talk to his friend, Art Droz. Art, a detective in the HBPD sex crimes unit and the husband of police artist Marilyn Droz, had already been assigned to the Samsoe case.

Droz, Robison told the college instructor, "has great interpersonal skills as well as a background in crime work. He might be able to help out." Although the instructor knew that Droz was a detective—and that Crappa didn't want to talk to any police officers—he nevertheless felt that Crappa was in such great need of help that she should speak to him.

The college instructor set up the meeting.

On February 7, Crappa first met Droz at the college. At the time she didn't know he was a detective. Psychologist Larry Blum was also present. Blum was connected to the county's juvenile diversion program, serving as their consultant and specializing in juvenile and adolescent problems. "It seemed natural and appropriate to have him be present during the interviews," said Droz, even though, at age twenty-one, Crappa was a bit older than a juvenile. "It was apparent that Crappa was having problems dealing with what she had seen and could not talk about it."

Crappa related a story about seeing a Datsun on June 21, 1979, and in a dream "she saw a man, who may have been wearing Levi's and a white shirt, sitting on a wall near the Datsun F-10." She made certain that Droz understood: "I don't know if I really saw it or if I just think I saw it."

Crappa also told Droz that on the night of June 29, 1979, when she and a co-worker were spraying fire retardant in a brushy area, her co-worker tossed her a long bone, "like an arm." In the evening she returned to the spot and had seen the decomposed body of a child near Mile Marker 11, with "clothes strewn about the area, a 'crusty' knife in a hole, and six .22 caliber bullet casings on the ground, which she picked up and threw away." She said that the remains were "pretty well decayed," "beyond recognition," and had no flesh.

On February 11, Crappa again met with Droz at the college. After being urged to talk about her feelings concerning what she had seen or thought she had seen in the mountains in mid-June, Crappa stated that she could not recall seeing a child near the Datsun F-10 or having seen Samsoe. She said she was not even sure whether or not she had seen a man next to the car. Crappa confirmed that she did, however see six .22 caliber shells, not rusted, next to the body, and a knife "in the hole" near the body.

Although originally Crappa said she didn't want to talk

to any police officers, when Droz told her he was a detective, "it really didn't seem to have made any difference to her," said Droz later.

On February 15, Crappa met with Robison and prosecutor Richard Farnell and offered more details about the events concerning the missing Robin. Crappa stated that on June 20—not June 21, as she had stated previously—she did in fact see a Datsun, as well as a man wearing a white T-shirt and Levi's pushing or "steering" a blond-haired girl. She also stated that she had gone to the murder scene on the night of June 29 and had seen a knife and children's clothing near the corpse.

On February 26, Robison and Crappa met again, and this time Crappa told more of her version of the story.

Robison asked Crappa if she could recall what she did on the evening of June 25. When Crappa was unable to do so, Robison said he would paint a hypothetical for her of what *could* have occurred. He suggested that it was *possible* that Crappa went to the spot where Robin's body was later discovered and it "smelled foul," and that was how she was able to locate the body later.

After listening to Robison, Crappa stated, "It's a real possibility."

In previous interviews, Crappa had adamantly denied ever having seen a corpse before June 29.

Chapter Sixty-five

In the nearly seven months since his arrest, Alcala, now thirty-six, had been serving time in the Orange County Jail.

As his day in court neared, Alcala was hopeful that a jury of his peers would see things his way: He was *not* guilty of murdering Samsoe.

The preliminary hearing was held in September 1979. Preliminary motions, or pretrial motions, began in early February concerning what information could or could not be admitted during trial testimony. One major point of contention was whether or not the judge would allow Alcala's prior offenses involving actual and alleged abductions and sexual attacks to be admissible. The defense forcefully argued that the prior incidents were "too remote, inadmissible, and irrelevant."

On February 15, superior court judge Philip E. Schwab came down with his ruling: The priors in question—the 1968 beating and sexual molestation of an eight-year-old in LA; the 1974 alleged abduction and molestation of a thirteen-year-old in Huntington Beach; the suspicion that Alcala was involved in a woman's death in 1977 in New York; and the 1979 abduction and beating of a fifteen-year-old girl in Riverside County—*would* be allowed in evidence.

The ruling was a momentous victory for the prosecution. Because there was little direct evidence linking Alcala to the Samsoe crime, the prior attacks would add credence to their case.

* * *

Like most everyone else planning to attend the opening day of the trial on March 6, Robin's mother, Marianne Frazier, paid special attention to how she looked. A short, slender redhead, she picked out just the right outfit and fixed her hair just so. She wanted to appear put together and sophisticated. She wanted to represent Robin's memory in the most positive light.

However, that morning Frazier did one thing that no one else did. She stashed a .25 caliber pistol in her straw purse. She planned to take it out, point it at the man accused of murdering her daughter, and pull the trigger.

Justice be damned. She knew what justice *really* was.

Every seat in Judge Philip E. Schwab's courtroom was taken by friends, teachers, immediate family, and relatives of Robin Samsoe, as well as by the media, who were out in full force. The story of the beautiful blond-haired, blue-eyed twelve-year-old girl who had gone missing on her way to ballet class tugged at everyone's heartstrings. Robin had captured the soul of California.

Alcala's mother was also in attendance. A tiny woman with white hair, she sat in the back row, fingering white rosary beads.

At a few minutes after nine a.m., Rodney Alcala was led into the hushed courtroom in cuffs and leg shackles. He looked at no one in the gallery but instead kept his eyes cast downward as he took he seat.

Schwab, presiding over his first capital case, welcomed the jury and the spectators and then discussed some points of law that needed to be paid attention to.

Sitting in the front row, Marianne Frazier opened her purse. The monster was less than twenty feet away. She put her hand on the gun. *It won't be hard to shoot him directly in the heart,* she thought. *Maybe if I kill him, I'll be able to get out from under this unrelenting misery.*

With the preliminaries out of the way, the trial was ready to begin. Frazier closed her eyes briefly, telling herself that she had plenty of time to do the deed—days and weeks, in fact—and that she wanted to listen to what the prosecution had to say.

In his opening argument, prosecutor Richard Farnell wasted no time telling his version of the story. After giving details about the case the jury would be hearing, Farnell said that in his opinion, the linchpin of the trial would be the testimony of one Dana Crappa, twenty-one.

Crappa, Farnell promised the jurors, would testify that she saw a man, later identified as Rodney James Alcala, with a young girl, later identified as Robin Samsoe, near where Samsoe's skeletal remains were found twelve days later.

Furthermore, said Farnell, Crappa would testify that seeing this man "forcefully steering" a little girl down a ravine seemed "strange" to her, but she didn't stop to investigate further because the man "stared at her and she was afraid."

Crappa would also testify, Farnell promised, that more than a week later, while she and a co-worker, William Poepke, were working in the mountains, Poepke tossed her what he thought was a deer bone—but which later was identified as a bone from Samsoe's body—and Crappa "freaked out." Farnell paused for effect. Then he added, "She *knew* then that that bone did not belong to an animal."

In the months since then, Farnell told the jurors, Crappa had suffered a nervous breakdown. She was plagued by the thought: *Had she said something sooner, could the outcome have been different?*

Farnell stated that during the trial he would call on other witnesses as well who would point the finger at Alcala as the murderer of twelve-year-old Robin Samsoe, including witnesses who had seen Alcala on the beach photographing Samsoe on the day she went missing. He would also call fellow prison inmates of Alcala's.

After foreshadowing his case, Farnell thanked the jury in advance for their attention and devotion. "By the time this trial is over," he told the twelve-member panel, "you will be certain, beyond a reasonable doubt, that Rodney Alcala was the man who murdered Robin Christine Samsoe."

Farnell had barely taken his seat when John Barnett stood up and dramatically began his argument. Vehemently disagreeing with Farnell that Crappa was going to be a defining witness, Barnett stated that Crappa's testimony should not be believed. He said it would be "a recent fabrication created by the firefighter to end harassment by the prosecution." Barnett agreed with Farnell that Crappa had, indeed, suffered a nervous breakdown and that she had been suicidal, but he said it was not because she felt overwhelming guilt that had she said something sooner, she could have prevented the murder. "Here is why Crappa's testimony cannot be believed," Barnett stated definitely. "Crappa has been so mercilessly barraged by the cops to *admit* that she had seen Alcala with Samsoe in order to support their case that she has become confused about what she saw or had not seen on those crucial June days."

In fact, Barnett continued, after forest ranger Poepke discovered skeletal remains on July 2, Crappa was shown a photograph of Robin Samsoe, and Crappa stated to the authorities that she had *never* seen that little girl before. Furthermore, stated Barnett, during Alcala's preliminary hearing in November, Crappa never once mentioned ever having seen either Alcala or Samsoe. And wasn't that testimony, asked Barnett, given closer to the time of the incident in question, more credible than testimony that might be offered at this trial, seven months later?

Finally, Barnett disputed the concept that any information given by inmates at the trial would be credible. "They are only testifying so they can have their sentences reduced," he said dismissively.

Barnett concluded his opening argument by strongly disagreeing with Farnell that his client had committed murder. Barnett was certain that at the end of the trial, the jury would agree with him and find so many holes in the prosecution's case that they would return a not-guilty verdict.

And with that, Barnett took his seat, and the trial was under way.

* * *

As anticipated, the most riveting witness called by the State was Dana Crappa.

On March 19, Crappa began what was expected to be a long testimony. Farnell asked Crappa to tell the court what her job was in June of 1979. A meek and troubled-looking young woman distractedly explained her duties. Then Farnell moved directly to the evening hours of June 20, 1979.

"Where were you, and what did you see?"

With head down and in a nearly inaudible voice, Crappa stated that she was employed as a firefighter in the Chantry Flats area and that evening, between 5:00 and 5:30 p.m., she was driving up the mountains. She paused before continuing. Everyone in the courtroom tensed as the silent seconds ticked by. No one was certain she was going to be able to continue.

Finally she spoke. She said that as she slowed her car down during a sharp curve, she noticed a Datsun parked on the side. She added that it was the same spot, less than three hundred feet from where Robin's body was found. There was also a man, she said, with dark brown hair and a medium build and a girl with long blond hair "a few feet" from the car, "walking toward the wash." After another nearly interminable pause, she continued: "The man was behind the young girl." He was not "pushing" or "shoving" her, said Crappa, but he seemed to be "forcefully steering" her up the gully. Crappa stated that the man turned around and looked "straight through me."

When asked what she did then, Crappa stared into space. After a few moments she answered.

"I continued driving to the barracks."

Farnell then asked her how she felt about what she had seen. Crappa stated that she thought something *could have been* amiss, but she wasn't so concerned that she felt the need to report the situation. After all, plenty of families have issues getting their children to go along on hikes.

Asked to give information about the car she saw that evening, Crappa was able to describe the car "in intricate detail," if painfully slowly. She said that she knew so much about it because she owned one just like it. "It was a 1976

Datsun F-10," she said, her voice now trembling, "and had distinctive smoke-tint rear windows. And a luggage rack." After another nearly interminable pause, she said, "It was parked on a turnout, near Marker 11." She said she was able to see it clearly as she maneuvered a sharp turn on Santa Anita Canyon Road.

After being shown photographs of a car that Alcala owned at that time, Crappa positively identified it as the one she saw that day.

Farnell then asked her if she had told anyone about what she had seen.

"No."

"Did you ever see that car again?" asked Farnell.

After a few tense moments, Crappa said in a whisper, "Yes."

She added nothing more, so Farnell urged her to explain the circumstances.

Crappa said, "I saw the Datsun again the following evening, June 21, between 8 and 8:30 p.m."

"Can you describe what happened?" Farnell asked, trying to pull the words out of her mouth.

Crappa, nearly breathless with anxiety, said that after purchasing groceries, she was passing Rendezvous Turnout and in order to avoid colliding with a car that had entered her lane, she had a near collision with a vehicle parked there.

"And where is Rendezvous Turnout?"

"About a mile and a half from where I saw the man, the girl, and the car the previous evening. Approximately one and a half miles up the road from Mile Marker 11."

"Was anyone nearby?" asked Farnell.

After hesitating for nearly a full minute, Crappa stated that she saw a "dark-haired" man standing nearby, leaning against a rock wall, wearing a white T-shirt that "appeared to be sort of dirty or have a stain" and a pair of Levi's.

Now Farnell was the one who hesitated, allowing the image sink into the jurors' minds.

"Five days later," Farnell then asked, "on June 25, what did you do?"

After a long pause Crappa finally answered. She admitted that on that date she returned to Marker 11 between 7:00 and 7:30 in the evening and walked up the ravine with a flashlight.

"And what did you see?" asked Farnell.

She said, "It was a body."

"What did you see about the body?" asked Farnell.

Slowly and with her head hanging down even lower, Crappa said, "It was missing hands and feet. It smelled pretty foul."

"What else did you see?" asked Farnell.

"It was bloated like an animal gets after it sits for a while, and pretty cut up."

"And the head?"

With slow emphasis on each word, she stated: "It had been decapitated. It was next to the body. Part of the face was gone," she stated, but she could not say for sure whether the hands and feet, which were missing, had been cut off.

Farnell asked her if she had seen anything near the body. Crappa tentatively said yes: She saw a blue-and-yellow tennis shoe and something that looked like shorts and a T-shirt. Tire tracks were in the area, she added. No, there was not a knife.

"And what did you do?" asked Farnell.

Crappa stated that she was horrified and left quickly. Once again, she said, she told no one about what she had seen.

Farnell continued with more assurance now that he had "breached the emotional barrier" that had prevented Crappa from testifying completely before. "Do you see the man who was pushing the little girl on June 20 in the courtroom?"

Her voice shaking, she said, "I'm not one hundred percent positive, but the individual that looks like the one I saw is here."

"Where is he?" pressed Farrell.

For the first time since taking the stand, Crappa lifted her head. Her eyes scanned the courtroom. "He's sitting next to Mr. Barnett," Crappa said in a barely audible voice.

Judge Schwab asked the record to show that the witness was pointing out Rodney Alcala.

"Now, Ms. Crappa," continued Farnell, "can you tell the court what happened on June 29?"

Again, after some hesitation, Crappa testified that on that date she was part of a spraying crew that included another ranger, William Poepke. Crappa stated that Poepke saw a pile of bones in the area and, believing they were from a deer and thinking it would be a joke, he tossed one to her. Crappa stated that she was horrified. She knew, she admitted, that the bone was most likely not from a deer.

"And then what happened?" asked Farnell.

Crappa told the jury that that night at around seven p.m. she went back to Marker 11 because she was haunted by what had happened and wanted to check out the area by herself. With her flashlight scanning the area, she said, she saw a shiny object. "It may have been a knife," but she couldn't say for certain, she said. The body, she testified, was now "drawn out" and skeletal. The right arm was missing. Some blond hair was nearby. A pair of shorts, a T-shirt, and a child's tennis shoe were also nearby. She said she picked up six .22 caliber shells and threw them away.

Farnell continued to probe. "What happened three days later, on July 2?"

Crappa stared into space. It didn't seem as if she had heard the question so Farnell repeated it: "Ms. Crappa. What happened three days later, on July 2?"

After hesitating a moment longer, Crappa finally stated that on that day her colleague Poepke found a skull at the same spot where he had previously seen the "deer" bones. He alerted authorities, she said.

After that, with Farnell feeling confident that Crappa had presented a credible—if achingly staccato—chronology of what had taken place near Mile Marker 11 in the San Gabriel Mountains between June 20 and July 2, Farnell said, "No further questions," and took his seat.

Barnett then began his cross-examination. Barnett walked right up to Crappa and asked her repeatedly, "Why have you concealed important information throughout this case?"

For the first time since she began testifying, Crappa spoke in a strong voice. She said she had been unable to give details about certain things earlier because of her compromised mental state. She added that when investigators first contacted her, she didn't think that anything she had seen was the least bit important. Furthermore, she said, she wasn't even sure that it was her duty to give any more information than exactly what was asked for.

Crappa admitted that as the intensity of the interviews increased, she was unsure even if what she *thought* she saw was *really* the truth. Finally, she said, she was in such a poor emotional state that she was physically and psychologically unable to come forward earlier.

Crappa stated that she had told no one until today that she had found a mutilated body on June 25 because she had formed a mental block that prevented her from disclosing certain facts. Barnett played tapes of Crappa's interviews with investigators in February, during which she denied returning to the spot prior to June 29.

"Was this a lie or was this the truth?" asked Barnett.

"Yes, I did *not* tell the truth," said Crappa

Then, under intense questioning, Barnett got Crappa to admit that on June 20 she had gotten "only a fleeting glimpse" of the man. She also admitted that the man she saw that day *resembled* Alcala but she was "not one hundred percent positive" it was him.

Hoping he had planted at least a seed of doubt in the jurors' minds, Barnett continued trying to whittle away at Crappa's credibility. He pointed out that during preliminary hearings, Crappa testified that she had seen the Datsun between 10:00 and 10:30 p.m. on the twenty-first—but in testimony over the past few days she changed that time to between 8:00 and 8:30 p.m. Showing the jury a phone bill in his hand, he pointed out that a call was made at 10:08 p.m. on the twenty-first to Alcala's girlfriend's phone number from Alcala's home phone, suggesting, said Barnett, that Crappa's initial recall of time was the truth—and since that was the case, Alcala certainly could *not* have been the person who was at the site at 10:00 p.m. on June 21, as Crappa had initially stated.

Barnett asked Crappa whether or not she had been truthful to the investigators.

"No," she responded, head down.

"No?" he said, feigning incredulity. "How many false statements have you made?"

After thinking it over for some time, Crappa said, "Seven, before the trial. However," she added, "during these three days of testimony, I have been, on the whole, truthful."

Barnett then asked, "Why did you tell various versions of what you saw, or didn't see?"

"From the very beginning," Crappa stated, "I was trying to find a way out. I didn't want to [testify.] Blaming it on my imagination was easier than actually saying I believed [what I saw]."

Crappa admitted that she had been petrified to come forth with evidence because of overwhelming feelings of guilt, depression, denial, and horror. She said she had recurring nightmares about what she saw, although the nightmares were never the same, causing her to question what, in fact, she had actually seen. She said she wanted to be absolutely certain of her facts before revealing anything.

When Crappa finished testifying, the day in court had ended and the exhausted spectators, attorneys, and Crappa could finally go home.

On the next day of testimony, over the defense's strenuous objection, Farnell stated that he intended to show that the defendant had a history of enticing young girls into his car, taking them to isolated places, and subjecting them to forced sexual activity and violence. Alcala's criminal record of sexual molestation of young girls," Farnell told the jurors, should be considered when deliberating Alcala's guilt or innocence. "The law states," Farnell said, "that if prior offenses are so similar that they identify the defendant as the culprit, then that evidence can be admitted."

Testimony concerning Alcala's conduct on prior occasions

was offered concerning Tali S. (short for Shapiro), Julie Johnson, and Monique Hoyt.

Toni Esparza and Joanne Murchland both testified that the defendant took their pictures on June 19, 1979, at Huntington Beach for a "bikini photo contest" and that he offered them a ride and marijuana and tried to get their phone numbers. Both stated that they called the police after the composite appeared to tell them that the sketch looked like the man who photographed them.

Lori Werts and Patty Elmendorf recounted a similar tale, saying that they encountered the defendant on June 20 at Sunset Beach. Farnell then showed the jury five slides that were found in Alcala's Seattle locker. They were all of Lori Werts roller-skating in a blue bikini.

Bridget Wilvert and Jackye Young testified that they, too, positively identified Alcala as the man who took photographs of Robin and Bridget on June 20 at Huntington Beach.

On the day Robin's mother was called to testify, it was as if all the air in the courtroom had been sucked out as the spectators watched a woman so obviously emotionally broken walk to the stand, her hands and legs visibly shaking.

Breaking down into tears, Marianne Frazier testified that the earrings found in Alcala's storage locker in Seattle looked just like a pair of her own earrings, which she thought Robin might have borrowed the day she went missing.

In a soft voice Farnell asked, "Mrs. Frazier, did you ever have a set of earrings that were just round, gold balls?"

"Yes."

". . . Did something happen to one of those earrings?"

"It broke. . . . Well, they were very inexpensive and I don't know how it broke. They were just—cheap. . . ."

"When a part broke off one of the earrings, did you do something?"

"I clipped the bottom of the other one off, and tried to clip both sides even, so that they could still be worn as little posts."

"Did Robin ever borrow any of your jewelry?"

"Many times."

"Did Robin ever borrow those particular earrings from you?"

"Yes."

"Did you see that particular jewelry at the police department?"

"Yes."

Mrs. Frazier testified that she believed the earrings in evidence were the ones she had owned.

After Frazier testified, Orange County Jail inmate Robert J. Dove was called to the stand. He stated that one day in jail, he overheard another inmate, Michael Herrera, and Alcala talking together. During the conversation, Dove testified, Alcala said he had only "slapped [Robin] unconscious" but never stabbed her. Dove also testified that Alcala later told him that "nobody seen me take her and they could never convict me without the film and the bike and they would never find the bike."

The inmate Michael Herrera then testified that while he and Alcala were in Orange County Jail, Alcala told him that when the little girl realized he wasn't taking her to her dance class, she started screaming, and it was then, according to Herrera, that Alcala bashed her time and time again on her head. Alcala also told him, said Herrera, that he forced Samsoe into his car. Once she was in the vehicle, Herrera testified, the girl was "worried, scared" and "wanted to get out." He said that Alcala told him that he had asked the girl if she had ever posed nude and she started crying and he started "slapping the shit out of her." Alcala said it was a "weird situation" and "a trip."

Continuing, Herrera stated that Alcala told him that when Robin became unconscious, he decided to take her to "some mountains." Herrera believed they were the San Gabriel Mountains. Alcala told him he left the bike behind a "Thrifty Drug Store or Thriftimart or some kind of thrift store," because Alcala felt that the police wouldn't find it there. Herrera concurred with Dove that Alcala denied shooting or stabbing the young girl.

* * *

In early April, the State rested its case. After having presented all the witnesses Farnell had promised he would during his opening statements, he felt confident that the trial was off to a great start.

The judge then asked the jurors to exit the courtroom. When the jury had exited, defense attorney Barnett asked the judge for a motion to dismiss all charges, stating that the government had failed to prove its case. The defense also contended that "prejudicial evidence had been presented which would prevent the jury from reaching a fair verdict."

Schwab denied the motion.

The defense specifically requested that the charge of kidnapping be dropped because no proof had been presented that a kidnapping had taken place. "To prove kidnapping," the defense contended, "you have to prove that force was used. But the evidence is that she was enticed into a car."

The judge respectfully denied the motion and ruled that the charge would not be dismissed.

Under the 1978 California death penalty law, if a special circumstance, such as kidnapping, occurred in the course of committing a murder, the defendant could be eligible for the death penalty. In the Alcala case, the jury would be able to consider giving Alcala the death penalty *if* it found Alcala murdered Samsoe after kidnapping her.

However, in a decision favorable to the defense, the judge granted the motion for dismissal of the charge of performing a lewd or lascivious act on a child under fourteen, stating that the prosecution had not offered enough evidence to support the charge.

Barnett was thrilled with the day's session. In speaking to reporters later, he said that the dropping of the molestation charge will "vindicate my client." He went on to say that Alcala could be considered a prime suspect in the Samsoe murder "only if it had been shown that he committed child molestation. His unique connection to this case has been severed."

* * *

On April 8, Barnett began his direct case by calling several alibi witnesses to show that Alcala could *not* have been the person who kidnapped or killed Samsoe.

Tim Fallen came to the stand first. He stated that he had been in the area of Huntington Beach on June 21 and saw Robin riding a yellow bicycle there—the day *after* Robin went missing. Fallen stated that shortly after the young girl went missing, a police officer was showing a picture of Robin to people in the neighborhood. He told the officer then that the picture was of the girl whom he had seen.

On April 9, three witnesses reported that they had had contact with Alcala on key days and key hours in the Samsoe kidnapping, which *proved* that Alcala couldn't have done the deed. Unfortunately for the defense, none of the three witnesses could be described as unbiased.

Alcala's sister, Christine De La Cerda, testified that her brother was at her home on June 20 from about 4:30 p.m. to 4:35 p.m., around the same time that Crappa stated she saw Alcala in the mountains. De La Cerda added that her three children spent time with him that afternoon and even "looked in his glove compartment for gum."

Another sister, Marie Toriano, offered into evidence a telephone bill showing that someone from Alcala's home— her brother—had called her collect at her home in Fremont at 5:54 p.m. on June 20. This, Toriano believed, refuted Crappa's testimony that Alcala was at Chantry Flats that evening. Alcala's mother denied having made the Fremont call.

Alcala's girlfriend, Elizabeth Kelleher, provided records showing that Alcala made a one-minute call to her on June 21 at 9:15 p.m. and left a message. At 10:08 p.m., the records showed, Kelleher made a call to Alcala and they stayed on the phone for nineteen minutes. That 10:00 p.m. time was the same time Crappa first testified she saw Alcala at Chantry Flats.

The defense then tried to further discredit Crappa.

Barnett called Poepke, the forest ranger who had worked alongside Crappa, to the stand. Poepke testified that he cooked a pizza dinner for Crappa "from [their] first paycheck." During the meal, he reported, Crappa mentioned that she had just had a near accident at Rendezvous Turnout. According to Poepke, they received their first check on June 13 or 14. Poepke said that Crappa never mentioned another accident at any other time when they were together. The implication was that Alcala might have been at the location in question earlier in the month of June, but certainly *not* on the dates that Crappa testified she had seen him.

The defense then called inmate Joseph Drake to testify. Drake, a jail buddy of Alcala's, testified that he, Dove, and Herrera had made up the "admissions" that Herrera testified to "only after viewing television and reading reports in the newspapers." They did so, he claimed, to strike an "informer's bargain" with the authorities.

In an attempt to create a plausible timeline of events on June 20, David Carpenter, a defense investigator, testified that he drove at the speed limit from Marker 11 to the Monterey Park residence of Alcala, leaving at 5:15 p.m. on a Thursday afternoon and using the most logical route. He stated that he arrived about 5:58 p.m. This time frame, he suggested, showed that the defendant could not have gotten home from Marker 11, where Crappa allegedly saw him between 5:00 and 5:30 p.m. on the twentieth, in time to make his 5:54 p.m. collect call to his sister in Fremont. "Simple mathematics demonstrates that the proof is not persuasive."

Barnett next called Dr. Albert J. Rosenstein to the stand. Rosenstein was a forensic psychologist hired by the defense to review Crappa's mental condition. Under questioning, Rosenstein said his review of trial transcripts and tapes of interviews of Crappa by HBPD detectives and a psychologist indicated that Crappa had been manipulated through low-level hypnosis. Rosenstein stated, "I feel to the highest degree of certainty" that Crappa's testimony was "confabulated," a process by which the witness fills gaps in memory with false and imaginary information, often implanted by others, and comes to believe in the truth of the reconstruction. Rosenstein said Crappa became a "victim of suggestion . . . a Manchurian candidate at a minor level" in her February meetings with Detective Art Droz and psychologist Larry Blum. Thus, he declared, nothing Crappa testified to should be believed. He said he thought the questioners had "lured" Crappa into believing the things that they had suggested, "hypnotizing" her into accepting what they told her.

To bolster this theory, Barnett introduced the tapes of the interviews with Crappa by Detectives Droz and Robison that suggested, according to Barnett, that Crappa had been "brainwashed" or otherwise led to construct false memories while she was in a suggestible state. He claimed they had planted "seeds" in her mind, intimidated her, and threatened her.

Under cross-examination, an angry Farnell asked Rosenstein how sure he was about his opinion. Rosenstein responded, "I don't feel I'm guessing."

When Farnell pointed out that Rosenstein, an Irvine-based psychologist who worked with returning prisoners of war from Korea in the early 1950s, served far more often as a defense witness than as one for the DA's office, Rosenstein retorted "I'm not a prostitute. I'm not a whore."

When asked, Rosenstein said he testified in court two or three times a week and had testified in Orange County between 100 and 150 times in the past.

"And how many times did you testify for the prosecution?"

"For about twenty-five or thirty of those cases, I was hired by the DA."

When asked why he testified so rarely for the prosecution, he said it was because he was expensive.

The jousting became so intense that several times Rosenstein had to ask Farnell, whose voice was raised in anger, to stop interrupting him.

On Wednesday, April 23, the defense rested its case. Alcala was not called to testify on his own behalf.

* * *

Final arguments began on Monday, April 28.

Walking right along the jury line and taking time to make eye contact with each member of the nine-woman, three-man jury, Farnell began by stating that Barnett's claims regarding Alcala's innocence were "ridiculous and [ones that] do not mesh with common sense."

Then, focusing on why he had brought in evidence and testimony about Alcala's past arrests and convictions, Farnell said that they were all perpetrated on girls. "It shows motive. It shows why he was kidnapping Robin, why he was taking her up to the hills, and why he had to kill her afterwards, so that she would not report him. It is important, we feel, to show you this so that you know that we don't just have a man down at the beach taking pictures of young girls."

Farnell continued, "There is a tremendous difference between a man down at the beach taking pictures of young girls and a man who is a sex pervert, who is a child molester, who is down at the beach taking pictures of young girls and trying to get those girls to go with him—especially when just a very short period of time before, after he tries to get a girl to go with him, he actually does get Robin Samsoe to go with him."

"The court will instruct you," continued Farnell, "that other offenses may be offered to show intent, to determine his method of operation, to determine a plan or scheme . . . similar to the method, plan or scheme . . . in this case, which would tend to further show the existence of the intent . . . and the identity of the person who committed the crime . . . and that is exactly what the testimony has shown."

In ending his testimony, Farnell urged the jurors to give Alcala the punishment he deserved.

In what seemed at first like a surprising way to begin a closing argument, Barnett stood up and labeled his client a "bad man." He said, "The People have proved that Mr. Alcala is a bad man. The People have proved that this is a bad crime." Continuing, however, he added with assurance, "But the People have *not* proved that Mr. Alcala killed Robin Samsoe."

Barnett stated that there was no physical evidence that Robin was abducted on June 20. He said there were no hairs. There were no fibers. There were no fingerprints. There was no blood. There was nothing, in fact, to link his client to the murder of Robin Samsoe.

The case was purely circumstantial, he said, and riddled with holes. Reiterating what he said earlier, the jailhouse informants were not to be believed because they had ulterior motives to say what they did. He said Crappa was not to be believed because she was an unreliable witness.

Barnett thanked the jurors for their time and attention and urged them to vote the only way that made any sense: not guilty.

With closing arguments completed, Judge Schwab spoke to the jury. He repeated the charges leveled against Alcala and told the jurors that their duty was a grave one. He wished them good luck.

April 29, 1980, was the first day of deliberations. The jury asked to have certain testimony given by Crappa read back to them.

At the end of the day, no verdict had been reached. It would be a sleepless night for Robin's mother and her entire family. Frazier was still carrying the loaded gun into the courtroom; it was still hidden in her purse. Now she was just waiting for the exact right moment.

On the second day of deliberation, April 30, the jury told the judge that they had reached a verdict.

With a mere eleven hours devoted to deliberations, it was apparent that the jury clearly saw the case as an open-and-shut one: Either Alcala was *definitely* innocent or *definitely* guilty.

The court was called back into session. Alcala's elderly mother and stepfather sat looking on, their faces contorted in pain.

After the spectators and jurors took their seats, the judge called the court to order. He asked the foreperson if the jury had reached a verdict. The foreperson stated yes and handed the papers to the court clerk.

"And how do you find the defendant regarding the first-degree murder charge with use of a deadly weapon?" asked the judge.

"Guilty of first-degree murder."

A cheer went up in the courtroom as family members and friends of Robin hugged each other in relief.

Alcala's mother, Anna Maria German, and Alcala's stepfather, Pedro, remained calm. Their faces, however, showed their pain.

After admonishing the gallery to remain respectful, Judge Schwab then asked, "And regarding one count of forcible kidnapping. How do you find the defendant?"

"Guilty," the clerk replied.

After polling the jury to make sure that each person had, in fact, voted guilty, the judge asked the jurors to return the following week for the penalty phase of the trial.

Afterward, German walked over to Barnett and thanked him, touching him on his shoulder. When asked later about her stoic attitude, German said, "I didn't cry because my boy's innocent." She added, "The twelve people are wrong. It is unjust."

Marianne Frazier hugged and kissed Farnell after the trial, thanking him for his hard work. Outside the courtroom she said, "I want the death penalty. I think he deserves it. He's been convicted several times."

The trial had lasted eleven and a half weeks. No one knew that Frazier had been bringing a gun to court the entire time.

Chapter Sixty-six

During the penalty phase, prosecutor Farnell called only two witnesses to testify, both Alcala's former parole officers.

One, Olivia Gomez, who was Alcala's parole officer in 1977, testified that after Alcala returned from a New York trip in 1977, he showed her several photographs he had taken of children in sexually suggestive poses.

Farnell was attempting to show that Alcala's string of crimes and unrepentant nature demanded that he receive the death penalty.

In closing arguments, Farnell described Alcala as a cold and calculating killer, "a man who stalks little girls for selfish, aberrant purposes. This beast, this conniving scum, stole Robin's life. What other penalty is appropriate for the murder of a little girl [besides death]?"

Barnett did not call any witnesses. He didn't call Alcala, he said, "because I didn't feel it would be profitable."

Barnett acknowledged that his client was a "sick and disturbed man. I cannot believe," he declared, "that you cannot say that [Alcala] suffers from a mental disease that causes him to switch from being a normal man one minute into an unpredictable, frenzied person the next. You don't need a psychiatrist to tell you that—just the way you don't need a weatherman to tell you which way the wind blows." Barnett added Alcala was "a man who never really grew up." He said that in his previous attacks on other girls, Alcala was driven by a frenzy he could not control.

Finally, in ending his closing argument, Barnett declared, "My client was tried on anger and fear. The aura of death pervades this courtroom." Then, after a pause, he asked sorrowfully, "Will death have its day today?"

On May 7 the penalty phase ended. Jurors got the case the next day.

After spending four hours and seventeen minutes weighing the case, at 4:05 p.m., the jurors sent word that they had reached a decision. After everyone was settled in the courtroom, Judge Schwab admonished the attendees to remain calm, regardless of the outcome.

Frazier, sitting in the first row as she had every day of the trial, tried to stop her body from shaking.

The judge then asked the court clerk, Arturo Guevara, for the jury's verdict.

In a loud and clear voice, Guevara declared: "Death."

"All right!" screamed Robin's mother. She then began sobbing so hysterically in the arms of the Huntington Beach police officer sitting next to her that he had to lead her out of the courtroom.

Appearing spent, the jurors responded in turn to the judge's question as to how he or she voted; yes, they replied, death was their verdict.

Alcala showed no emotion.

Others in the courtroom hugged one another in support.

Judge Schwab set June 20 as the date for sentencing. The irony of the day—exactly one year after Robin Samsoe's disappearance—was lost on no one.

Outside the courtroom, several jurors were visibly distraught. It had been a grueling several months and, in the end, they had "ordered" the death of another human being. Weeping, two of them embraced the fragile and emotionally spent Frazier.

In speaking to the media about their decision, the jurors stated that they were never in disagreement as to Alcala's guilt. They were split, however, as to whether he should be charged with second-degree murder—murder with intent but without premeditation—as four of them believed, or first-degree murder—murder with intent or malice aforethought—as the other eight voted at first. Asked what evidence most convinced them of Alcala's guilt, one juror stated that it was the earrings in the storage locker. Another said that it was Crappa's testimony. Still another felt it was the testimony of several different witnesses, who all claimed that they saw Alcala taking Robin's picture at the beach on the day she went missing. Another juror said it was no one thing. "It was a lot of little things."

One juror said the group took three or four votes before agreeing on the death penalty, believing that was what state law required them to do.

Frazier told reporters, "Robin didn't die for nothing," she said through tears. "He [Alcala] deserves it."

When asked later, both the defense and the prosecution believed that Crappa's testimony, in which she identified photos of Alcala's car as the one she saw on the turnout, and the fact that she testified to having seen a body on June 25, were the most damning of the trial.

Farnell called the death sentence for Alcala a "hollow victory, since I would doubt we'll ever see anybody executed in California until we get a new [State] Supreme Court." Farnell said that the governor could commute a death sentence after twelve years and, if the governor did so, Alcala could at that point be released on parole. "The last execution in California was in 1967," he added.

Barnett stated, "Mr. Alcala will not be put to death if I can help it." He added that "appeal issues are strong" and indicated he would file one in the Fourth District Court of Appeals in San Bernardino.

A few days later, when Robin's mother was interviewed, she said, "[Alcala] was blowing kisses at me across the courtroom, and I thought I was going to lose my mind. I thought I was going to go crazy, you know. And I reached into my purse and I was going to grab it, you know, and I thought, 'I can't do this.' "

Frazier admitted that throughout the proceedings, while she had her hand in her pocketbook, poised on the gun, she debated nearly every minute whether or not to shoot Alcala and just get it over with.

"The only thing that kept me from doing it," she stated, "was the thought that Robin would have been upset if her brothers and sister didn't have a mother at home with them."

When Farnell was interviewed, he stated that he was pleased with the outcome, believing that death was the only appropriate punishment for Alcala's crime. But, he wondered aloud, "is death sufficient for this defendant?" He told a reporter, "From what I know of Mr. Alcala, there are probably many more victims we don't know about." Farnell believed that Alcala would prove to have been a serial killer.

In responding to critics who wondered how he could possibly defend such a heinous person, Barnett said, "In every jury trial, there are actually two trials. One trial is of the defendant; the other is a trial of the system—our system of justice."

Barnett, a thirty-two-year-old husband and father of an eight-month-old son, told a *Los Angeles Times* reporter that during the trial "his wife had to stop seeing some old friends because of the intensity of community feelings about the gruesome death of Robin Samsoe."

But, Barnett said, he and his wife "believe in the correctness of Barnett's defense of criminal defendants." After all, it is the law that anyone in the United States who is accused of a crime is entitled to a defense.

On June 20, once again the court was in session, this time to hear Judge Schwab's decision as to whether or not he would agree with the jury's recommendation of death for Alcala.

The judge spoke sternly and solemnly. "It is fair to say that the evidence disclosed that the defendant in a premeditated manner stalked his prey for a number of days. The defendant not only has a prior felony conviction [for child molestation], but there are also distinct similarities to this case. . . . This is a particularly vicious and cruel crime."

Schwab also spoke to the point of whether or not Alcala was mentally ill, rejecting the defense's plea that Alcala not be put to death because he is mentally disturbed. "He is a man of depraved character," said Schwab, "but he is able to appreciate the difference between right and wrong."

Schwab then agreed with the jury's decision on death. He stated that Alcala's death would take place in the gas chamber.

And with that, Alcala was remanded to San Quentin prison.

No date was set for the execution, pending an automatic appeal to the state supreme court.

Chapter Sixty-seven

On July 11, with the ink barely dry on Alcala's death penalty conviction for the murder of Robin Samsoe, the Los Angeles County district attorney's office filed murder, burglary, and sexual assault charges against Alcala for the slaying of Jill Parenteau. The Parenteau homicide had taken place on June 14, 1979, just six days before the Samsoe murder. Deputy DA Richard Size said, "It will be a special-circumstances case, which means we will seek the death penalty."

The key element in pointing the finger at Alcala, said Size, was that two types of blood were found at the scene. "One type was the victim's, but various subgroups of the other blood matched the blood of [Alcala] to a degree that would eliminate ninety percent of other humans."

According to information the investigators now had, Alcala and Parenteau had met at a bar, but she was not interested in going out with him. She reported to friends that once she made it clear to him that she had no interest in him, she began receiving obscene phone calls. When matched with Alcala's whereabouts, phone records indicated that the calls came to her telephone number when Alcala was in town—but abruptly stopped every time he left town.

In the end, prosecutors alleged, Alcala had broken into Parenteau's second-floor apartment and viciously beaten, raped, and strangled her.

Chapter Sixty-eight

In September 1980, although Alcala had already been sentenced to die in the gas chamber, he nevertheless was brought from San Quentin to stand trial in Riverside for the 1979 rape and beating of fifteen-year-old Monique Hoyt. That case was still open in Riverside, and that jurisdiction needed to close its own cases.

During the trial, law enforcement officials from Riverside County testified that Alcala picked up Hoyt on February 13, 1979, as she was hitchhiking in Pasadena. Hoyt, they said, ran up to them the next day in a "beaten, hysterical state" and identified the defendant as her assailant.

The trial was short, and at the end Alcala was pronounced guilty of the charge of rape.

During the penalty phase, the prosecution played the tape-recorded interview the police had had with Alcala after he was brought to the station regarding the Hoyt incident. Alcala confessed to the police because right after the incident the police had Monique Hoyt with them and they could see her condition. Also, they discovered pictures on Alcala's camera with "before" photos of Hoyt, unharmed. Alcala "copped out," or confessed, because he knew they had him cold.

The jury heard Alcala describe how he took Hoyt to a dirt road in the mountains, photographed her in the nude, took pictures as they performed simulated sexual acts, and then, when consensual activities ceased, choked Hoyt until she was unconscious, tied her wrists and ankles with rope, and, after she revived, stuffed her shirt in her mouth to force her to stop screaming. He admitted he also raped her. It didn't take long for the jury to deliberate. Alcala was sentenced to nine years for the rape.

PART
VIII

PART

VIII

Chapter Sixty-nine

Nearly eight months after Alcala's death sentence was handed down, his state-appointed appeals attorney, Keith Monroe, filed an appeal in February 1981 contending that two grievous mistakes had been made in Alcala's trial: One, too much weight was given to the testimony of jail informants Michael Herrera and Robert J. Dove, whose testimony Monroe contended was highly suspicious. Two, some potential jurors had been removed because they admitted that they did not agree with the death penalty, and that, declared Monroe, was "an arbitrary decision," because federal law requires that those who disagree with the death penalty be permitted to serve as jurors.

To support his point of view about the unreliability of jailhouse informants, Monroe claimed in his brief that both Herrera and Dove were heroin addicts. Monroe wrote that Herrera first became an informant in 1974 after having been convicted in 1972 of heroin possession. According to Monroe, Herrera knew he would get a break if he informed. Monroe added that Herrera had been convicted of two counts of robbery in 1975.

Monroe wrote that Dove, also an inmate at Orange County Jail, lied to prosecutors in the hopes of receiving special treatment. According to Monroe, Dove admitted that he, Herrera, and two other inmates made up the story to get favorable treatment regarding their own cases.

Monroe further pointed out that "there was no corroboration at the trial of anything the inmates said, except by each informant corroborating the other" as to whether or not Alcala said he had forced Samsoe into his car (as Herrera had testified), or that he slapped the girl until she was unconscious (as Dove had testified), or that Dove had seen Herrera and Alcala talking in jail (as Dove had also testified).

After reviewing the appeal, the Supreme Court of California came down with its decision. The court believed that there was at least the *possibility* that Dove and Herrera had lied, so it ruled that Orange County Superior Court could hear new evidence from Dove. The issue, as the court saw it, was that *if* Dove had, in fact, lied under oath, *did* his testimony make a difference in Alcala's June 1980 sentencing?

The widely publicized hearings gripped the LA area for five days, beginning on April 10, 1981. Would this man, whom many believed to be a cold-blooded killer, a vicious child molester, and a possible serial murderer, be granted a new trial?

When Dove appeared in front of Judge Schwab and was asked about his testimony during Alcala's trial, Dove admitted that he had, in fact, lied. He stated that he and other inmates had banded together to say that Alcala had told them he had kidnapped Robin Samsoe.

Angry, the prosecutor, Richard Farnell, questioned Dove: "If you all made up so much of the story, then how come many parts of your testimony corresponded with established fact?"

Dove shrugged. "I guess they were just coincidence. Maybe," he added, "some things could have been true because I heard them or read about them." Dove continued, "I went to my cell one night and stayed up all night and wrote a bunch of crap."

Joe Drake, another jailhouse informant, corroborated Dove's testimony that he, Dove, and Herrera made up a story implicating Alcala as the kidnapper of Samsoe.

It was beginning to look like Dove's testimony at Alcala's trial *was* crucial, because if it proved *not* truthful, then there would be no evidence that Alcala kidnapped Samsoe—and thus no "special circumstance" to put Alcala on death row.

Was Alcala about to get another free pass?

Chapter Seventy

While the appeal of the Samsoe conviction was taking place, the Parenteau case was still front and center on the caseload of the LAPD.

Finally, after nearly a year, a decision came down as to whether or not Alcala would go on trial for the 1979 murder of Jill Parenteau.

He would not.

The reason? John Mulqueen, an Orange County inmate and buddy of Alcala's while they served time, was considered a crucial witness in the Parenteau case. His statements were to provide the only evidence linking Alcala to Parenteau's murder. But it had been discovered that Mulqueen had lied in another case in which he served as the State's key witness, and as such, he could not be considered a "credible witness."

As a result, the case was dismissed.

Orange County prosecutor Farnell was enraged. "Just because Mulqueen lied in another case down here in Orange County, I don't see it as an ethical problem because we use known liars and crooks a lot as informants. The test is whether we can corroborate or support what a snitch says."

Both LA County deputy DA Robert Cohen and Detective Gordon Bowers said they didn't plan to abandon the Parenteau case. Bowers said that Mulqueen's testimony was "very valid" and could only have been known by someone who knew Parenteau's murderer. Simply because Mulqueen perjured himself in another case, argued Cohen and Bowers, did not mean he would not be a credible witness in this case.

Chapter Seventy-one

On May 28, 1981, Judge Schwab ruled on whether or not the special circumstance of kidnapping in the Samsoe case would be dismissed, based on the testimony of Dove.

If the court ruled that Dove had told the truth, then the kidnapping charge would *not* be dismissed—and Alcala could still face the death penalty.

If the court deemed that Dove had lied, then the kidnapping charge would be dropped due to insufficient evidence.

In the much anticipated decision, Schwab stated that there had been no "perjured evidence introduced during the trial, and that even had there been, that was not a substantial consideration regarding Alcala's guilt."

The special circumstance of kidnapping would remain.

Alcala was returned to San Quentin's death row.

The prosecution was elated, as were Robin's family and friends.

Monroe said he would appeal the judge's ruling to the Supreme Court of California.

PART
IX

PART
IX

Chapter Seventy-two

For the three years since Alcala's appeal had been turned down, Alcala spent each and every day in a cell in San Quentin.

However, all that was about to change.

On August 23, 1984, the Supreme Court of California, the highest court in the state, wrote a decision in response to an automatic appeal of Alcala's 1980 murder conviction and death sentence.

In a five-to-one decision, the supreme court held that the "trial court committed a reversible error in admitting into evidence the defendant's prior crimes, which were *not* so similar to the present case as to establish a peculiar pattern to prove the defendant's identity as the perpetrator; nor did those prior offenses establish intent, plan or scheme, or motive.

"Inasmuch as the jury may well have been influenced by improper consideration of the crimes, which were highly prejudicial in their nature, it appeared reasonably probable a result more favorable to defendant would have been reached absent the error."

The opinion continued, "The alleged similarities among the offenses are common to a substantial portion of the population of child molesters, including the use of charm or deception, transportation to places of privacy, and violence. There was no peculiar pattern in defendant's past conduct that established his identity as the girl's killer by setting him apart from the general class of violent sex offenders against children. . . .

"We will conclude that the convictions and special circumstance finding must be reversed, since the admission of prior offenses constituted prejudicial error on those issues."

In other words, the Supreme Court of California gave Alcala the best forty-first birthday present he could ever get: Alcala's death sentence was reversed.

One dissenting judge, Associate Justice Stanley Mosk, offered his opposing view. He wrote that the prior crimes *were* similar enough to have been allowed as evidence and added that there was "no miscarriage of justice" in Alcala's conviction.

"I cannot conclude, with the assurance of my colleagues, that the admission of evidence of prior offenses committed by defendant was erroneous. . . . There were sufficient similarities in the prior offenses, all against female children, to permit their introduction on the issue of identity. That the prior offenses against little girls did not result in a killing is not sufficient justification to find dissimilarity and to conclude that the trial court improperly exercised its discretion in admitting the evidence. I would affirm the conviction on the ground that there has been no miscarriage of justice."

In spite of Mosk's dissent, Alcala was returned to pretrial status and recharged with the crimes. It was as if his entire trial in 1980 had never taken place. Alcala had yet another chance at freedom. He and his defense team were in a celebratory mood.

At the same time that the court reversed Alcala's death penalty conviction, it rejected the "defendant's contention that the double jeopardy clause [a defense that states a defendant cannot be tried a second time for the same crime based on the identical set of facts] barred retrial of certain allegations because the valid evidence at the first trial was legally insufficient to support them. We will also hold that defendant may be retried on all counts of the current information regardless of asserted irregularities at his preliminary hearing."

In other words, although Alcala and his defense team had hoped that "double jeopardy" would save Alcala from having to be retried at all, the court saw it differently and Alcala *would* have to be tried again.

In spite of this setback, appeals attorney Keith Monroe was ecstatic, stating that the evidence against Alcala was "very, very speculative." He said Alcala "certainly has got a far better chance of being acquitted" after the high court's reversal of the original conviction.

James Enright, Orange County's chief deputy DA, strongly disagreed with Monroe, saying that the reversal was a "horrible decision" and was a result of the liberal supreme court that Governor Edmund G. Brown Jr. had appointed. Enright, along with prosecutor Farnell, expressed confidence that Alcala would be convicted in a new trial, although they acknowledged that the supreme court's ruling and other factors would make it more difficult. "Evidence of [Alcala's] past crimes," said Enright, had been "a very vital link in establishing [Alcala's] mode of criminal conduct."

PART
X

PART

X

Chapter Seventy-three

As Alcala's second trial date neared, Chief Deputy DA James Enright expressed his thoughts. "It's really needless to have to go through this again, certainly in the Alcala . . . case. But that's the [Chief Justice] Rose Bird Court for you." But, he added, "If we have to, we'll retry every one the Supreme Court sends back. It's difficult. You have to round up all your witnesses again and you have to put your victims' families through the whole thing all over. But you do it because the death penalty is the only just verdict for these guys."

Rose E. Bird, the first female appointed to the California Supreme Court, served as its chief justice from 1977 to 1987, after being appointed by Governor Edmund "Jerry" Brown. Bird was known for her liberal views and unwavering opposition to the death penalty, which caused many to revile her as being soft on crime. During her tenure on the court, she reviewed sixty-four death penalty cases that came up for appeal. In every single case, she and her fellow justices overturned the ruling—including Alcala's.

Bird was the only chief justice ever *not* to be retained by the electorate. Justices are appointed to twelve-year terms by the governor of California and run unopposed on ballots during retention elections; these are held every four years, at the same time as a general election, and the voters choose between electing the incumbent judge to another term or voting that the judge not be retained. Bird was criticized, not only for being an ideologue who wasn't able to suppress her own convictions in favor of the law, but also for being a "terrible administrator," who—before her appointment as chief justice—lacked prior judicial experience.

Alcala's appeals attorney Keith Monroe had his own thoughts on the 1984 reversal. "If you were to ask me whether Rodney is capable of a crime like this, my heavens, yes. It would not surprise me at all to learn that Rodney killed that little girl. But did the evidence at the first trial prove that he did? I say no."

Deputy DA Tom Goethals, who would serve as prosecutor during Alcala's next trial, saw some hurdles ahead but felt that, ultimately, he would be successful. "Even if we convince the jury [Alcala] is guilty of murder, we still have to convince them there were special circumstances involved." However, he added, "if we are successful in that, I don't think it will be too tough, considering Alcala's past, to convince a jury he should get the death penalty again."

On April 23, 1986, Alcala's second trial began. Judge Donald A. McCartin called the court to order. After the charges were read and the jury settled in, prosecutor Goethals began to make the state's case.

"I think you, ladies and gentlemen, will relive through the evidence presented, one of the most notorious and horrendous crimes probably in the history of this county." He paused, glared at Alcala, then scanned the jurors. "You will see through the evidence presented to you, that the man seated here in front of you in court, nicely groomed, conservatively dressed, apparently mild-mannered, is not the same Rodney James Alcala with whom Robin Samsoe spent the last few hours of her life."

Goethals then recounted the outline of his case: Seven years ago, a thirty-five-year-old Alcala kidnapped twelve-year-old Robin Samsoe, "twenty-three years his junior," not far from her home in Huntington Beach and brutally murdered her in the mountains above Los Angeles. "Samsoe," said Goethals, "was less than five feet tall. She weighed under 100 pounds."

After pausing for a moment to let those details sink in, Goethals went on. "Alcala got Robin into his 1976 Datsun and drove her forty miles away to the mountains above LA County, and up Santa Anita Canyon Road, a desolate mountain area. After removing her from the car, he steered her up an even more remote area and into the underbrush. There, he killed her . . . and left her body for the mountain animals."

He paused once again, allowing the nauseating image to sink in before concluding his remarks by saying, "I will show you how after Robin never showed up for her ballet class and the next day the police interviewed [her girlfriend Bridget] Wilvert, a sketch was made and it was shown on all TV stations and people started coming forward, identifying the same man: a tall, thin, curly-haired man named Rodney Alcala."

Goethals stated that Dana Crappa, former firefighter, would be a key witness during this trial, as she had been in the earlier trial, and that her testimony would help convince them of Alcala's guilt. Crappa, Goethals stated, had seen a blond-haired girl and a man where Samsoe's remains were later discovered, as well as a car that looked just like the one Alcala drove.

Goethals stated that he would call on two jailhouse informants to testify that Alcala told them he had kidnapped the young girl.

Feeling confident that his case was airtight, Goethals thanked the jurors and said that he believed that, at the end of the trial, they would return the only verdict that was appropriate: guilty of murder.

After Goethals took his seat, defense attorney John Patrick Dolan began his opening statement. In strident tones, he put forth the three major problems with the prosecution's case that he intended to focus on during his defense: the police and prosecutors, for "badgering, cajoling, and intimidating" Crappa; the jailhouse informants, for their lack of credibility; and the prosecution itself, for putting forth evidence that "no one in his right mind" would use to convict Alcala.

Dolan told the jurors that during the trial he would shed some light on "a little game that's been going on at the Orange County Jail for years, called 'buy your way out of the jailhouse.'" In this game, he claimed, "jailhouse informants seek out defendants whom they learn the prosecutors are having a hard time convicting. Then they fabricate evidence to incriminate these folks. And why? So that in exchange, they get some help in their own cases." He described the informants that would appear for the prosecution as heroin addicts "who would sell their grandmothers' false teeth to get out of jail."

Dolan concluded by making some admissions. "Yes," admitted Dolan, "Alcala was on the beach that day. And yes, he could have taken Robin Samsoe's picture. But," he added forcefully, "that's all he did."

The trial then got under way. During most of it, much of the same evidence that was presented during the first trial was presented once again.

However, there were some surprising differences. Right before Crappa was called to testify, and outside the presence of the jury, Crappa spoke to Judge McCartin, saying that she did not remember any of the events that took place while she worked as a firefighter. She added that she did not even remember what she had testified to at the preceding trial. She said that she could not be called as a witness.

Goethals was outraged. He immediately argued that Crappa should be examined by a doctor in order for her to be deemed "medically unable" to testify.

However, McCartin ruled that Crappa was, in fact, incapable of appearing as a witness during this trial, but that her earlier testimony could be read aloud to the court.

Now Dolan was outraged. He stated that McCartin's decision "was an errant ruling, to say the least. . . . It's really a fraud on the jury as far as I'm concerned because [Crappa's] demeanor on the stand was so important. They've really got us over a barrel. But we can't come unglued here. We'll just have to do the best job we can. This is a critical case. They're trying to execute this man." Dolan believed that Crappa's lengthy pauses and "bizarre performance" during her first trial could not successfully be translated if her testimony was simply read aloud; therefore, the jury would not have the opportunity to see her totally discredited.

In another stab at discrediting Crappa, defense attorney Dolan contended that Crappa had been hypnotized by a police interviewer who made suggestions about details of the case, and that Crappa's testimony at the first trial was a result of that hypnosis.

McCartin saw it differently. He ruled that here was no evidence to conclude that Crappa had been hypnotized.

Outside the court, Goethals verbalized his anger: "We had lengthy pretrial hearings where police investigators and even the prosecutor in the first trial denied that Dana Crappa was hypnotized. Perhaps the defense believes that these people lied under oath as part of a criminal conspiracy."

During the trial, the prosecution called Frederick Williams, a former fellow inmate of Alcala's in the Orange County Jail.

Williams, who was still in custody, recalled a conversation he had had with Alcala during Alcala's first trial. Williams testified that Alcala, in recalling a demonstration for the jury of how he might have placed Robin's bike in his car, "was sort of laughing to himself, making fun of the jury as if they were not too competent." According to Williams, Alcala said that the police, who were doing the demonstration, "were all acting like a bunch of ducks trying to get the bike in the car and weren't doing too good of a job of it. Those guys looked like a bunch of morons." Williams testified that Alcala had told him that when he placed Robin's bicycle inside the vehicle, he "just threw it in there like a snap." According to Williams, Alcala also told him that Robin "kicked and clawed like a wildcat."

During the trial, the prosecution relied on a variety of circumstantial evidence, since there was no physical evidence directly connecting Alcala to Samsoe. Patty Elmendorf testified that Alcala was the Sunset Beach photographer who had taken pictures of her on the afternoon of June 20; Lorraine Werts testified that a slide later found in Alcala's locker was of her roller-skating at Sunset Beach on June 20; Jackye Young testified that Alcala was the photographer whom she had seen on June 20, wearing a striped collarless shirt and taking pictures of Robin Samsoe and Bridget Wilvert; Joanne Murchland and Toni Esparza both positively identified Alcala as the man who had taken their pictures.

The prosecution also presented evidence that Alcala straightened his hair three days after Samsoe went missing, and cut his hair a few days later—suggesting that after he had seen a composite drawing of himself, he wanted to change his appearance.

However, Alcala's girlfriend, Elizabeth Kelleher, testified that Alcala's changing of his hairstyle in the days following Samsoe's disappearance had *nothing* to do with the publication of composite sketches, as the prosecution had contended. Rather, she stated, she had been encouraging him to change his appearance for some time.

To support Alcala's claim of innocence, the defense presented witnesses to offer an alibi for Alcala's whereabouts on the day Samsoe disappeared. Employees at Buena Park's Knott's Berry Farm testified that they remembered seeing Alcala at the park near the date of Robin's disappearance, applying for a job as a photographer for a disco dance contest to be held there later in the week. However, none could pinpoint the exact date as June 20.

The defense pointed out that neither Robin's fingerprints nor any other physical evidence linked to Robin were found inside Alcala's vehicle. Several "experts" testified that none of the clippers supplied by Robin's mother could have made the cuts that appeared on the earring. However, an "expert" prosecution witness testified there was a "strong probability" that one of the earrings seized from the Seattle storage locker was trimmed with the nail clippers provided to the defense by Robin's mother—and therefore belonged to Robin.

Sharon Gonzales, a co-worker of Alcala's at the *Los Angeles Times*, stated that she believed she had seen the defendant wearing such an earring *before* the Samsoe murder. However, she later admitted that the gold ball earring she testified that she had seen Alcala wearing was a different size from the one recovered from the Seattle storage locker.

Testimony favorable to the defense came from a friend of Alcala's sister Christine De La Cerda, who claimed that he had seen Alcala over forty miles away at an automobile auction at the same time as Esparza and Murchland claimed Alcala was taking pictures of them.

Phone records entered into evidence showed that Alcala had made phone calls from his home to two businesses, at 2:19 p.m. and at 2:46 p.m. on June 20, the day Robin Samsoe disappeared.

Another sister of Alcala's, Marie Toriano, claimed that her brother had phoned her from his home at 5:54 p.m. on June 20.

Alcala's mother, Anna Maria German, had presented detectives with a phone bill that showed that on June 20, at 9:41 p.m, a forty-minute call had been made from her house phone to Alcala's girlfriend in Long Beach.

After each attorney presented closing arguments, telling the jury that there was only one possible verdict that was appropriate in this case, the trial ended and deliberations began.

Hoping for a verdict immediately, Robin's mother, Marianne Frazier, who had attended every day of the four-week trial, was disappointed at the end of day one when no decision was announced.

Her spirits sank even lower the next day when still no word was heard from the jurors.

On the third day, still no verdict was announced.

What could they be thinking about? Frazier wondered. Obviously the jurors weren't all convinced that Alcala was guilty. Frazier couldn't stand that thought. Would he escape justice *again*?

Finally, on the fourth day of deliberations, on May 28, the six-man, six-woman jury returned their verdict.

The judge asked clerk Gail Carpenter to read aloud the jury's decision regarding the murder allegation.

After looking it over, she spoke the word with finality: "Guilty."

Frazier collapsed in tears.

The judge then asked the clerk to state the jury's decision regarding the counts of false imprisonment and use of a deadly weapon, a knife.

"Guilty."

The judge continued, "And as to the special circumstances of kidnapping during which the murder was committed. What did you find?"

"Guilty," said Carpenter in a strong voice.

As soon as Frazier heard the final guilty decree, her best friend, Donna Farley, who had come to the courtroom with Frazier every day, embraced her friend. Finally, Frazier's day had come.

The judge then told Alcala to return to the court on June 9, when the same jury would hear the penalty phase of the trial, and ultimately recommend life in prison without the possibility of parole—or death.

Once outside the courtroom, Frazier told reporters, "I just thank God. Maybe now my daughter can go to sleep for the first time in seven years. Maybe the rest of my family can go back to life." She said that she had been afraid that perhaps the jury would not convict Alcala this time because of all the information that the jury was not allowed to hear, based on the supreme court's decision. Frazier's friend Donna Farley stated that justice had been served "despite Rose Bird and the Supreme Court."

Goethals was ecstatic. He promised the court that Alcala's prior convictions would be "the first thing jurors would hear in the penalty phase of his trial." He was permitted to do this because Alcala had already testified in his own defense, thus allowing for cross-examination about his prior offenses.

The defense, on the other hand, felt that the verdict was an errant one, believing that there was "overwhelming evidence" to appeal the conviction.

On June 9, the penalty phase began.

Outside the presence of the jury and in front of Judge McCartin, Alcala read from a forty-nine-page paper he had written concerning his attorneys. He wrote that they were "unprepared and unwilling" to provide him with an adequate defense and that he had severed his relationship with them and would not cooperate with them in the future. As a result of their incompetence, the document stated, he was asking that his case be dismissed.

After listening carefully to the document, Judge McCartin respectfully denied Alcala's request.

Later, Goethals said, "It didn't work and the judge saw right through it. It was a ploy by Alcala to stay off Death Row for as long as possible."

After the judge's ruling, the penalty phase began in earnest.

True to his word, Goethals began by bringing up prior incidents in Alcala's history that would help make the case for a death penalty decision. Goethals declared that Alcala was the worst of the worst, a person "who preys on totally defenseless young girls." He stated, "The defendant is the epitome of malevolence. He is a sexual carnivore, and the meat he thrives on is our children."

To bolster his case, Goethals brought two witnesses to the stand. Tali Shapiro., now twenty-six, recounted how she was eight years old when Alcala kidnapped, raped, and beat her into unconsciousness. Monique Hoyt's father stated that he was testifying because his daughter was still so traumatized that she couldn't bring herself to come to court. He explained that his daughter had been kidnapped, raped, tied with ropes, and gagged by Alcala. Hoyt declared that Alcala had already been found guilty for that crime and sentenced to nine years.

When defense attorney John Patrick Dolan spoke (apparently Alcala had not entirely severed his relationship with his lawyers), he began by asking Alcala to address the jury as to what he felt an appropriate sentence would be. Sitting in his chair as he had during the entire trial and speaking unhurriedly and softly, Alcala stated that his thirteen-year prison record "shows I am absolutely harmless. I am not a threat to hurt anyone." Alcala admitted that he had a history of molesting young girls; possessing child pornography; having violated his parole; and raping and beating a fifteen-year-old girl. However, he vehemently denied that he ever met Robin Samsoe. "Please don't kill me. I don't think I should die for something I didn't do." He appealed to the jury to send him to prison for life, arguing that he was "absolutely harmless" away from children.

Alcala's mother, Anna Maria German, then testified. In tears, she said she believed in the innocence of her son, adding that he had always been a good son. She said he was always quiet and studious. He was always kind to her. He had served in the Army. She begged the jurors to spare his life.

Dolan also called witnesses who testified that Alcala was a model prisoner and a skilled typist who could serve well as a prison clerk.

Dolan told the jurors that if they decided on death, any lingering doubt in their minds would come too late. "Furthermore," he added, "even if you feel he killed the girl, a life in prison without parole would keep Alcala off the streets."

On June 19, the jury began deliberating whether it would be life or death.

The next day, the jury came back with a verdict—exactly seven years to the day after Samsoe went missing.

"And what is your verdict as to life in prison without the possibility of parole, or death?" asked the judge.

"Death," declared the foreperson.

Robin's mother cried, "Oh God!" She was steadied by her fiancé, Harry Connelly.

Outside the courtroom, Frazier hugged Joyce Carey, the jury foreperson, and said, "Thank you. My daughter deserved this."

Jurors who were interviewed cited the testimony detailing Alcala's crimes committed on other young girls as key to their decision. Jury foreperson Joyce Carey said, "The big thing among all of us was the brutal crimes inflicted on three young girls. We think Robin must have suffered tremendously."

One juror said that hearing Alcala's mother on the stand supporting her son was the one thing that "made our decision an extremely difficult one."

Formal sentencing was set for August 20. In California, the judge had the right to change a jury's decision of death to life in prison without the possibility of parole if he or she saw fit. However, up until that time, no judge had ever reversed the jury's decision in Orange County.

Two months later, on August 20, 1986, the court was once again called into session. As always, Frazier was there to witness what she hoped would be the final chapter in the heartbreaking saga concerning her daughter's death.

Before handing down his own judgment, Judge McCartin read aloud some poignant moments from Alcala's history:

In 1968, he brutally beat and raped an eight-year-old girl.

In 1971, he was caught and sent to prison.

He was paroled.

In 1974, he was caught smoking dope with a thirteen-year-old.

He was sent to prison.

He was paroled.

In 1979, he attacked and raped a fifteen-year-old.

He was sent to prison.

He was out on bail when he killed a twelve-year-old.

During the penalty phase of the trial, continued McCartin, Alcala had owned up to his past crimes but declared he had reformed.

"It is clear," stated McCartin, "that nothing in Alcala's past has made an impression on Mr. Alcala."

Before McCartin pronounced his decision, Goethals told the judge that Robin's mother would like to speak to the court.

McCartin, however, respectfully denied the request, saying, "There has already been enough emotion. . . . I think everybody has had enough of this particular case." He went on to say that he was denying the request partly out of respect for Alcala's mother, who was also in the courtroom.

McCartin ended the court session by saying that he concurred with the jury's decision of death for kidnapping and killing Robin Samsoe.

Alcala stared straight ahead as he listened to McCartin's words. Alcala's mother left the courtroom in tears, speaking to no one.

Outside the courtroom, shaking and in tears, Frazier told reporters, "My baby can rest in peace. It's long overdue. It should have happened years ago. I'm glad my daughter's death served a purpose and he'll get his just deserts. I can't wait for it to happen."

Then, speaking to her family, she said, "It's finally over. Let's go home."

Alcala would now be returned to death row at San Quentin and an automatic appeal of the death sentence would take place.

Deputy DA James Enright stated, "This was a good trial. I am confident this verdict will not be overturned."

But Alcala seemed to have nine lives.

PART
XI

Chapter Seventy-four

A March 25, 1990, headline in Orange County's *Daily Pilot* read: "A Date with Death: OC Child Killer Steps Closer to Death as Executions Resume."

The article stated that a convicted killer on California's death row, Robert Alton Harris, was scheduled to be executed in the gas chamber the following week, and if that came to pass, others on California's death row might see the Grim Reaper a lot sooner than they had expected—including Rodney Alcala.

However, few on the row were losing any sleep about the possibility. California had not used the gas chamber in twenty-three years.

The "Date with Death" article—the title was a morbid reference to Alcala's 1978 appearance on *The Dating Game*—was based on a *Daily Pilot* reporter's in-depth interview with Alcala. To find out what San Quentin death row inmates felt about the impending execution and other issues related to death row, reporter Janet Zimmerman had contacted Alcala. But before he would agree to the interview, he required that Zimmerman first read his four-hundred-page petition for a new trial and then pass a fifteen-minute quiz that he would administer, "concentrating on fine points of evidence presented at the trial."

Zimmerman passed the test.

In her two-hour interview, Zimmerman asked Alcala to describe his feelings about being on death row. He responded,

"It feels like that night in the early sixties when the back tire of my motorcycle blew out and I struggled to regain control as I careened down the Long Beach Freeway. It's like that instantaneous fear you feel. You can feel the same thing here. 'My God, I'm on Death Row.' That's pretty frightening."

It sounded like Alcala was describing death row as some kind of thrill ride, one that he might even have been enjoying.

Alcala said he spent his days in his five-foot-by-eleven-foot cell researching legal issues regarding his case and filing court motions for the right to have dental floss, baby oil, and toothpicks—items prison officials do not allow inmates to have, stating that they could aid in an escape. He was allowed a typewriter in his cell, on which he had written his own appeal to the state supreme court. The court had not yet ruled on it.

Four hours per day, six days a week, Alcala said, he could leave his solitary confines and go to the yard, where about forty other inmates hung out. Three days a week he might run laps on a small outdoor track or do aerobics in his cell. He took a shower three times a week, with hands cuffed. Sometimes he played backgammon or Scrabble with fellow inmates.

"If you had told me twenty years ago I'd be on Death Row and be playing games with killers, I'd say you were crazy," Alcala told Zimmerman.

Alcala had a color TV, which inmates were allowed if they had the funds to buy one or if someone gave them one as a gift. The TV had headphones but no speakers. Alcala said he never watched violent movies shown on the prison cable channel. Instead, he tuned into sit-coms and adventures that had no violence in them. One of his favorite movies, he said, was *When Harry Met Sally*.

Alcala kept a picture album containing photographs of his mother, his two sisters, and his brother in more joyful times.

Alcala told Zimmerman that there were 278 other men awaiting the same fate: death in the gas chamber. However, he was optimistic that he would never see that day—in spite of what they said about Robert Alton Harris's fate.

"They never keep their word around here," he pronounced with certainty.

It took two years, but Alcala's prediction about the fate of his death row companion turned out to be wrong. Harris— who had sadistically murdered two teenage boys in San Diego before robbing and terrorizing a bank full of people— was executed in San Quentin's gas chamber on April 21, 1992. It was the first execution in California since 1967.

Chapter Seventy-five

On December 31, 1992, the Supreme Court of California affirmed Alcala's 1986 conviction and death sentence.

The court acknowledged that some minor errors had, in fact, been made during the guilt phase of the 1986 trial, but it determined that these errors were "harmless and had not prejudiced defendant's trial in any fashion." The court noted that none of the defendant's assertions of error during the penalty phase had any merit and concluded that the "defendant had received a fair and untainted trial and that the Constitution did not require more."

Once again Associate Justice Stanley Mosk dissented—this time, in favor of the defense. His primary reason concerned the prosecution's key witness, Dana Crappa. He felt that the judge should have required Crappa to testify during the trial instead of simply allowing her previous testimony to be read aloud.

The dissent was officially recorded, but for the time being, Alcala would remain on death row, wiling away his time with his Scrabble board, typewriter, and color TV.

Chapter Seventy-six

In 1994, while on death row, Alcala penned what he thought of as a true-crime book, titled *You, the Jury*. The three-hundred-plus-page book was published by Buquor Books of Fremont, California. Buquor was Alcala's legal surname. Fremont was the home of his sister, Marie.

On the cover, in large capital red letters was YOU, THE JURY, followed by these words in smaller letters: *are about to hear the evidence. You have two duties: to determine the facts of the case from the evidence revealed in this trial and not from any other source; and to apply the rule of law to the facts as you determine them, and in this way to arrive at your verdict.*

Below that, in all capital red letters read: A MAN ON CALIFORNIA'S DEATH ROW CLAIMS HE'S INNOCENT, THE VICTIM OF A LEGAL SYSTEM GOING AWRY. HERE'S THE EVIDENCE. YOU'RE THE JURY. YOU DECIDE.

Completing the cover appeared four images, from left to right along the bottom: a photograph of Alcala, with big hair, a sly smile, and the words *An Unintended Victim*; two composite drawings done by Marilyn Droz in 1979—a side view and a front view of Alcala—and the words *A Possible Suspect*; and a photograph of a confident blond-haired Robin Samsoe with the words *The Intended Victim*.

The book was Alcala's attempt to prove his innocence of the murder of Robin Samsoe. It contained the transcript from the second trial, along with Alcala's own notes refuting the testimonies of witnesses and the statements of the prosecutors, maps, and pleas for readers of the book to come to their own thoughtful conclusions.

"Twelve-year-old Robin Samsoe is dead," he wrote in his self-published tome. "That her life ended abruptly is a tragedy, made more so by her youth. . . . She was victimized by an unknown assailant, and lost her life. . . . The killing of a child brings rage to all of us. It very easily blocks attempts, even in the most reasonable of us, to separate fact from emotion. . . . In our search for truth, we should be guided by reason, not emotion."

Referring to himself in the third person, he claimed, "An innocent man agonizes on California's Death Row."

Alcala maintained that "no one knows what circumstances caused Robin to go from Huntington Beach to a desolate spot near Mile Marker 11 on Santa Anita Canyon Road in the mountains above Sierra Madre; that neither the cause nor the time of Robin's death could be established; that Rodney James Alcala never even met Robin; and that Rodney had absolutely nothing to do with Robin's murder."

Alcala concluded *You, the Jury* by stating there was "no evidence linking Rodney to the disappearance and murder of Robin Samsoe . . . [T]he People have attempted to deceive you. . . . Fundamental American fairness requires that I get a fair trial, unlike the trial I got in 1986. That trial continues to mock, with apparent impunity, our unequaled American system of justice and our great Constitution."

You, the Jury included a seven-and-a-half page list of witnesses; a three-and-a-half-page list of illustrations; an eight-page index; and many footnotes. It also included a seventy-one-question yes/no survey that readers could fill out and send to Alcala at San Quentin, telling him what they thought of the book. Also in the book was an order form that a reader could fill out requesting another copy of the book for $24.50.

Chapter Seventy-seven

Since 1992, when the Supreme Court of California ruled that Alcala's 1986 trial was "fair and untainted," Alcala had spent all his days in his cell at San Quentin. Disappointed, he nevertheless filled his time reading and researching the law and serving as the in-house lawyer for other inmates on death row.

Nine years slowly passed. From all prison accounts, Alcala was a model prisoner. He never had a violation. He worked in the law library as a clerk.

Then, on March 30, 2001, a higher court issued an unexpected and shocking reversal: Alcala's conviction in the second trial was once again being overturned.

Really? Some people who were watching the case closely thought: *What kind of justice system could allow this to happen* two *times—on technicalities?* Others felt that true justice was unfolding just as it was supposed to do in a democratic country where strict laws exist as to what and what was not admissible in a trial.

Federal district court judge Stephen V. Wilson of Los Angeles wrote an opinion stating that during Alcala's 1986 trial, Judge Donald A. McCartin of Orange County Superior Court did, in fact, commit several game-changing errors:

McCartin, the opinion declared, "precluded the defense from developing and presenting" evidence from Dana Crappa by allowing her testimony from the 1980 trial to be *read* to the jury without the witness being on the stand.

Further, the opinion concluded that McCartin had ruled incorrectly when he did not allow psychologist Ray William London to testify for the defense. London had listened to hours of taped police interviews with Crappa and was set to testify that her statements "appeared to be induced."

Furthermore, Alcala's lawyers should have been allowed to introduce a psychologist's testimony that cast doubt on Crappa's amnesia claim.

Finally, the opinion stated, Alcala's attorneys did not call a witness to support Alcala's alibi that he was interviewing for a job as a photographer at Knott's Berry Farm when Robin Samsoe disappeared.

As a result, the ruling concluded, "the Court grants the petition and orders that the State of California either grant Alcala a retrial consistent with the United States Constitution or release him from custody."

At fifty-seven, Alcala was once again poised for another shot at freedom.

Was he the luckiest man in the world, or what?

After Judge McCartin was told of the ruling, he was outraged. "What do I think about it? I was thinking I could do the execution myself." He continued, "It's insanity," adding that there was no evidence that the authorities performed hypnosis on Crappa.

Alcala's sister, on the other hand, was thrilled. Krissy, fifty-four, of Whittier, stated, "Oh my God. I'm ecstatic. I cannot believe this. It's about time." She added, "There's just no evidence that ties [my brother] to this. You think the system of law protects the innocent, but it doesn't work that way."

Krissy was eager to voice her indignation. Notwithstanding Alcala's conviction for child molestation following the brutal rape of Tali S. and his conviction for rape after the vicious attack on Monique Hoyt, Krissy had steadfastly stood by her "innocent" big brother for years.

Chapter Seventy-eight

When Robin's mother, heard that Alcala's conviction had been overturned, she screamed, "Oh, no!" In anguish she choked out, "My God, how many times are they going to put us through this hell? This is just so unfair!" Then she broke down in sobs.

Robin's mother had remarried since the second trial and was now Marianne Connelly. That night she wasn't able to sleep at all, and the next day Connelly was taken to Riverside County Regional Medical Center. She told the doctors, "I'm a mess. I need help just to get through the day. . . . I am scared, just so very scared."

Connelly's friend, Patricia Rose, had accompanied her to the hospital. "We'll get through it," she comforted Connelly. "I'll help you get through it."

"How?" asked Connelly disbelieving. "This is just too much to ask. No one should have to go through this a third time."

That day, when she returned home from the hospital, reporters were waiting. Connelly gathered all her energy to focus and began to speak. "You've heard enough about Alcala," she said. Now she wanted people to know about Robin.

Connelly said that she wanted them to have an idea of the kind of girl Robin was. She said that for over a year, every Saturday morning, Robin would prepare breakfast for her and serve it to her in bed. "The food would be artfully placed on a tray, with a daisy.

"She never called me Mom," Connelly continued. "Her name for me was Pretty Lady. She told me she wanted to have red hair, just like mine. Robin's hair," said Connelly, "was almost white. I told her that people spend lots of money to try to get hair like hers, and she said, 'But, Pretty Lady, I want to look like you.'"

Connelly reported that two years before Robin died, Robin had had surgery on her esophagus, and after that Robin told her mother that if God got her through it, she would spend one hour in church for every hour that she danced. "Robin lived up to that promise."

Connelly told reporters that she had worked three jobs as a single mother to raise four children. Two years before Robin died, the family had left Wisconsin and moved to California to get a new start. "We chose Huntington Beach because it seemed like a nice, safe place to raise children. I can't help but think I drove Robin to her death," she said with tears running down her cheeks. Connelly explained that she no longer read newspapers or watched TV after seeing her daughter's pictures plastered all over the media. She filled her days with friends, antiquing, volunteering, and enjoying her remaining children and nine grandchildren. "Each of my children has a daughter who resembles Robin," Connelly said. "Each one asked me to name their daughter after Robin," but Connelly admitted she had declined. There was only one Robin.

Regarding the overturning of the conviction, Connelly said, "I didn't think Alcala had any appeals left. I thought I was waiting only to hear the date he'd be executed." Then, speaking about the trials, she said, "The first time, I don't think it was even as bad. You're in a lot of shock. The second time, you know everything and you get scared. You have to see him every day . . . I don't know. I just don't know. I don't think I'm ready for this."

Then, after a long pause in which Connelly seemed as if she might fall apart, she said with a faraway look in her eyes, "Robin was our angel. There was always an aura of peace and tranquillity about her. And now we're all so overwhelmed."

Chapter Seventy-nine

In its March 2001 ruling overturning Alcala's conviction in his second Samsoe trial, the U.S. District Court gave the State of California 120 days to either retry or release Alcala. In response to this ruling, the State petitioned the Ninth Circuit Court of Appeals for a reversal of their ruling.

In 2002, a new California state law allowed law enforcement and corrections officers to take samples of DNA from prisoners, using "reasonable force" if a prisoner refused to give a sample voluntarily. Once obtained, a prisoner's DNA profile would then be entered into the state's DNA database. Investigators could use the database to search for DNA profiles that matched crime-scene evidence—even from cold cases.

This was a momentous decision for law enforcement officials. Now, finally, they would be able to compare DNA evidence from crime scenes with DNA of prisoners—and hopefully find some matches and solve some cases.

Over the years while he was in jail, Alcala had railed against the unfairness of implementing such a program.

In 2003, two years after his conviction was overturned, Alcala was feeling, if not optimistic, then at least hopeful: He was going to have a new trial. He was going to have another shot at freedom.

Matt Murphy, Orange County senior deputy DA, who focused solely on homicides, was the prosecutor slated to try

Alcala for the third time for the Samsoe murder. Admitted to the bar in 1993, by 2003 he already had important wins to his credit.

There was the double murder case 2003 in which Vincent Cheung killed his former boyfriend and his lover. He was convicted and sentenced to death.

There was the murder in 2003 of a woman from San Clemente by a man she met on the Internet but who a month later refused to move out of her home. He was convicted and sentenced to twenty-five years to life.

At the time, Murphy was a boyish-looking thirty-six-year-old whose healthy, outdoor good looks belied a razor-sharp tongue and bulldog tenaciousness. He *would* win his cases by doggedly pursuing every angle and leaving no stone unturned.

One day, as Murphy was planning various scenarios for what he would present to the jurors to permanently nail Alcala, he received a call.

"You sitting down?" asked his boss, Orange County DA Tony Rackauckas.

"I will now," responded Murphy. "What'cha got?"

"Something big. Just got a call from [Los Angeles County DA Steve] Cooley's office. They got a match!"

"Care to tell me who? What case?"

"Yup. Your boy, Alcala."

"What'd you get?"

"DNA links him to Wixted. Nineteen seventy-seven murder. Malibu. Semen."

Murphy was glad he was sitting down. When he got off the phone, he was speechless. His first clear thought was: *How many more will we get?* His second thought was to contact the Los Angeles County DA's office right away—and start working with them.

Alcala was now linked to another killing. Only, this time it wasn't a circumstantial case. It was a DNA case!

As a result of the DNA hit, the Los Angeles County DA's

office filed murder charges against Alcala on June 5, 2003, alleging that he killed Georgia Wixted while committing two other felonies—burglary and rape—thus making it a special-circumstances case. If convicted, Alcala would be eligible for the death penalty.

Although it was unusual, prosecutors in Orange and Los Angeles counties began to pool information and resources and to work together to figure out the breadth of Alcala's rampage. They combed through cold-case files in search of any murders from the 1970s that matched the MO of the Georgia Wixted case. Wixted was a nurse who worked at the Centinela Hospital and failed to show up at work on December 15, 1977. The MO was deeply disturbing. The key elements of the Wixted attack were that the assailant had broken into the victim's apartment in Malibu in the middle of the night; smashed her skull with a claw hammer; repeatedly strangled her; raped and sodomized her; and callously posed her dead, battered, and bloodied body.

How many cases like that could there be?

When Anne and Al Michelena of Irvine, sister and brother-in-law of Georgia Wixted, heard the news about a DNA match, they were shocked. For a quarter of a century the mystery of who had murdered her sister had kept Anne anxious and troubled every single day.

"For the past twenty-five years," said Anne, "I've been constantly looking over my shoulder, not knowing what I was looking for or who I was looking for. It got to the point where I thought I would never know, but I never stopped wondering."

With the DNA news linking Alcala to Wixted, it looked like Alcala might soon receive the punishment he deserved.

However, on the seemingly never-ending roller-coaster ride that had become Alcala's life, on Friday, June 27, 2003—around three weeks after Alcala's DNA was matched to DNA found on Wixted's body—Alcala received some good news.

The Ninth Circuit Court of Appeals upheld the 2001 federal district court's decision to throw out Alcala's conviction and death sentence for the Samsoe killing—thus denying the appeal made by the warden of the California State Prison at San Quentin, Jeanne S. Woodford, to overturn the decision.

"The judgment granting the inmate's petition for a writ of habeas corpus was affirmed," stated the announcement from the Ninth Circuit. "We conclude, as did the district court, that the deficient presentation of Alcala's alibi and the exclusion of Dr. London's testimony [which "deprived Alcala of an important opportunity to discredit the *only* eyewitness who allegedly could place Alcala with Samsoe at the scene of the crime on the evening of June 20"] was each on its own an error sufficiently prejudicial to grant Alcala's petition . . . . [Along with] the deficient failure to investigate the crime scene, the cumulative impact of these errors severely undermines our confidence in the jury's verdict. We affirm the conditional grant of Alcala's petition."

The ruling was signed, "U.S. Court of Appeal decision for the Ninth Circuit, D. W. Nelson, Senior Circuit Judge."

Alcala would, indeed, be retried for that case.

When Deputy Attorney General Adrienne S. Denault, who argued the case before the appeals court, heard the news, she said she was "incredibly disappointed. We think the court is wrong and that justice has not been served in this case." Denault said that the decision would be appealed to a larger panel of the Ninth Circuit Court of Appeal—or to the Supreme Court of the United States, if necessary.

After Deputy DA Tom Goethals, who had prosecuted Alcala during the 1986 trial, heard the news, he said, "This is unbelievable. It was one of the most satisfying convictions of my career, because I truly believe that Mr. Alcala is a very dangerous man." He continued, "No doubt, he'll have to be tried again, but after twenty-two years, it won't be that easy."

Brent Romney, a professor at Western State University College of Law in Orange County and a former deputy district attorney, concurred: "Live witnesses, their memories no longer fresh, are generally less effective than they were at the original trial. They can refresh their memory by reading the prior testimony, but there's more opportunity for the opposing counsel to cross-examine concerning very minor details that have been lost over time."

When Robin Samsoe's brother, Robert, now thirty-seven, heard the news, he was enraged and appalled. "Two juries can't be wrong. He's the one who killed my sister. [The appeals courts] have no feelings for victims."

Upon hearing the news, Judge McCartin who had presided over Alcala's 1986 trial, stated: "I am furious. Those ***** [on the Ninth Circuit Court] always find something to reverse. The Ninth Circuit Court is a bunch of hacks and college professors who never tried a case themselves, and they're all against the death penalty."

McCartin saw little hope that things would change anytime soon. "One can do nothing to get rid of these guys. Federal judges are appointed for life, and barring death, retirement, or impeachment and conviction by Congress, they can't be booted out."

On October 7, 2003, Alcala was brought before superior court judge Francisco (Frank) Pedro Briseño, who would be presiding over Alcala's third trial. Briseño was a retired U.S. Marine Corps colonel and former prosecutor.

That day, for the third time, Alcala pleaded not guilty to killing Robin Samsoe.

Then, on October 17, 2003, Alcala made a motion to act as a lawyer in this third trial.

In his motion, Alcala, now sixty, wrote that he had reviewed every single detail of the Samsoe trials for the past seventeen years and felt he could help his attorney, David Zimmerman, with his defense.

"I feel I'm wasting my time sitting in my cell doing nothing," Alcala told Briseño,

Briseño stated that he would consider Acala's request for cocounsel status.

Alcala's new trial was set to begin in the spring of 2005.

PART
XII

PART
XII

Chapter Eighty

In 2004, Los Angeles detectives who were working on cold cases may have felt they had died and gone to heaven.

Another DNA match was found—and it didn't bode well for Alcala.

Decades earlier, investigators had discovered semen on the body of Jill Barcomb, eighteen years old, originally from Oneida, New York, but then living in LA. Her dead body had been found posed in the Hollywood Hills in November 1977, just as Wixted's would be the next month. The DNA from the semen turned out to be a match to Alcala's.

This DNA hit came as a complete shock to investigators. For nearly thirty years, they had believed that Barcomb—who had been viciously beaten, strangled, and raped—was a victim of the Hillside Strangler, in spite of their protests otherwise.

And now there were three counts against Alcala.

The body count meant that Alcala could now, by definition, be declared a serial killer.

PART
XIII

Chapter Eighty-one

Alcala's third trial for the murder and kidnapping of Robin Samsoe was set to begin in October 2005, and Alcala was poised to help himself. He was aiding one of his court-appointed attorneys, George Peters, to prepare. (Peters had taken over the case from David Zimmerman, who had represented Alcala on his first appeal and recently passed away.)

In spite of the recent DNA matches linking him to the murders of Jill Barcomb and Georgia Wixted, Alcala, sixty-two, was focused *only* on the Samsoe case. He wasn't going to spend any time at all defending himself against the LA cases.

However, before the trial began, Alcala received some *really* bad news that temporarily halted his focused research.

An Orange County grand jury came down with an indictment against him, and this time the evidence seemed irrefutable. It turned out that authorities had found DNA and other forensic evidence linking him to *two more* victims.

The two new victims were Charlotte Lamb, a legal secretary, who was murdered in 1978 and whose body was found thirteen miles from her home in a laundry room in El Segundo; and Jill Parenteau, a supervisor in a data-entry company and also a college student, murdered in 1979 in her apartment in Burbank.

And now there were five.

* * *

"The DNA hits were like turning a light on in a room," said Captain Ray Peavy, head of the homicide bureau for the Los Angeles County Sheriff's Office. "Suddenly an unsolvable case is now solved. [Alcala] was running around Southern California looking for prey. He looked for innocent victims who couldn't put up much of a fight."

"He belongs right up there in a list of serial killers," said LAPD detective Cliff Shepard, who was in the department's cold-case unit. "His being behind bars since 1979 probably saved a lot of lives."

Tony Rackauckas, the district attorney for Orange County, agreed, saying that Alcala's arrest in Samsoe's death was "the only reason he stopped killing. I think that the ability of law enforcement to analyze DNA is the greatest breakthrough . . . since the two-way radio. We knew Alcala was a vicious, merciless killer. But we didn't realize that he was a serial killer to this extent."

When the grand jury was convened in Orange County to hear all the new forensic evidence against Alcala, prosecutors from Los Angeles County joined forces with the Orange County DA's office to make the case. Los Angeles County deputy DA Gina Satriano helped present the evidence in court as part of a cross-jurisdictional collaboration. Prosecutors from both counties believed the grand jury needed to hear the *whole* story about Alcala and the murders of Charlotte Lamb, Jill Parenteau, Georgia Wixted, and Jill Barcomb. To that end, seventeen witnesses were called.

Satriano stated that testing *definitively* linked DNA found on earrings in Alcala's Seattle storage locker to the DNA of Charlotte Lamb; that DNA in semen recovered from Lamb's body was a positive match to Alcala; and that Alcala's palm print matched a print lifted from a brass bed railing at the scene of the murder of Georgia Wixted.

Revealed also was that some of the blood taken from the robe and bed of Jill Parenteau pointed to Alcala. "Alcala could not be excluded . . . and the combination of serological factors was so rare that it would only be present in 3.5 percent of the population."

Moreover, semen swabs taken from the murdered bodies of Georgia Wixted and Jill Barcomb were a definitive match to Alcala's DNA profile. The chance of that DNA profile belonging to someone other than Alcala was one in a billion.

Satriano asked that Alcala's dental records be retrieved from San Quentin because, according to Satriano, evidence of a bite mark on Jill Barcomb's body had been preserved by the coroner in 1979, and Satriano wanted to see if it was a match to Alcala. "The bite nearly severed the victim's right breast nipple," she stated.

After hearing all the evidence against Alcala, the grand jury came down with an indictment. Although Lamb, Parenteau, Barcomb, and Wixted had all been murdered in Los Angeles County, the grand jury held open the possibility that prosecutors could consolidate all *five* cases—including that of Robin Samsoe—and try Alcala in Orange County. Proceedings were already well under way there for his third trial in the Samsoe case.

Orange County DA Rackauckas said that combining the Samsoe case with the LA cases would allow the counties to pool resources and shorten the survivors' already lengthy wait for justice.

George Peters, Alcala's lawyer, strongly disagreed with the idea of combining the cases. "By trying the Samsoe case separately," said Peters, "the jury would be able to see the Samsoe case in isolation and not be prejudiced by hearing about the other cases."

When Samsoe's mother heard about the DNA hits, she said that if Alcala had been executed after his first death sentence, the other victims' families might never have known who killed them. "The new charges might allow the families to get some closure." However, she added, "I'm saying that strictly to be noble, I'm sure. I just wish he was gone."

Anne Michelena, Georgia Wixted's sister, said, "It makes

me feel a sense of justice knowing that DNA technology can do this." Anne and her husband, Al, believed that the charges would give hope to other families as well.

"I just regret that most of my family didn't live long enough to hear the news," Anne said.

Chapter Eighty-two

On November 22, 2005, Alcala, sixty-two, entered an Orange County courtroom wearing glasses, a denim jacket, jeans, and a red plaid shirt. He pleaded not guilty to the torture, rape, and slayings of four LA women. The Los Angeles County district attorney's office made the decision to bring the LA cases to the Orange County grand jury. Then the LA County district attorney's office moved to consolidate their cases with the Orange County case. The judge granted the consolidation.

Judge Briseño scheduled a hearing for January 13, 2006, at which time he would rule on whether or not the charges against Alcala would be consolidated into one trial in Orange County, using prosecutors from both Orange and Los Angeles counties' district attorney offices.

The prosecutors' contention was that Orange County could try the Los Angeles County cases based on a 1998 law that stated that serial killers charged with murders in different counties can be tried in one county. Orange County deputy DA James Mulgrew, who was handling the motions in Alcala's case, stated that the law recognized that "serial killers do not consider county lines when they perpetrate their crimes."

During the January hearing on whether or not the five murders could be joined into one trial, Alcala's lawyers, George Peters and Richard Schwartzberg, argued that the Samsoe trial should be separated from the others, stating that the statute allowing for consolidation was new and that no settled case law regarding it had been issued.

However, they would not prevail.

A May 25, 2006, headline in the *Los Angeles Times* read: "Judge OKs Merging 5 Trials for Murder." The article began, "A man accused of killing a 12-year-old Huntington Beach girl as well as four LA area women in the 1970s will be tried in all five cases in Orange County at once, prosecutors said Friday."

Attorney John Patrick Dolan, who had once represented Alcala, called the ruling by Judge Briseño "a big victory for the prosecution." Dolan said that after Alcala's second conviction in the Samsoe murder was overturned, the case against Alcala "was paper thin. But lumping the cases together makes the prosecution's case much stronger." Dolan continued, "If you're a juror and you hear one murder case, you may be able to find reasonable doubt, but it's very hard to say you have reasonable doubt on all five, especially when four of the five aren't alleged by eyewitnesses but are proven by DNA matches."

LA County prosecutor Satriano believed that combining the cases would show a fuller portrait of Alcala to the jurors. "Hopefully," she said, "the jury will get to see who he is."

Chapter Eighty-three

To prosecutors in both counties, Alcala was a serial killer. But even within this rare, sociopathic breed, he was something more—a narcissist for one thing, and that was just one of the multiple diagnoses Alcala was given by court-appointed mental health experts.

According to the *DSM-IV*, a person with "narcissistic personality disorder (NPD) must exhibit at least five of the following: a grandiose sense of self-importance; fantasies of superiority; a sense of entitlement; concern only with his/her own ends; inability to empathize; often envious; often haughty."

But, according to the authorities, there was still more to the psychological profile. Alcala was not *simply* a sociopath and a narcissist: He was also a sexual sadist whose insatiable appetite for brutality and cruelty was what eventually got him caught.

The *DSM-IV*'s definition of sexual sadism is that it "involves acts (real, not simulated) in which the individual derives sexual excitement for the psychological or physical suffering of individuals (including humiliation) of the victim. . . .

"When sexual sadism is severe, and especially when it is associated with antisocial personality disorder, individuals with sexual sadism may seriously injure or kill their victims."

Did these traits fit Alcala? The prosecutors were going to do their best to prove so.

Chapter Eighty-four

Despite the growing body of forensic evidence against Alcala, the road to justice continued to be haphazard. On February 28, 2007, the optimism prosecutors felt about merging the five murder trials into one was quashed when, in response to Alcala's petition to separate the four LA murders from the Samsoe case, the Fourth District Court of Appeal decided that Alcala would have two trials.

They would not, however, be the two trials that Alcala was hoping for.

In their summation, the justices wrote: ". . . Alcala argues that a fair trial is absolutely impossible if he is forced to face the 'glass mountain' of evidence that all five murder cases would build. That point is hard to deny. The Barcomb and Wixted crimes do not share all the marks of similarity as do the Parenteau, Lamb, and Samsoe murders; and they possess the DNA evidence Alcala argues is unfairly insurmountable."

The court of appeals then ordered that the Wixted and Barcomb cases be severed from the Robin Samsoe trial but that the consolidated cases involving Samsoe, Parenteau, and Lamb could go forward as a single trial.

The prosecutors were deeply dissatisfied with this judgment, believing all the cases should be tried together. The defense was also dissatisfied that any of the Los Angeles County cases were going to be consolidated with the Orange County case. The defense immediately appealed to the

Supreme Court of California, and the prosecution joined in the appeal.

How many more years, prosecutors wondered, would the families of Georgia Wixted and Jill Barcomb have to wait before getting their day in court?

Chapter Eighty-five

The Daring Case Killer

Despite All, Cantcon has had to wait three decades a lie the outstil.

How many more convictions court workstool what be families of Grayson Moore and Jill Barcomb have to await before getting their day in court?

Chapter Eighty-five

On June 11, 2008, the roller-coaster ride continued. There was yet another reversal. The California Supreme Court ruled *against* the 2007 decision to separate the trials into two. The court wrote that Alcala would *not* have two separate trials but would stand trial on all five cases simultaneously in Orange County. The California Supreme Court's conclusion was the following:

"As the People observe, there is nothing unfair about the defendant facing an overwhelmingly high likelihood of conviction based on admissible evidence and permissible inferences [DNA and serological evidence]."

In their eighteen-page ruling, the state's highest court stated that the cases were similar enough to warrant a single trial. They cited the fact that all of the victims were white and young; all were found partially or totally nude; all had been sexually assaulted; all had received blunt force trauma to the face; and all occurred within a nineteenth-month period.

As a result, wrote the California Supreme Court, "The judgment of the Court of Appeal is reversed. A single trial on all five murder charges may proceed in Orange County."

When this latest decision came down, the Orange County DA's office was ecstatic. An official statement from the deputy DA read, "We are gratified. Had the cases been split up, families of some of the victims would not have seen justice . . . for at least another decade." The statement continued, "Robin Samsoe has had to wait three decades to get justice. The court correctly recognized that a serial murder case involving five young women in two neighboring counties with common characteristics . . . should be tried together."

Alcala's defense team was enraged. They stated that the prosecution was unfairly "piling on Alcala with a mountain of evidence in cases that were not that similar." Defense attorney Richard Schwartzberg added that the district attorney's office wanted to try four "exceptionally strong" LA cases to bolster the "exceptionally weak" Samsoe case.

PART
XIV

PART
XIV

Chapter Eighty-six

In 2009, there was no question that Alcala's trial for the murders of Samsoe, Wixted, Barcomb, Lamb, and Parenteau would proceed. Alcala, however, had not yet finished monkeying with the justice system. That year he began repeatedly filing appeals to Judge Briseño to be allowed to represent himself in his upcoming trial:

On April 17, 2009, he filed a request; it was denied on May 29.

On June 3, he filed another request; it was denied again.

On July 2, he again requested to proceed in propria persona; it was denied on July 24.

Alcala was not simply petitioning to act as co-counsel, as he had in 2003. Now he was requesting to act in propria persona, meaning that he would act—without backup—as his own lawyer. *Why not?* he reasoned. Hadn't he been working as a de facto jailhouse attorney for years?

Alcala believed that his court-appointed lawyers had been ineffective and that he could do a better job of representing himself. However, most everyone else who had followed Alcala's case closely felt differently, citing the fact that Alcala had been defended by three of the top attorneys in Orange County—John Barnett, John Patrick Dolan, and David Zimmerman—and more recently by specialists in death penalty matters, George Peters and Richard Schwartzberg.

Was this an instance of Alcala's narcissism in action?

Was he convinced that he was smarter, more effective, and more qualified than a real attorney? Some observers of the proceedings weren't so sure. No doubt Alcala was a narcissist, but it was also possible he was acting strategically. Michael Molfetta, a defense lawyer with no affiliation to the case, commented that he believed Alcala wanted to represent himself so he could "muck up the system so [as to ensure] he dies a natural death." He felt that Alcala thought his best chance at avoiding the death penalty would be to keep his case in appeals for thirty years—and considering it had already been thirty years since Robin Samsoe was killed, Molfetta's theory did not seem implausible.

When Briseño ruled on July 24 that Alcala *must* permit his court-appointed lawyers, George Peters and Richard Schwartzberg, to represent him, Scott Burns, executive director of the National District Attorneys Association, agreed with Briseño's decision. Representing oneself, he said, is "like someone saying 'I want to engage in a complicated surgery on myself.'"

Richard Dieter, executive director of the Death Penalty Information Center, concurred. He said that the "biggest reason cases are reversed is poor representation by an attorney." When you serve as your own attorney, Dieter stated, "it's difficult to complain about the quality of your representation if you knowingly, willingly represent yourself." And by law, when you represent yourself, you waive any right to later appeal that you had ineffective counsel.

Larry Welborn, who reported on the Samsoe case over the years for the *Orange County Register*, weighed in on Alcala's desire to represent himself in court. Welborn stated in a September 28, 2009 article titled: "Serial-Murder Suspect Gets His Wish, and It May Come Back to Haunt Him" that Alcala's representing himself "reminds me of another old adage: He who has himself for a lawyer has a fool for client."

But, as was the case in so many of Alcala's previous dealings, the roller-coaster ride was just getting under way. After Briseño made his July 24 ruling, Alcala appealed the decision to the Fourth District Court of Appeal. On September 14, 2009, the district court came down with what was to be the final ruling on the matter of self-representation. It granted Alcala "pro per" (short for "in propria persona") status. According to the district court's ruling, "Defendants have a constitutional right to defend themselves unless they are mentally incompetent or if it would unjustly delay the trial."

So, strange as it seemed, Alcala would serve as his own defense attorney in his upcoming trial, pitted against Orange County senior deputy DA Matt Murphy and Orange County senior deputy DA and motions expert Jim Mulgrew—who wrote the brief regarding the joinder of all the murders to be tried in Orange County and argued it in front of the California Supreme Court—and Deputy DA Gina Satriano of Los Angeles County.

In December 2009, Rodney Alcala, along with Satriano and Murphy, began jury selection. Satriano would be presenting the Los Angeles County cases and Murphy would be handling the Samsoe case for Orange County.

Satriano's background as a district attorney included several high-profile cases, including Courtney Love's assault and possession charges; Mel Gibson's drunk-driving incident; and Paula Poundstone's child-endangerment charges. Satriano knew something about playing hardball, having played professional baseball for three women's teams (her father, Tom, was one of the original Los Angeles Angels catchers/third basemen). Satriano was primarily a pitcher for the Colorado Silver Bullets, the first women's professional baseball team in the United States since the 1950s. She taught at Pepperdine and had appeared on several TV shows, including *Oprah* and *Day One*, on ABC. She was also the Stuart House coordinator for the Los Angeles sex crimes division.

One feature of this jury selection stood in stark contrast to most others: As defense counsel, Alcala spoke directly to prospective jurors and asked them questions. Once empaneled, these same jurors would ultimately decide whether Alcala would live or die.

"The danger with a pro per," said Murphy later, "is that prospective jurors are going to feel sorry for him because you have a situation in which there are two experienced attorneys and a guy representing himself. You have to be very careful that you don't leave anyone on the jury who will feel sorry for him, because at the end, we want to argue that he is not the underdog. The victims are the underdogs."

Late on January 5, 2010, the two prosecutors and Alcala agreed on a seven-man, five-woman jury and on three men and two women to serve as alternates.

Chapter Eighty-seven

On January 11, 2010, the third trial for Rodney J. Alcala was set to begin. In this one, however, not only would Alcala be representing himself, but he would also be standing accused of four *other* murders besides that of Robin Samsoe.

When Marianne Connelly arrived at the courthouse, reporters asked her how she was feeling. "Oh my God," she said weakly. "It's starting all over again. Everyone says I need to go on with the rest of my life, but how can I when my beautiful daughter is in her grave and her killer keeps getting more trials?" Connelly stated that she hoped to attend every day of the trial. "How can I not go? I need to know what is going on." However, she was afraid she might not have the strength. "I hope I can do it for Robin," she said, "but I'm getting a little weak. I'm getting tired."

Along with Connelly, more than one hundred spectators piled into the eleventh-floor courtroom. Several media organizations had asked if they could video opening statements, and Judge Briseño said they could. All of the local news stations had been running with the story. It seemed that all of Southern California was poised to see if justice would be meted out, once and for all.

Alcala, now sixty-five and wearing a tan sports coat, blue shirt, and a striped blue tie, sat next to his court-appointed investigator, Alfredo Rasch. Rasch's role was to assist the defendant in his defense by interviewing witnesses, serving subpoenas, and performing any other tasks the defendant might need from outside the jail world, since, of course, he was in custody. On the desk in front of Alcala was a laptop computer.

Aaron Mintz was the court reporter. Impeccably dressed and laser-focused on his work, he alone transcribed each and every word of the proceedings each and every day. Sitting below and in front of the judge with a Stentura 8000 stenograph machine on his desk, he had his fingers poised to record everything that transpired. All in all, the transcript numbered 6,640 pages. "You have to listen with your hands. If you listen with your brain, you won't be fast enough. It's got to be an automatic response," he said.

Mintz remarked that because this was a "pro per" case, the defendant wouldn't have free rein to walk around the courtroom, for security reasons. So, said Mintz, Alcala stayed seated and Murphy and Satriano stayed seated or stood at the podium during the trial.

"When you work on a death penalty case," said Mintz, "you do what they call a daily transcript. Monday's proceedings are turned in to the attorneys on Tuesday. I e-mail the proceedings periodically throughout the day to a scopist, who edits them and sends them back to me. Then I proofread the transcript, print it, and it is ready for attorneys."

Mintz takes his job seriously.

"A tape recorder is not as good as a court stenographer," Mintz explained, "because there is no better microphone for deciphering the spoken word than the human ear. Tape recorders pick up all sounds accurately, but they can't tell you if they don't understand a word or if someone mumbles. I have the ability to stop proceedings and ask to repeat. And I have to. I dispassionately preserve the record. I am protecting all the parties involved—the judge, the witnesses, the lawyers. We protect the record."

After welcoming the jurors, Judge Briseño told them that because the defendant had entered a plea of not guilty, they were here to "hear the evidence and the law and to make a decision, if you're able to."

The clerk then read the charges: murder during the commission of the kidnapping of Robin Samsoe; deliberate, premeditated murder with torture during the commission of the burglary, robbery, and rape of Jill Parenteau; deliberate, premeditated murder with torture during the commission of the burglary, robbery, and rape of Charlotte Lamb; deliberate, premeditated murder with torture during the commission of the burglary, robbery, and rape of Georgia Wixted; and the deliberate, premeditated murder with torture of Jill Barcomb.

The judge told the court that the State wished to make an opening statement but that Alcala, acting as his own defense attorney, wanted to hold off making opening remarks until he began his defense.

And with that, the prosecution began its remarks. Satriano started by giving a chronological overview of the case. Dressed in a tailored suit, Satriano spoke alternately softly and louder at times. She stood at a podium in front of the jury and looked each one of them in the eyes. Her kind face and soft demeanor immediately sent out welcoming vibes to the jurors. First, Satriano detailed the horrific sight that police encountered in the Hollywood Hills on November 10, 1977, when the body of Jill Barcomb was discovered. Then Satriano described how, just over one month later, the Los Angeles County Sheriff's Department had found Georgia Wixted dead in her Malibu apartment, bloodied and bruised.

As Satriano spoke, a PowerPoint presentation was displayed on a large screen, showing vivid, gruesome crime scene photographs of each victim. These were juxtaposed with snapshots showing happy times in each victim's young life.

Satriano noted similarities between Barcomb and Wixted's deaths: Both had suffered multiple bruises and deep cuts to their scalps; both had suffered multiple cuts to their chest and extremities; both had ligatures around their necks; both had multiple tears from impact to their mouths; both were strangled so hard that many of the small blood vessels in their eyes had ruptured from the pressure.

"And like Jill," said Satriano, "almost every one of Georgia's injuries was inflicted upon her body while she was alive, while her heart was pumping the blood through her system."

Satriano stated that DNA was found on both women. "The murderer left a part of himself . . . but technology was not yet available to solve these crimes in the '70s, so this investigation also grew cold and eventually this case also went unsolved."

Satriano then detailed how six months after Wixted's body was found, Charlotte Lamb's body was discovered on a "cold, empty concrete floor . . . with [the deceased's] breasts propped up . . . absolutely naked. The only item of dress found was a single sandal shoe with a long lace, but the shoe was not on Charlotte's foot. The lace of the shoe was tied tightly around her neck as a ligature, with the sandal itself dangling off to the side of her strangled dead body."

As with the other two bodies, Satriano continued, ligature cuts deep in her neck caused the blood vessels in her eyes to rupture. As with the others, there was trauma to the genitals, to both the anal and vaginal openings. As with the others, Satriano stated, most of the torture was inflicted while "she was alive, while her heart was still pumping the blood through her system."

But it wasn't only the killer's MO that matched the previous cases. The evidence was similar too. "Again sperm was found in her vaginal cavity and again, the person who did this left a part of himself at this crime scene inside Charlotte Lamb's body. But," Satriano continued, "the technology wasn't available, and the case investigation grew cold."

A year after Lamb's murder, Satriano told the jurors, "Jill Parenteau was found dead inside her apartment bedroom." Again, she was completely naked. Again, her shoulders and upper back were propped up by pillows, exposing bare breasts. She was posed on her back, on the floor, directly facing the bedroom door, her legs spread wide open.

As with the others, Satriano told the jurors, Parenteau was "strangled to such a point that many small blood vessels in her eyes ruptured. The trauma to her head was sufficient to cause bleeding into the under-surface of her scalp. Ligature marks were found around her neck. And, once again, the injuries were inflicted upon her body while she was alive.

"And once again," Satriano intoned, "the person left part of himself at the scene. But nothing could be matched until many, many years later."

Satriano had one more murder to describe. All the jurors were spellbound by her words, unable to take their eyes off the woman who was detailing some of the most horrific incidents they had ever heard of. "Less than one week after Jill Parenteau's murder," Satriano continued, "a twelve-year-old girl, Robin Samsoe, went missing on her way to her ballet lesson that day in Orange County."

After giving details about the discovery of Samsoe's remains, Satriano told the jurors about the media frenzy that followed; about the composite showing a suspect with long, curly hair that ran 24/7 in newspapers and on TV; about how, a few days after Samsoe's disappearance, Alcala changed the carpet in his Datsun; about how, less than a week after Samsoe's disappearance, Alcala straightened his hair and then cut it into "a Rod Stewart–type style" after having had long hair for some ten years; and about how Alcala made plans to leave the area, telling some people he was moving to Dallas and others to Mexico.

"As with Jill Barcomb's body," continued Satriano, "Robin's body was also found off a dirt road, in a remote brush-filled mountainous area." However, her body was discovered "two long weeks after Samsoe went missing." Because of the late discovery and the decomposition of the body, along with its exposure to the elements and animals, Satriano stated, little biological or trace evidence was found with the body.

Satriano paused. Her face clearly showing the anguish she felt for the victims and their families. She then told about Alcala's driving to Seattle, "where he knew no one, had no job, had no place to live, and told no one, including his mother, where he was going." There, she said, Alcala rented a storage locker.

Meanwhile, said Satriano, the Huntington Beach police continued looking for the suspect in the composite and started receiving many phone calls. After putting together a "six-pack" photographic lineup and showing it to witnesses, people began pointing to one man as the photographer who had been taking photos of young women and girls in their bathing suits at the beach on June 20, 1979, the day Samsoe disappeared.

The man was Rodney Alcala.

Ultimately, continued Satriano, Alcala was arrested on July 24, 1979, and charged in Samsoe's murder. The police searched his home and car and, among other things, they noticed a receipt for a storage locker in Seattle, Washington, dated after Robin's death.

A short time later, police flew to Seattle to look at the contents of the locker. In it, Satriano stated, they found many of Alcala's personal items as well as a silk pouch containing women's jewelry. When earrings from the pouch were shown to Robin Samsoe's mother, she recognized one of them.

Meanwhile, continued Satriano, over the years, another earring from that same silk pouch sat on the shelves of the Huntington Beach Police Department evidence room "without challenge, without controversy, until technology caught up."

When DNA analysis became available, stated Satriano, detectives working on the case sent out the entire pouch for testing. "After twenty-seven years, DNA evidence on a rose earring with a diamond stud in the middle found in the silk pouch matched that of Charlotte Lamb's DNA profile."

Satriano wrapped up her remarks by saying that in addition to offering irrefutable DNA evidence, prints, and blood evidence from the crime scenes linking Alcala to the murders, she would also show that DNA evidence found on earrings in Alcala's pouch belonged to Lamb.

Having presented the crux of the prosecution's case, Satriano told the jurors that this might be a lengthy trial, that some things might be difficult for them to see and hear, and that deliberations could be disturbing due to the serious nature of the charges—but she was grateful and thankful for their time and careful attention.

"At the end of the trial," she concluded, "we will ask you to use your common sense, apply the evidence to the law, and find Rodney Alcala guilty of all the charges against him. Thank you."

Satriano, in a clear, logical, and vivid manner, had created a striking recap of Rodney Alcala's past deeds. However, throughout her opening remarks, Alcala, with eyes peering directly at Satriano from behind black-rimmed glassed, showed no emotion—not even when slides of the gruesome, bloody murder scenes were projected on the screen in the front of the courtroom. From time to time, with his left hand—Alcala was left-handed, a fact that would come into play later in the trial—he jotted down notes at the counsel table.

After a break, the afternoon session began.

The prosecution's first witness was Jill Barcomb's brother, Bruce. He described how his sister had left upstate New York and arrived in Los Angeles full of hope and excitement about her new life. He said that Jill "was the one I was closest to in the nest . . . I genuinely missed her [after she moved out of the house and began living with their sister Debbie]." Barcomb said that when Jill called him from LA, she said she "had no fears for her life nor concerns of harm. She was actually herself in California."

Choking back tears, he said that he heard about Jill's murder the same night he had been at a party, where, when some friends of Jill's friends asked him how Jill was doing, he replied, "I just talked to her. She is out in California having a good time."

Barcomb said that now, more than thirty years after her death, he still missed her.

When the prosecution finished questioning him, Bruce

Barcomb braced himself. For years and years he had not known the identity of his sister's murderer, and now he would face the man who he was certain had killed her. Everyone in the courtroom was wondering what kinds of invasive and offensive questions Alcala might ask.

Alcala, however, quietly said that he had no questions, and Barcomb was permitted to step down.

Satriano next called Kirk Mellecker, a detective in the Hollywood Homicide unit, who investigated Barcomb's murder. As Mellecker described the condition of Barcomb's beat-up, bloodied body, Satriano showed the jurors photographs of the crime scene. The photographs were so disturbing that many of the jurors averted their faces.

One photo showed Barcomb's own pant leg wrapped around her neck. Another photo showed fingernail marks on Barcomb's neck: Barcomb had made the scratches herself. Mellecker explained, "When someone is being strangled, they are trying to get that thing out, getting their fingernails in there." Barcomb, Mellecker observed, was "plucky" and had fought hard for her life. One photo showed "her lips were swollen, her teeth were broken, there were three gaping wounds on her forehead . . . you could look in and see the skull." In another extremely graphic picture, Mellecker pointed out that Barcomb's anus was torn and the whole area was bruised. "Just as she was dying," Mellecker said, "she was being sodomized and that little bit of blood eventually oozed out onto her fingers." In addition, Barcomb's pubic hair had been singed, "so some flaming instrument was placed between her legs and into her vaginal area and close enough that it actually singed the hair along the left side of her vagina."

Mellecker's final opinion was that Barcomb was alive during the beating, while her right nipple was severely mutilated, while three different ligatures were put around her neck.

Regarding the position of her body when police found her, tucked up almost into a ball, he stated, "She did not just end up like that. She is not going to end up the way she is in that package, if you will, of being tucked up together, having her hand up almost pointing to her rectum and having that blood oozing down her fingers. . . . That was the final staging, posing of Jill, so that whoever found her when the sun came up or discovered her body, she would be degraded and, of course, the person would be shocked, and, of course, it's all part of the crime scene."

After a short break, the jury returned and Alcala spoke to the judge. He said he was going to object to Mellecker's testimony on three grounds: One, Mellecker was not qualified to make the statements he had made and that only a licensed doctor or forensic expert who performed the autopsy could; two, Mellecker "had no personal knowledge of the victim, yet he described the victim's behavior or reaction"; and three, "most of [Mellecker's] answers were in a narrative form. He kept on going on and on, and they required only a short answer."

Judge Briseño considered Alcala's words and then respectfully told Alcala that the next time he felt he needed to make an objection, he must do so at the relevant point in the proceedings, so the judge could rule on it at that time.

Briseño then asked Satriano to give more of a foundation as to why Mellecker was qualified to testify about the things he had.

Satriano called Mellecker back to the stand. He stated that his law enforcement career spanned over forty years and that his field of expertise was homicide. During that time, he said, he had attended innumerable autopsies at the Los Angeles County coroner's office. "I've been to schools and conferences, where death, homicide, and the reactions of bodies to different injuries and to the ante-, peri- and postmortem phenomenon were discussed." He had "taught areas of homicide since 1980"; had been to blood-spatter school; and "had been in charge of well over one hundred crime scenes." When he worked for the FBI Behavioral Analysis Unit, he said, he went out to crime scenes both nationally and internationally. "Personally," he said, "I have witnessed over a hundred autopsies and stood in on autopsies for other officers."

After Mellecker finished detailing his areas of expertise, Alcala began his cross-examination. He asked Mellecker if any witness claimed that Barcomb was wearing earrings "that evening or that night or that day."

"No," responded Mellecker.

Alcala then said that a lot of the "blood stuff" Mellecker mentioned "would take a doctor to testify about."

Mellecker disagreed but acknowledged that a doctor could go into greater detail.

Alcala objected to the detective's labeling the victim as "plucky." Alcala added, "You didn't even know her."

Again the judge admonished Alcala to state his objections when he felt that something objectionable had occurred, not later.

Alcala had no further questions.

The prosecution proceeded as Nick Sanchez, criminologist with the LAPD, was called to the stand. He testified he had received an "oral reference sample and anal slides" in July 2005. The samples had been taken from Jill Barcomb's body in 1977. Sanchez found that the anal sample included sperm and blood and was a mixture from two individuals. With Barcomb as one contributor, said Sanchez, the genetic marker of the other was "approximately one hundred billion times more likely to occur if Alcala is the second contributor."

Alcala had no questions.

When Joseph Lawrence Cogan was called to the stand, he stated that he had been the assistant medical examiner for Los Angeles County in 1978 and that he had performed the autopsy on Charlotte Lamb, then known as Jane Doe number 64.

The cause of Lamb's death, said Cogan, was strangulation. He remarked that the body seemed to have been posed; that the struggle had taken place over a long period of time; and that because Lamb was a healthy young woman, there would have been enormous pain and suffering. He alluded to Lamb's being repeatedly strangled and intentionally allowed to revive, only to be strangled again. This, he said, would have caused Lamb to experience "great anxiety and stress, especially when put in a situation, then out of it, then through it again. It's very psychologically stressful."

Alcala had no questions.

Zaffar Shah then testified about finding Charlotte Lamb's body in the laundry room of his apartment complex. In a matter-of-fact tone, in response to "Can you tell me what happened in the early morning of June 24, 1978," Shah said, "I had clothes in my hand. I walked in. I saw a naked woman lying faceup."

"And what did you do after seeing that?" asked Satriano.

"I went to the apartment manager, and his wife was a nurse. She came over and she said there was a dead lady there."

Shah did not flinch at all during the very short testimony he gave.

Alcala had no questions.

Following Shah, William Gaynor testified that he had been deputy sheriff investigator of homicide scenes for LA County when he was called to Shah's apartment complex in 1978. Gaynor told the court that he had found a young female there, lying on her back on the concrete floor of a laundry room. She was nude, and "it appeared that she was strangled with a shoelace that was attached to a shoe." Asked what he saw, he replied that when he looked directly at the body from the doorway, he and the other detectives "saw her pubic area straight up towards the neck and her head."

On cross-examination, Alcala had only one question for Gaynor: "Did any of the people say that Charlotte Lamb had been wearing earrings the day she died?"

"I don't recall that," said Gaynor.

Next James Fraracci testified that he and Charlotte Lamb were friends and that they had last spoken on the phone on

Friday, June 23, 1978. He said that one day, after he had not been able to get in touch with Lamb for a while, a woman called him and said that she had gotten his name from Lamb's phone book and that Lamb hadn't paid her rent. The woman reported that all of Lamb's things were in her apartment, but there was no indication that Lamb was around.

Of course, Fraracci said, he was distraught. Later, a card was placed on his door saying, "Please call me." It was signed, "The Police Department." He called and soon thereafter went to the police department with his mother. A police officer asked him, "Is this the girl we are talking about?" He showed Fraracci a picture of Lamb's bloodied and strangled body.

Shocked, Fraracci hung his head and said yes.

The police then asked him if he knew Rodney Alcala. He said no.

Throughout his testimony, Fraracci had to pause to compose himself.

Alcala did not ask Fraracci any questions.

The prosecution then moved on to the circumstances surrounding the murder of Georgia Wixted. Steve Renteria, senior criminalist for the LA County Sheriff's Department, testified that in May 2003 he analyzed the DNA on an anal slide taken from Wixted's body and found the probability of it *not* being Alcala's DNA was "one in two trillion." He elaborated on the significance of this statistic: "Assuming the world population, which I checked yesterday on [the] census website, is 6.8 billion, there would have to be 147 Earths, all with 6.8 billion people, and if all of them were unrelated, I would expect at most to find one person that had that DNA."

Alcala had no questions for Renteria regarding his findings.

The prosecution called Phil Bullington, a lieutenant assigned to the homicide bureau in the LA County Sheriff's

Department in December 1977. He had supervised the investigation of Georgia Wixted's murder.

Bullington described going to apartment 8 at 22647 Pacific Coast Highway in Malibu and noticing that the screen was missing from the center window and seeing a wooden box below the window, which he learned was "not where that box normally was kept." He determined that that was the entry point of Wixted's apartment.

"What did you see when you entered the apartment?"

"Well, the first thing is . . . the victim lying on the floor. . . . The bed was pretty well saturated in blood, all over the sheets and mattress. There was a pillow there that was soaked with blood. There were blood smears on the brass railing around the bed. There was blood splatter on the wall above the bed."

"Was she wearing any clothing?"

"None."

"How were her legs positioned?"

"The lower part of her body, her knees were drawn up, she was laying on her right side with her knees drawn up."

Bullington then described that there was a pair of shoes on her left side . . . and there was blood on just about everything." He said there was "a claw hammer, wooden handle" found next to her body. He said there was a nylon stocking around her throat.

"Did you notice anything around the vaginal area?" Satriano asked.

"There seemed to be a lot of damage to it, and a lot of bleeding."

"Did you notice any earrings on the victim?" asked Satriano.

"Not that I recall."

Alcala then cross-examined Bullington, asking if he had interviewed anyone regarding the case. Bullington said he had not, but that others he knew had.

"During any of those interviews," asked Alcala "did those people report that earrings were missing from Ms. Wixted's apartment? Were there any interviews in which earrings were mentioned by the people?"

"I can't recall that, no."

"No more questions," said Alcala. "Thank you."

Other forensic experts were called to testify. Dale Falicon, a fingerprint technician for the LA County Sheriff's Department, testified to having matched a palm print found on a brass bed railing at the Wixted crime scene to that of Alcala.

Alcala cross-examined Falicon and asked one question. "Could the palm print have been distorted by the curvature of the railing?"

"There might be some minor distortion, but the unique characteristics of the print would still be readily identifiable," responded Falicon.

Joan Shipley, who had been a deputy medical examiner for LA County in 1977, testified that she performed the autopsy on Wixted. She stated that quite a bit of force had to have been used to crack Wixted's skull the way it was bludgeoned and that all the injuries to her neck were caused before her death, as were lacerations to her labia. Farther inside the vaginal opening, Shipley stated, there was a two-inch tear, which meant that something had penetrated the vagina. Shipley opined that the penetration was much more severe than a penis entering the vagina. It could have been "an object, an instrument."

Alcala asked her no questions.

Also testifying was Wixted's friend and colleague, Barbara Gale, who gave details about their friendship and their job at Centinela Hospital. Gale recalled how they often rode to work together, since they worked the same shift, and how sometimes after work they would go out together.

Gale recalled that the last time she saw Wixted was at Brennan's Pub celebrating a friend's birthday. After the place closed, Gale testified, Wixted drove her home. Gale recalled how proud Wixted was of taking "a step in her independence and self-sufficiency" by renting an apartment on the beach in Malibu. "It's a dream come true."

Gale testified that Wixted failed to pick her up for their shift the next afternoon and that she eventually called the police, who went to check out Wixted's apartment.

On cross-examination, Alcala asked, "During any of the talks you had with detectives, do you recall giving them any information as to whether or not Ms. Wixted was wearing earrings on the night that you last saw her?"

"No."

Anne Michelena testified about the trauma she has felt ever since her big sister, Georgia, was killed. Growing up, "we shared a room," she said. "Our mom was a single mom, and my brother and sister were a little bit older than I. . . . [Georgia and I] were very close." She said that Georgia had been in a car accident about six months before she moved into her own place "so she was finally recovered and moving on and getting back to being independent."

"Did she ever mention the name Rodney Alcala to you?" asked Satriano.

"Never."

"The person in the tan suit to my right, prior to her death, had you ever seen that man before?"

Hardly able to disguise the disgust she felt at looking at Alcala, she responded, "No."

On cross, Alcala asked Michelena if she had seen her sister on the day she died.

"No."

"Then you can't say whether or not she was wearing earrings that day, can you?"

"No," she replied, clearly annoyed at the question.

The next witness was Katherine Franco, who testified to her lifelong friendship with the fourth murder victim, Jill Parenteau. She said they had been to the Handlebar Saloon in Pasadena several times. When asked if she recognized anyone in the courtroom from the Handlebar Saloon, she said she did and pointed to Alcala. She said that she and Jill had seen him at the saloon maybe four or five times. "He would just try to talk with us and ask either of us to dance." She said that they had talked about him and Jill said she wasn't interested in him.

Franco testified that when she spoke with Jill on June 13, she was excited because she was going to a Dodgers game with a friend, Dan Brady.

Then, with tears streaming down her face, she said she never spoke to her friend again.

"Back in 1979, were you asked to look at a group of eight photographs by Detective Bowers?"

"Yes."

"Did you recognize any of the people?"

"Yes. I picked out Alcala."

"In 2003," asked Satriano, "were you asked by another detective, Detective Comstock, to look at a group of photographs?"

"Yes."

"Did you recognize one person and write your name below his picture?"

"Yes."

"And who was that?" asked Satriano.

"Rodney Alcala, the defendant. Him."

And with that. Satriano said she had no further questions.

Alcala began his cross-examination.

"You testified that you believed that she wore earrings, but you're not sure she wore earrings, or what—exactly what did you mean when you said I believe she wore earrings?"

"I mean I'm not absolutely one hundred percent positive that she wore earrings, but I think she did."

"And in 1979, did anybody ask you about earrings at the interview?" asked Alcala.

"I do not remember," replied Franco.

"Okay. And in 2003, did they ask you about earrings?" persisted Alcala.

"I do not remember," replied Franco crisply.

"Thank you," said Alcala.

* * *

Gordon Bowers, investigator for the Burbank Police Department, stated that he had investigated the murder of Jill Parenteau in 1979. When shown a photograph of the apartment where Parenteau's body was found, he pointed out that a screen had been cut in order for the perpetrator to enter the apartment. "It had been cut vertically along the left-hand edge and then across the top to make a flap." He noted that it was "unusual to be cut on the left. Normally a right-handed person, which most people are, would do cutting with their right hand, and it would be awkward with your right hand to cut on the left-hand side of the screen. So I suspected this person was left-handed."

Bowers went on to detail the disarray in the apartment, including the fact that a jewelry box was open "on the top of the dresser." He stated that Parenteau's bloodied and bruised body appeared to be posed, adding that "when you're standing at the door [you are] looking straight between her legs at her body, with her shoulders propped up with the pillow." He told of a "cord that ran around under her body over toward her neck." He stated that he saw ligature marks around her neck and suspected that nylons, lying near the body, had made the marks. He noted that teeth marks appeared to be around her breasts.

On cross, Alcala asked Bowers about the jewelry box: "Did there appear to be anything out of order? Did you interview anybody . . . who provided information that some of her jewelry was missing?"

Bowers said no.

"So you never had any reports on missing jewelry, missing earrings?"

"We have no reports of that."

On January 21, Satriano called Dr. Sharon Schnittker to testify. She stated she was coroner for LA County in 1977 and that she performed an autopsy on Jill Parenteau. After giving horrific details about the kinds of injuries Parenteau suffered—extensive hemorrhaging of the scalp, with multiple blows from something like a hammer, all "definitely caused before death"; ligature marks most likely made from fabric and knots; aspirated blood in the airway; red areas in each corner of her mouth; bruises on the tip of her tongue; abrasions on the breasts; and bruising and abrasions on her arms and knees—Schnittker said that the cause of Parenteau's death was "ligature strangulation."

On cross, Alcala asked about the tears to Parenteau's mouth, which Schnittker surmised were caused by forcible oral copulation. "Could her mouth have been stretched in some other way to cause that type of injury?"

Schnittker said that it could have been caused by a soft cloth gag tied somewhere around the head.

"If it were from forced oral copulation," asked Alcala, "would it indicate a large-diameter penis, or would it be consistent with a small-diameter penis?"

After trying to answer the question in a number of different ways, Schnittker finally said, "I think generally if oral copulation were consensual . . . you would probably not get the abrasions at the corner of the mouth. I don't have any idea of what the size of the penis would be, other than I would say within the realm of a normal, you know, ninety-eight percent of size of penises."

"Okay," said Alcala. "Now let's consider a possibility here. Let's say you have a toasted hero sandwich, right? Sort of like a French piece of bread, sliced down the middle, down the center, and with some salami or whatever in there, you're putting that into your mouth, could that scrape, in other words, how, to what extent was [*sic*] the scrape marks on the edges of the mouth?"

"Very small."

"So it's consistent, then, with sticking a hero sandwich into your mouth, you know what I'm talking about, a hero sandwich. It's like a loaf of bread slit down the middle. It's rounded, toasted. You put it in their [*sic*] mouth, they are pretty big, wide, you bite on it, and it could have scraped, cause those type of marks, is that—"

"I wouldn't think so," replied Schnittker.

"Have you ever had a big hero sandwich?"

"Sure, I've had a lot of big sandwiches."

"They are bigger than the mouth."

"Right. You do not tend to injure yourself as a general rule intentionally. You're not forcibly jamming it down your mouth. You tend to take a bite-size piece."

This line of questioning continued until finally Alcala said, "Thank you. No more questions."

On redirect, Orange County prosecutor Matt Murphy took the floor. He asked Schnittker if she had examined the remains of Samsoe. She said she had, but when she did so, the remains had not yet been identified as those of Samsoe. Schnittker testified that, from the remains, she was unable to determine a cause of death.

Alcala then re-cross-examined her, asking her if it was correct that neither the cause of death nor the time of death had been determined. Schnittker said that was true.

"Then the death could have occurred on any of several dates around the twentieth, right?"

Schnittker agreed.

Murphy then began his direct questioning, focusing on the Samsoe case. He first called Lorraine Wetzel, who stated that her maiden name was Werts. She said that she had been almost sixteen on June 20, 1979, when she and her friend Patty were skating and a man asked if he could take their pictures for a contest. "He got out of the car and he came up to us and was asking us if we would let him take some pictures . . . because he was in a contest with a class and was sure he was going to win if he had some skating shots." Wetzel then identified several pictures of herself in her bikini that she said had been taken that day. She said that after the man took some pictures "he started asking me some real personal questions that made me a little uncomfortable." Wetzel said that she and her friend immediately skated off and that the man drove off toward Huntington Beach.

Alcala then cross-examined Wetzel for a long time, asking

questions about the direction in which he supposedly walked toward her, the direction in which his car was supposedly parked, and the direction in which he supposedly drove away. Her responses always included the fact that Alcala was, without question, the photographer who took her picture that day: "I know that I saw you get out of a car. I don't remember exactly where you were parked. . . ."

Alcala did not dispute the fact that he was the photographer who took pictures of her, concluding his remarks with: "Now we know exactly where it was where you were, where you and I were talking, and that you skated off."

Patricia Elmendorf was called next. She said that on June 20, she and her friend Lorraine Werts were roller-skating at Sunset Beach. She was sure of the date because she kept a calendar of things she did. She liked to keep a calendar, she said, because "it keeps me focused and I still do it to this day."

When Alcala cross-examined her, he once again asked about the direction his car was supposedly facing and which direction she skated off in.

Toni Wainscott, formerly Toni Esparza, testified that Alcala took her and Joanne Murchland's pictures at the beach on June 19.

"And you're absolutely positive, no doubt in your mind whatsoever, that I was the person that took photos of you?" asked Alcala.

"Absolutely," she responded.

Murphy called Bridget Goldstein, formerly Bridget Wilvert. Goldstein recounted what had happened on June 20: how Robin had come to her house; how they lay out on her deck; how they cooked food for lunch; how they walked to the beach; how a "gentleman walked up . . . and my initial reaction was he just wasn't dressed right for the beach"; how he asked to take their pictures for a photo class; how he "leaned in close and put his hand on Robin's knee, posing her"; and how "up popped my neighbor . . . Jackye Young . . . and said 'Girls, is everything okay?' "; and how the photographer was "shocked" and "immediately tipped his head down" and walked away "very quickly."

Goldstein then recalled how she never saw her friend again after Robin rode off on Goldstein's bike in order to get to her ballet class on time. "[Robin] did not want to miss ballet. She wouldn't have gone anywhere else. I mean, I lived for gymnastics, she lived for ballet."

Alcala cross-examined Goldstein for about twenty minutes regarding her encounter with the photographer, trying to plant a seed of doubt that he was, in fact, the person she had seen that day on the beach.

He then asked her if she had ever seen Robin wearing earrings, but before she answered, he read from a report Goldstein had given to detectives directly after Robin's disappearance in which she said, "I never really saw any jewelry on her."

Goldstein said that was, in fact, what she had said, but added, "I mean, at twelve, I wasn't really looking to see if friends had jewelry on."

Several times Alcala asked Goldstein to stand up, go to the easel, and look more closely at one picture or another. In fact, during the trial, he asked many other females to do the same. However, he rarely asked a male to stand up.

Richard Sillett testified that he saw a photographer walk by him "about five to ten feet" away on June 20, 1979, while he was "survey party chief for the city of Huntington Beach." When asked if he saw the photographer in court, Sillett identified Alcala.

On cross, Alcala asked Sillett why he didn't get in touch with the police before July 10 if he was so sure he had seen the photographer whose picture was in the papers.

"Because I was stewing about it, I believe. I was thinking it over because I knew it was a serious thing."

Ruth Ikeda, forensic scientist in the DNA section of the Orange County crime lab, testified that DNA on the rose earring found in Alcala's storage locker matched that of Charlotte Lamb, and the "random match probability is one in one hundred billion that it was Lamb's." She testified that she could not get any DNA results from the gold ball earrings. She said that testing on two gold studs "were consistent with Rodney Alcala's standard," and she could not determine any other DNA on the earring.

Jackye Young was called to the stand. She said she had known Bridget Wilvert (now Bridget Goldstein) because "I was their neighbor" and because Wilvert used to play with her nieces. Young recalled that on June 20, she walked up to two girls on the beach, one of whom she thought was her niece but who turned out to be Robin Samsoe, and the other who turned out to be Bridget, because she "didn't think they needed to be with this gentleman taking pictures of them."

Young described how when she approached the trio, the man ran off, looking back over his left shoulder. "I preached to the girls rather sternly . . . and I took the little girls to my neighbor, Bridget's, house."

When asked if the man who was photographing the girls was in the courtroom, Young pointed to Alcala.

On cross, Alcala tried to get Young to admit that she didn't see "both the left and right sides" of his face as she had testified earlier. Young disagreed, saying that she saw the right side of his face when he briefly looked up at her upon hearing her speak to the girls.

Alcala said, "So it's your testimony today that you helped or that you provided the information for that composite [done by Marilyn Droz], is that correct?"

"Yes. And I seen you. I chased you away from those girls. It was you!"

On redirect Murphy asked, "Is there any doubt as you sit there now that Mr. Alcala is the man that you saw on the beach that day?"

Young looked directly at Alcala and said, "There is no doubt in my mind. . . . I seen his face. He looked eye to eye with me. There's not a day that goes by that I don't have a flash about you and those girls."

On January 25, Marianne Connelly, now sixty-six, was called to testify. Looking a combination of defeated and defiant, she walked slowly to the stand, shoulders and head up high. Senior deputy DA Matt Murphy asked her about her daughter and Connelly gave full details about what a wonderful child she was. Connelly recalled how the police came to her home and asked if she could identify a shoe found at the crime scene. That was when she knew Robin was never coming home, she said, clearly distraught.

Murphy elicited that since the time of Robin's death, Connelly had struggled with life and had even sought "refuge in some substances over the years."

When Alcala cross-examined Connelly, he asked her to look at a picture he was projecting.

"Were you the one that gave the police that picture?"

"I was her mother. Of course I did," Connelly replied angrily.

Then, after showing other photographs of Robin, he asked, "Did you notice on the picture, the one on the far left, her hair is a lot longer than the one on the right?"

"Is she not allowed to get a haircut?"

"No, I'm just—"

"What difference does that make?" she screamed.

"We'll go on to something else," said Alcala. "You testified that Robin would borrow your earrings. Were her ears pierced?"

"Yes."

"And who pierced them?"

"I believe that I took her to some place where they pierced them when she was about two years old."

"Two years old?"

"I don't remember where it was."

"She was only two years old?"

"Yes."

"She had her ears pierced for ten years?"

Exasperated, Connelly yelled, "Yes."

"Now, do you have photographs of Robin?"

"Of course I do. . . . That's all I have left of her."

"Do you have any photos of your daughter wearing earrings?" Alcala asked.

"I don't know what you're getting at," she shouted. "Those are my earrings. . . . You know whether she had earrings on, don't you?"

Finally, Connelly had been pushed to the limit with Alcala's cross-examination and said, "Please stop. I've answered your questions. I've been living this torture for thirty years."

Briseño called a recess to try to calm Connelly down. He told her, "It's going to be a difficult day to come up and take questions from the person that you feel is responsible for taking a life." But, he reminded her, however she may feel, Alcala still had certain constitutional rights, and he asked Connelly to try to have patience.

After the jury returned, Alcala continued his cross-examination of Connelly.

"Around 1977 to 1980, did you suffer a conviction for public assistance fraud in Kenosha for a misdemeanor?"

Barely able to contain her anger, she replied, "The charges were dropped."

"Around April the second of 1977, did you suffer a conviction for retail theft of a Kmart in Kenosha, Wisconsin?"

"No."

"On October 20, 1992, did you suffer a felony conviction for possession and transportation of narcotics?"

"Yes."

"On April 9, 2002, did you suffer a misdemeanor conviction for burglary?"

"No."

"Between July the twenty-fourth of 1979 and June of 1980, did you take a loaded .25 caliber pistol in your purse into a courtroom in which I was appearing?"

"Yes . . ."

"Thank you."

"I'd like to finish my sentence."

"Pardon?"

"Yes, I did bring a gun. But I thought the law would do their job much better than I could, and my children needed me, the ones I had left. So I didn't even take it out of my purse."

"Thank you."

And with that, Alcala said he had finished his questioning, and Judge Briseño said the court could take a recess.

When Craig Robison, lead detective on the Samsoe case, was called to the stand, he outlined his involvement with the case. "At first, it was a simple missing-persons investigation that developed into a homicide. She was twelve and we were trying to find her." Robison reported how he had had Bridget Wilvert come down to the station to help Marilyn Droz prepare a sketch of the man who had taken her and Robin's pictures on the beach.

Robison, looking at the remains of Robin that were projected on the screen, identified that those were, in fact, the skull and remains he saw when he combed through the crime scene area. He testified that the shoe and "an entire head of blond human hair" were also found. At a later date, he stated, detectives discovered a beach towel that Robin's mother identified as the towel belonging to her daughter, as she had the shoe.

Robison stated that many tips had come in to the police department suggesting that the photographer whose composite was being shown could be Rodney Alcala. Robison said he arrested Alcala on July 24 and took him down to the police station. Other officers went into Alcala's house with a search warrant, said Robison, and one of them, Sergeant Jenkins, saw a receipt for a storage locker in Seattle on a table and jotted down information that was on it. He wasn't able to collect the receipt because it was not specifically listed on the warrant.

Robison told Murphy that he listened to a tape recording

of Alcala talking to his sister, Christine De La Cerda, in which Alcala told her about the storage locker and she asked what she could do.

Robison said that the next day officers went to Alcala's sister's house because they believed she might know something about the locker.

"Was she cooperative with you?"

"No."

However, Robison went on, he and other detectives decided to book a flight the following day to Seattle to check things out. When they got there, they went to the specific locker—24 in the E building at Safeguard Mini-Storage—which Alcala had rented on July 11, 1979, for one month. Robison said that in the locker they found many items, including hundreds of photographs, several of which turned out to be of Lorraine Werts (now Wetzel), and a jewelry pouch that included a pair of gold studs as well as a small rose earring with a little diamond in the middle.

When cross-examined by Alcala, Robison admitted that he had never found any photos of Robin or Bridget or Toni Esparza or Joanne Murchland.

Murphy asked Robison to describe interviews he had with Connelly. Robison said that when he first told her that they had found her daughter, she begged to see her. "She was weeping."

Murphy said, "You had to explain to her that she couldn't go and actually see her daughter, is that correct?"

"She wanted to see her for the last time, and for obvious reasons, we couldn't let her."

Projected on the screen was a photograph of the meager remains of Samsoe. Murphy said, "When her remains were recovered, obviously whoever murdered this girl left her for the animals to eat, and there were no earlobes left to see if her ears were pierced."

"That's true," said Robison.

On cross-examination, Alcala once again asked countless questions about earrings.

* * *

On February 2, after the prosecution had rested and three weeks after the trial began, Alcala gave his opening statement. Sporting black glasses, long, shaggy, grayish hair, and the same sports coat he had donned since the trial started, he began: "About 10,820 days, five hours, and fifteen minutes ago, Robin Samsoe left Bridget Wilvert's apartment on Bridget's bike. Neither Bridget nor Robin's family saw Robin again. About thirty-three days and sixteen hours later, I was arrested and charged with Robin's murder. I've been incarcerated since then—about nine years in the Orange County Jail and almost all of the rest of it on San Quentin's death row."

Alcala continued, often talking aimlessly while attempting to counter the allegations against him concerning Samsoe. During his entire opening, he never mentioned the charges against him in the other four murders.

Alcala then showed the jury a video that he projected onto a screen from the laptop at his table. He called it "The 6 Minute 15 Second Window of Opportunity." The clip was intended to "prove" that he did not have that window of opportunity to kidnap Samsoe because, at the time she went missing, he was at Knott's Berry Farm, applying for a job.

He went on to proclaim that the gold ball earrings recovered from the Seattle storage locker belonged to him, not Samsoe. Although he did admit he had been at Sunset Beach the day Samsoe went missing, he was not the photographer whom people have been identifying. In fact, he claimed, he looked nothing like the composite sketch the police had come up with.

After he had been speaking for an hour and was in the middle of giving intricate details about his Olympus camera, Judge Briseño interrupted him and pointed out, "This is supposed to be an outline of the case."

"I apologize," said Alcala. "I see I've gone way over my time, and I was just rambling there and going on. I've pretty much covered what I want to say. . . . So I apologize for rambling on towards the end there, but I think—I wasn't looking at the clock, and so I'm completing my opening statement now, and thank you for listening to me."

Alcala called his first witness, Bruce Moran, who stated he was employed by the Orange County Sheriff's Department crime lab in 1980 as a tool mark and firearm identification expert.

Alcala asked Moran about the pair of gold ball earrings found in Alcala's storage locker that Connelly had identified as belonging to her. (Connelly had said she recognized them because of a unique cut she had made to the earrings with a nail clipper.) Moran said that after examining the cut marks, it was his opinion that the nail clippers submitted by Connelly were capable of making the type of marks observed on the earrings. However, after Alcala pressed him, Moran stated that he could not exclude the possibility that another similarly marked tool had made the cut marks.

Alcala called Marilyn Droz to testify. She confirmed that she had made the only composite drawing regarding the "incident" and that she had done so with information supplied by Bridget Wilvert.

It was unclear what Alcala was trying to point out by calling Droz to the stand, since he didn't follow up Droz's statement with any questions.

When Murphy asked Droz about her background, she stated that all told, she had drawn around four thousand police sketches. Droz said that Bridget Wilvert was "excellent" in helping her prepare the sketch and cooperated in every way. She said she had created the sketch the day after Robin went missing.

Next, Alcala called his former girlfriend, Elizabeth Kelleher Moore.

"Good afternoon, Mrs. Moore. You knew me in 1979, is that correct?"

"Yes."

It appeared to courtroom attendees interviewed after the

trial that Kelleher was still smitten by Alcala. According to the prosecution later, "She was cooperative with us. At points, she was clearly remembering things that benefited Alcala, specifically that she remembered seeing gold ball earrings in his bathroom. However, when pressed, she backed off and became more realistic about her recollections."

After testifying that they saw each other frequently from the time they first met on April 13, Kelleher gave details about June 19, 1979. She said that on that date she helped Alcala prepare folders to bring to Knott's Berry Farm. "Rod was interested in photographing, getting a photography business going . . . so doing photos of the contestants at Knott's Berry Farm [was something he wanted to do]."

Alcala then skipped to July 3—not asking one question about June 20, the day Robin Samsoe went missing. Kelleher told about a costume contest she and Alcala went to on July 3 and about a Bee Gees concert they attended on July 7.

When Murphy cross-examined Kelleher, she said that they had been dating for about three months before his arrest.

"And during that time . . . you guys got along pretty well?"

""We got along really well."

"Just so we're clear, this is a romantic relationship?"

"Yes."

Kelleher admitted that she was in love with Alcala at that time. She said that at one point he told her that he was leaving for Dallas, and on July 8 she actually helped him pack his car. The next time she saw him was on July 14, and he said he had been to Dallas. Kelleher said Alcala never mentioned having gone to Seattle.

"When did you see a change in his hair, as far as it being straight?" Murphy asked.

"On the twenty-third."

Kelleher said he had done such an awful job of straightening his hair that he asked her to cut it on June 26.

She also testified that they shopped together for new carpeting to put in the back of his car on July 21. Alcala, she said, had complained that the old carpet smelled bad.

When asked if she had been with Alcala on June 20, Kelleher said she had not. She also testified that during the time they spent together, she did not recall him wearing earrings, nor did she recall seeing any earrings among his personal possessions.

Two people with whom Alcala worked at the *Los Angeles Times* testified that Alcala had worn earrings, although they could not remember what kind. One of his co-workers, Sharon Gonzales, testified that the earrings Alcala had worn when he worked at the *LA Times* appeared similar to the ones in the jewelry case found in the Seattle locker.

On February 9, 2010, Alcala showed the jury a twenty-second video clip from a 1978 episode of *The Dating Game*. This was the episode in which Alcala had appeared as Bachelor Number 1. Before he ran the clip, he warned the jurors, "You have to watch really closely when it plays because it's just a flash. You'll see a flash of my hair going up and a flash of gold. Two little specks, you'll see that." He was referring to the earrings he maintained he wore when the show was taped—which he stated were his—but which the prosecutors contended Alcala took from Samsoe in 1979.

However, as the video played, Alcala did not pause it to allow the jurors to see the earrings in question. When it was done, he admitted that the resolution on the clip was poor and it *could* look like he was wearing one long earring instead of the two he claimed he was wearing.

After the *Dating Game* demonstration, the jury was in for another strange show: Alcala called *himself* as a defense witness. For the next five hours Alcala, defense lawyer, asked questions of Alcala, defendant:

"Rodney, would you please tell us about your hair?"

"Would you tell us what you did on June the fifteenth?"

"Rodney, what did you do on the sixteenth?"

"Mr. Alcala, after you spent time with your sister and her kids, what did you do?"

"Okay, Mr. Alcala, what did you do next?"

"What was the next phone call you made, Mr. Alcala?"

"What was the next thing you did, Mr. Alcala?"

"Okay, Mr. Alcala, so that completes Tuesday, June the nineteenth. What did you do on June the twentieth?"

Alcala, the defendant, answered each question.

Alcala went into excruciatingly minute detail about what he had done on all the days *surrounding* June 20—including showing phone records concerning those dates—but he never said much about what he had done *on* June 20. As for the crucial time when Robin had presumably been kidnapped, Alcala simply said that he had gone to Knott's Berry Farm, gone home to change clothes, and then gone out on a date: "That was pretty much my day on June 20."

On February 10, the prosecution began its cross-examination of Alcala and for two hours relentlessly grilled him.

Matt Murphy asked Alcala, "Why did you lie to police [about taking photos of girls on the beach] if you were an innocent person? If you're innocent, truth is your best friend." Murphy then asked again if Alcala had lied to investigators when they interviewed him about June 20.

Alcala hemmed and hawed about not having lied. Finally, after Murphy asked Alcala several similar questions, Alcala admitted that he had, in fact, lied to investigators about what he had been doing on the day Samsoe went missing.

Murphy, not giving Alcala an inch, got him to admit that he had been in the area photographing girls in bikinis on the day Samsoe went missing; had cut and straightened his hair; had installed new carpet in his car; and had taken many items to a storage locker in Seattle a few days after Samsoe went missing.

By choosing to testify in his own defense, Alcala opened up the possibility of being cross-examined about his prior offenses. Although the introduction of his prior offenses had caused his 1980 trial to be reversed, during this trial these offenses were allowed to be introduced because Alcala had taken the witness stand. (When the priors were originally introduced against him, since he had not testified in the guilt phase, it was considered "character evidence or propensity to commit the crime." Once he testified, then the priors were introduced for credibility purposes, which is allowed. According to Murphy, "Once you take the stand, courts are far more willing to allow evidence of that type so the jury can assess the defendant's credibility.")

Alcala admitted that he had been convicted in LA County in 1971 for a molestation that took place three years earlier and that he had also been convicted in Riverside County in 1980 of a rape that occurred in 1979.

During some of Alcala's remarks, Connelly could not bear to listen to him and had to leave the courtroom. During one of those times while she was in the hall, a reporter asked her how she was doing. "I feel so frustrated and helpless because I can't speak my mind and he gets to say anything he wants. Where's the justice in that? I've gone through thirty-one years of this and there is no end in sight. I've spent half my life crying."

On February 11, during more relentless cross-examination, Murphy suggested that Alcala had knocked Robin Samsoe off her bike so he could abduct her.

"I never met Robin Samsoe. I never met her," Alcala barked.

"I have one more question," Murphy snapped back. "When you were bashing in her teeth, was she crying or was she already unconscious?"

In a louder voice, Alcala insisted, "I never met Robin Samsoe."

Murphy then asked, "Can you explain, how did earrings containing the DNA of Lamb end up in your locker in Seattle?"

After a long pause, Alcala finally replied, "Not at this point. I will explain it to the jury . . . ." He trailed off.

Alcala rested his case later in the day on February 11. He did so without having mounted any defense against the LA cases and after focusing solely on the Samsoe case.

* * *

Closing arguments began on February 22.

The prosecution's recitation lasted a day and a half.

During his closing argument, Murphy's goal was to show that Alcala had committed all the murders with "premeditation and deliberation" and that there was more than enough evidence—DNA and otherwise—to prove that beyond a reasonable doubt.

Standing at the podium, facing the jury and looking at all the jurors, Murphy stated, "It takes about ten minutes to strangle a healthy [person] to death. He had plenty of time to think about what he was doing. Anytime you're talking about strangulation, you're talking about a first-degree murder . . . . He's got time to contemplate . . . that's premeditation and deliberation. . . . The defendant is guilty of first-degree murder if he acted willfully, deliberately, and intending to kill."

Then, pointing directly at Alcala and raising his voice, Murphy lambasted Alcala, calling him a "hunter" with no soul or feeling. "You will never see cases with more brutality," he said. "All of these victims put up resistance and he punished them for it. . . . He tortured his victims because he enjoyed it. He enjoyed posing his victims in horrific postures after he brutalized them, and probably took photographs of their bodies. . . . Alcala is a predatory monster. Don't feel sorry for him."

In one graphic description, Murphy pointed out that all four of Alcala's adult victims had been found nude; one was raped with a claw hammer; all were strangled, allowed to regain consciousness, then strangled again "to prolong the agony."

Murphy said that something put a stop to this hunter. "Modern science caught up with Rodney Alcala. All of a sudden, Robin was no longer alone. For two decades, one point six nanograms of Charlotte Lamb had sat on a cold, dark shelf in an evidence room, waiting for DNA testing to be invented."

After a poignant pause, Murphy added that Samsoe and

Lamb were linked. "Alcala murders women and steals their earrings." Then he added, "Listen to what Charlotte Lamb is telling you."

Murphy ended by saying, "Robin Samsoe's day in court is today. You make sure that [Alcala] is held responsible for what happened to that little girl."

Throughout Murphy's closing remarks, all eyes were riveted on this man whose carefully selected words and alternatingly loud and soft cadences portrayed an uncompromising picture of a cold-blooded, soulless killer.

Now it was Alcala's turn.

In a low, steady voice Alcala told the jurors that Murphy's entire case was based on "magical thinking" and that the evidence against him was "a bunch of gimmicks and lies." Throughout his three hours of argument, he never once defended himself against the four LA murders, three of which were linked to him by his own DNA. Alcala's demeanor never changed during the entire trial. His behavior and tone of voice were very consistent: He was respectful and soft-spoken and showed little, if any, emotion.

Alcala stated that Connelly fabricated the story about the earrings simply to point the finger at him. "I'm not trying to make Mrs. Connelly into a bad person. She deserves your empathy and your sympathy because she lost her daughter . . . but it does not give her the right to make up a story."

He pointed out that witnesses who saw him photographing on the beach on June 20 had wildly different descriptions of him: dark-skinned, light-skinned; 175 pounds, 150 pounds; tall, short; wearing stripes, wearing a solid color.

Alcala then gave Murphy a nod for a job well done, but he stated that Murphy "played a little loose with the facts."

Alcala concluded his closing with "If you think I was willfully false in any part of my testimony, I can't think of what it could possibly be. I think I've gone on long enough. I think that covers everything and I'll conclude my final arguments."

However, Alcala had not, in fact, covered everything. He had almost totally ignored the four murders that took place in Los Angeles County.

Deliberations began on February 23.

They didn't take long. On February 25, the jury came back with a verdict.

When Judge Briseño asked court clerk Susan Hauer to read the verdict aloud, Alcala sat straight in his chair. His hands were clasped tightly in front of him. He didn't flinch.

Aaron Mintz, court reporter, continued to dutifully record each and every word.

"And how do you find the defendant, Rodney Alcala . . . ."

Mintz typed out, "Guilty, beyond a reasonable doubt" of five counts of first-degree murder and one count of kidnapping. He also typed that the jury found true, beyond a reasonable doubt, five special-circumstance allegations, including torture, rape, kidnapping, and multiple murder. Alcala, once again, was clearly eligible for the death penalty.

Although Alcala showed no emotion as the verdict was read, the victims' families did, embracing and kissing one another.

Robert Samsoe said that his family was satisfied, but he stated that it was not a victory yet. "Until they inject him or shoot him or hang him, it's not over because of the appeals process." He added, "Robin didn't die for nothing. Her death stopped a maniac."

Bruce Barcomb said that over the years he had almost given up hope of ever finding the killer of his sister. "DNA technology never entered my mind."

Parenteau's friend Nancy Casserly stated, "There's not a memory from my childhood that doesn't include Jill. There's no justice, no closure, just a small bit of satisfaction that she had her trial and someone was held responsible."

Don McCartin, the eighty-four-year-old retired judge who had presided over Alcala's second trial, said, "Poor

Mrs. Samsoe. This is her third trial, and she would've been better off if they gave him life without parole and forgot it. I felt so sorry for her having to go through it again."

Now all that remained was the penalty phase.

From Mintz's vantage point, Alcala didn't react when he heard the guilt or death verdicts. "His hands were clasped, **Mintz** said. "This is a very usual reaction. Most of the time, defendants just sit still. They expect it."

Chapter Eighty-eight

Tuesday, March 2, was the first day of the penalty phase, at the end of which Alcala would hear the jury's verdict as to whether he would receive the death sentence or life in prison without the possibility of parole.

Actress Charlize Theron sat toward the back of the courtroom in the middle of a row during many days of the penalty phase, not attracting any attention. When asked later why she attended, she said she was doing research for a role. In 2003, Theron had played Aileen Wernos, the serial murderer, in the film *Monster*.

For the prosecution, Gina Satriano made an opening statement. She reminded the jurors that the five special circumstance murders they had heard about and ruled on in the guilt phase of the trial were not Alcala's first acts of violence. Nor were they his first sexual assaults of females. Nor were they his first assaults of a young girl and a teen. She asked what weight would they give to the torture and murder of each female? What weight would they give to the grief and loss each family member suffered?

After once again giving details about each crime and about the families' losses, she thanked the jurors for their attention and ended with: "For what he has done, does he deserve a punishment any less than that he gave his victims?"

Briseño then asked Alcala if he wished to make a statement.

"No, I don't, Your Honor."

The prosecution called family members to the stand to testify.

Monique Hoyt, now forty-six years old, recounted how Alcala had raped her on Valentine's Day in 1979—when she was fifteen years old. Throughout her testimony, Hoyt, always soft-spoken, was unable to keep herself from shaking and needed a police officer to sit next to her. She kept her hand on her forehead to hide Alcala from her sight. When she was given a photo of her bitten torso and asked to identify herself, she folded the photograph and instead used it as a larger screen to obliterate Alcala.

Alcala then cross-examined her. "Do you remember that I apologized in the car after the attack?"

Continuing not to lay eyes on him, she said, "An apology was meaningless."

"But I did apologize to you."

"It was fake."

"But I did apologize to you, did I not?" Alcala said in a louder voice.

"Yeah, but you killed those other people."

"No further questions, Your Honor."

Tali Shapiro testified about being attacked, raped, and nearly killed by Alcala in 1968—when she was eight years old. She spoke with confidence as she told the jurors that although she didn't remember the attack, she remembered the car ride and how afraid she felt as soon as she got in. "I remember wanting to jump out of the car, but I respected my elders, so I stayed."

She said she remembered walking up to Alcala's apartment to see some pictures he was going to show her.

She said that in terms of having recovered from the incident with Alcala, "Trust in people? Forget about it. Commitment to people? Forget about it."

When cross-examining Shapiro, Alcala apologized. "I sincerely regret what happened. I apologize for my despicable behavior," he said.

Although she stared straight at Alcala, Tali said nothing. "No further questions, Your Honor."

Celia Saunders, Charlotte Lamb's sister, recalled a terrible moment of realization at Charlotte's funeral. She had pulled Lamb's high collar down when Lamb was in the casket "and I saw the rope marks or something around her neck, and it was purple, just purple." Lamb's sister Carolyn was also deeply grieved over the markings she observed on Shug's neck. "Our sister looked like a porcelain doll, dressed in the lovely white, high-collared nightgown provided by our youngest sister, Janie, for the funeral. I was grateful that our dad was not alive . . . he couldn't have borne it. Our mother suffered greatly, both physically and emotionally from this ordeal. Our dad died in 1970 and Mother passed away in 1993."

Alcala had no questions.

Michael Wixted, Georgia's older brother, remembered having been called to clean up his sister's apartment after her death and the sight of all the blood overwhelmed him. He said, the scene "took me to my knees and caused me to go outside and vomit and then come back in and do the duty that I was there to do."

Wixted's sister, Anne Michelena, recalled that she and her brother had to put their mother in a mental facility soon after Georgia's death. "She spent the rest of her life under a psychiatrist's care and she was hospitalized several other times for mental issues." Michelena continued, "She couldn't accept it."

Alcala had no questions.

Dedee Parenteau said that when she heard of her baby sister's death, "I just collapsed to the ground. It's like something left my body."

She continued, "My mom passed away last November and the last ten months of her life she had developed Alzheimer's. One day she said, 'I have a son and I have two daughters, right?' And I said, 'Well I'm your daughter, Mom,' because I didn't want to bring up Jill. She said, 'I have another daughter, but I don't know where she is. Maybe you can help me find her.' "

Alcala had no questions.

Maurice Barcomb, Jill's oldest brother, recalled how he had to look at his sister Jill's body, even though his parents said he shouldn't, because "I could not live my whole life knowing or not knowing was that my sister [in the casket] or wasn't it my sister." He described what he saw when the mortician opened the casket and he "couldn't believe his eyes."

Alcala had no questions.

Bruce Barcomb recounted memories of his sister and then said that the night her casket was flown back to Oneida, he had a dream. "Despite her skull [being] kind of crushed in, kind of sewn together, very vivid, very discolored, she told me she was going to be okay, it was okay."

"She was taking care of you in your dream as well [as she did in life]?" asked Satriano.

"Exactly. Saying goodbye."

Alcala had no questions.

Robert Samsoe spoke next. He described how Robin's death totally destroyed their family. It ended his childhood at thirteen when he had to take care of his mother. "I miss her every single day. I miss her every single night. . . . And I just miss her so bad."

He said that during this trial, his family learned about the other victims and the horrific ways they died. Samsoe's heart broke for them.

Alcala had no questions.

It was now Alcala's turn to present mitigating evidence.

Alcala's court-appointed psychiatrist, Richard Rappaport, took the stand. He stated his practice was primarily limited to forensic work, so he testified in both civil and criminal matters, and that he was an associate clinical professor of psychiatry at the University of California, San Diego. Alcala asked him how he was involved in this case. Rappaport stated that he was sent "a large volume of documents . . . and I was asked to do a psychiatric examination of you at the jail . . . and to do a report." Among the reports he received, he stated, were two written by court-appointed psychologists who, like him, offered insights into Alcala's psychological situation.

According to Rappaport's analysis of Alcala, Alcala suffered from "borderline personality disorder," which, the doctor suggested, might explain why Alcala couldn't remember murdering Barcomb, Wixted, Lamb, or Parenteau. The psychiatrist stated that borderline personality disorder is primarily characterized by profound instability in personal relationships, poor self-image, impulsivity, intense fear of abandonment, and radical mood swings. It can sometimes be accompanied by "brief psychotic episodes," said Rappaport, in which a person is "out of touch with reality and may not actually realize what they are doing as wrong or right." If Alcala had felt he was being rejected by one of his victims, for example, said Rappaport, it might trigger a "violent delusional state." If any terrible things happened when he was in such a state, Rappaport added, "he blocked them out as a coping mechanism," and this is sometimes referred to as "dissociative amnesia."

During cross, Murphy asked the doctor if the two other psychologists who evaluated Alcala concurred with his opinion that Alcala suffered from borderline personality disorder. No, Rappaport responded, they had a different diagnosis. Both reported that Alcala suffered from "narcissistic personality disorder."

After disagreeing with Rappaport's diagnosis of borderline personality disorder, Murphy went through point by point of the definition of the condition and asked Rappaport for examples from Alcala's life to substantiate each. Rappaport struggled to do so. In fact, he agreed that Alcala seemed to have loving relationships with his mother and sisters; that nowhere was it documented that he had "unstable interpersonal relationships"; that Alcala exhibited no signs of impulsivity, had no recurrent suicidal thoughts, exhibited no self-injurious or self-destructive behaviors, had no reports of great mood swings, had no reports of engaging in physical fights, either in school, the army, or prison, and had never had a psychotic breakdown in the thirty years he had been on death row in San Quentin or at any other time.

"So basically, then, what we are talking about is the only psychotic breakdowns are as he's raping and murdering women, is that right?" asked Murphy.

Rappaport said, "I don't know if you can say 'as,' but okay, I guess that's the best way to put it."

Murphy suggested, "There is a more sinister subtype of the 'antisocial personality disorder' and the main characteristic of these narcissistic personalities are grandiosity, extreme self-centeredness, and a remarkable absence of interest and empathy for others. . . . And if that doesn't nail Rodney Alcala, I don't know what does." Murphy added that the person suffering from extreme narcissism often has good social functioning and is highly intelligent and creative. These attributes were far different, said Murphy, from those attributed to people suffering from borderline personality disorder.

Then, one by one, Murphy showed examples of how those criteria applied to Alcala. For example, he mentioned that Alcala had a "normal sexual relationship" with his girlfriend, went out to dinner with her and her parents, and went to the movies; so Alcala was able to have normal relationships with women. Murphy also showed "proof" of Alcala's intelligence, as evidenced in his superior school grades and IQ scores, and his creativity, as evidenced by his photography skills.

Rappaport did admit that Alcala "had a sexual perversion. The idea of being sexually involved with pre-pubescent or pubescent children, young girls, and so forth, is a perversion." Rappaport reported that Alcala "talked to me about his preferences for young girls because they were fit, because their bodies are tight . . . which is a characteristic he admired in his mother, who was a caretaker. . . ." Rappaport posited, "What he might have felt at the same time is the resentment toward those characteristics and those abilities. So I don't know exactly how it worked for him, but I think it certainly is a possibility that those phenomenon [sic] did take place."

Rappaport testified that he interviewed Alcala for three or four hours and took a chronological history of his life. He admitted that he never received, and therefore had not reviewed, any of Alcala's military records.

Murphy asked if Alcala had told him that he didn't remember the four murders (not including Robin's) that he was being accused of.

"He told me he doesn't [remember] and I don't have any information to contradict that," said Rappaport.

Murphy got Rappaport to admit that Alcala did, however, tell him about Tali Shapiro, Julie Johnson, and Monique Hoyt.

"Hmm, Dr. Rappaport," remarked Murphy, "wasn't it odd that Alcala was able to remember the crimes he had already served time for, but not the others?"

Rappaport suggested that because those "other" acts were so "distasteful and reprehensible," there "is a strong need of [his] ego to reject memories of such events."

However, Rappaport was at a loss to explain why Alcala was able to remember such "distasteful and reprehensible" events as what he did to Tali, Julie, and Monique. Clearly, Murphy was implying that Alcala did not suffer from any type of amnesia. Rather, he was a clever man who would only admit to having done what he had already been accused of and served time for.

When asked about Alcala's life, Rappaport reported that the defendant had been given many advantages. The defendant presented no evidence that he had ever been the victim of abuse, suffered a head injury, or experienced psychiatric problems at any time in his life before he began raping, torturing, and murdering women and girls, stated Rappaport.

After Rappaport finished testifying, it was Alcala's turn to present evidence favorable to himself. Since no one came in person to testify, Alcala began by reading aloud from transcripts of his 1986 trial, in which his mother said she loved him; that he was never a problem; that he was "quiet, but a good boy, very studious"; and that he was sensitive. Alcala also presented written testimony from several Department of Corrections officers who praised him as being a model prisoner, as well as testimony from two friends who called him a "fine human being, a man very much worth saving."

After all their testimony had been read, Alcala rested his case.

The People did not have any rebuttal.

Finally, the evidence in the penalty phases was complete. The judge said, "Final arguments are set to begin on March 9."

In Murphy's seventy-two-minute final argument, the prosecutor told the jury, "This is your question to answer: Does this defendant, given who he is and what he has done, really deserve punishment that is less than what he inflicted upon his victims? Based on his adult life choices to brutally assault and/or murder the seven females—two children, two teens, and three women—does he really deserve the *gift* of leniency? What has he done to earn it? Ask yourself: Did this defendant show mercy for his victims during his crimes? To deserve mercy you must show mercy."

Murphy called Alcala "an evil monster with a narcissistic personality who raped, tortured, and killed because he enjoyed it." He was a hunter, said Murphy. "He is not hunting deer or pheasant. He is hunting people." He went on to say that the more the victims suffered pain, "the more he enjoyed it."

Murphy then added details about the way the women died. He choked them with his hands, waited for them to come to, and then strangled them again. "It is a staggeringly horrific way to die," said Murphy.

Murphy reiterated what he had said during the guilt phase: that Alcala did not suffer from borderline personality disorder. Rather, he was a "narcissistic personality with antisocial traits. What does that mean? That means he is an evil monster who knows what he's doing is wrong and doesn't care. That's what that diagnosis means."

Further discrediting Rappaport, Murphy said, "Dr. Rappaport, for $500 an hour, is hoping that you, ladies and gentlemen, are fools. The final question on everything from Dr. Rappaport is, do you believe this garbage? Because this is garbage."

Murphy then told of the serious nature of the decision the jurors would be making. "The right decisions in life are often the most difficult decisions to make. It takes courage to do the right thing." Murphy told the jurors, "You speak for the conscience of this community. Hold Alcala responsible for exactly what he did, and you make sure the one appropriate penalty is the one that's given to him."

Alcala then spoke on his own behalf, urging jurors to spare his life. Sitting at the table where he had sat during the entire trial, he said that if they had any lingering doubt about his guilt, they must return a not-guilty verdict.

"By giving me the death penalty," he said, "you become a wannabe killer in waiting. Your desire to become a part of that elite group of citizens, your desire to share in the killing of a human being, is eloquently expressed by Arlo Guthrie."

In a freakish twist, Alcala then played a clip from Arlo Guthrie's 1967 song "Alice's Restaurant" containing the following lines:

'Kid, see the psychiatrist in Room 604.' And I went up there, I said, 'Shrink, I want to kill. I mean, I wanna, I wanna kill. Kill. I wanna, I wanna see, I wanna see blood and gore and guts and veins in my teeth. Eat dead burnt bodies. I mean kill, kill, kill, kill.' And I started jumpin' up and down yelling, 'kill, kill,' and he started jumping up and down with me and we was both jumping up and down yelling, 'kill, kill.'"

While the music was playing, Robert Samsoe got up and walked out of the courtroom.

The exact point of the music seemed lost on the jurors. Their response seemed to be a mixture of puzzlement and revulsion.

Alcala went on to admit that the rose earring, which

presumably belonged to Charlotte Lamb, had Lamb's DNA on it; but he said, that was not *proof* that they were actually Lamb's—although he gave no details as to what, exactly, would constitute proof.

Alcala told the jurors, "The death penalty would mean years, fifteen or twenty, of appeals and the high probability that the sentence would be reversed. A sentence of life in prison without parole," he argued, "would end this matter now." Concluding his argument, Alcala said, "This is probably the most important decision you will ever make. Choose wisely."

Throughout his closing remarks, Alcala never raised his voice. He remained calm the entire time.

The judge then told the jurors, "It is the law of this state that the penalty for a defendant found guilty of murder of the first degree shall be death or imprisonment in the state prison for life without the possibility of parole in any case in which the special circumstances alleged in this case have been specifically found to be true.

"Under the law of this state, you must now determine which of these penalties shall be imposed on the defendant."

The jurors were then remanded to the jury room to try to reach a verdict.

Although some feared it might be a long wait, it took the jurors only about an hour to reach their decision.

After they returned to their seats, Judge Briseño said, "I've been advised that you folks have reached a verdict."

Juror Number 9, the foreperson, replied, "Yes, Your Honor."

After handing the verdict to the court clerk, the clerk read the decision.

"We, the jury in the above-entitled action, determine that the penalty to be imposed upon defendant Rodney James Alcala shall be death."

A voice screamed out from the courtroom, "Yes!" It was the relieved voice of Robert Samsoe.

Applause rang out.

It was March 9, 2010.

PART
XV

Chapter Eighty-nine

On March 30, 2010, once again, Briseño's court was filled to overflowing, as extra seats had been brought in for victims' families, friends, relatives, law enforcement members from Orange and Los Angeles counties, and the media.

"This is a hearing on sentencing," stated the judge. "Mr. Alcala has been convicted of first-degree murder of Jill Barcomb, Georgia Wixted, Charlotte Lamb, Jill Parenteau, [and] Robin Samsoe, and the jury has found the special circumstances of multiple murder, kidnapping, torture, rape, and oral copulation to be true. Mr. Alcala has advised the court that he is not filing on his own behalf a motion for a new trial.

"However," Briseño continued, "in every case where a verdict of death is returned, the defendant is deemed to have made an application to modify the death verdict. The trial judge independently reweighs the evidence and determines whether, in the judge's independent judgment, the weight of the evidence supports the jury's verdict."

After a deafeningly quiet pause, the judge offered his "independent judgment." He said, "After careful review of all the evidence before the jury and an independent reweighing of the factors in aggravation [and] mitigation . . . I have determined that the factors clearly support the jury's verdict that death is the appropriate penalty. The motion to modify the punishment to life without the possibility of parole is denied."

Alcala showed no reaction at all.

After that, the judge spoke to the people in the court-room, saying that any family members of the victims would now be permitted to "step forward and make whatever statement they wish to make."

Bruce Barcomb was the first to speak. He stated that he "was the sixth child born out of eleven to Maurice and Joyce Barcomb. Jill was born fifth, and she was my older, yet smaller sister, by eighteen months. To this day, with the exception of Jill's homicide committed by Rodney, all of her siblings live to experience her justice at this trial."

Barcomb told the court that he was closest to his sister Jill. "She was always a source of comfort, support, and joy to be around. Her smile was always contagious."

He said that on the night he was told that his Jill had died, his "life was irrefutably changed forever in that moment."

He recalled how, when he approached his sister's closed coffin at the funeral home, "I prayed with all my heart through tears that she wasn't dead. But as this court has shown, that was clearly not the case. She was brutally tortured, raped, and savagely murdered by you, Rodney."

Barcomb continued, holding back tears. "At this trial, I got to look again upon her face, something I never thought I would see in this lifetime . . . and I was glad to say good-bye to her and see her face. . . . I had forgotten just how petite and young her beautiful face was, even in death."

Then, speaking directly to Alcala, he said, "While you continued to drink, drug, rape, and murder, I was left trying to find peace as a senior in high school, not having any idea how to deal with the front-page news of my late sister. Her unsolved case lingered in the media for nearly three decades."

Barcomb said he was grateful to the LAPD and for DNA technology. Addressing Alcala, Barcomb said he was grateful because together they had "identified you solidly as her killer." When Barcomb learned in 2005 that Alcala's DNA had been linked to his sister's murder, Barcomb told the court he began to write Alcala in prison, asking him to confess to his crimes. Quoting from one of his letters to Alcala,

Barcomb wrote: "Own your truth. Give up your dead. Let your victims' loved ones have some peace, and maybe you might have a little peace knowing that in the end, you finally attempted to make some humanitarian gesture for people's lives you have irrefutably harmed forever."

Then, looking directly at Aclala, he continued: "You have denied your truth and my four written requests asking you to forgo this frivolous trial process. You have hidden like a coward from your truth, even at this trial. Despite the overwhelming evidence, not once did the word 'guilty' come from your lips. . . .

"The DNA evidence for Jill was one in one hundred billion for you, and your ego couldn't say 'guilty' or 'I did this.' . . . My sister died curled in a ball, beaten, breast brutally bitten, raped, head bashed in with a rock, strangled, savagely sodomized, while a few of her fingers touched her privates, bleeding from her anus, and a few drops of blood dripping onto her hand.

"There's murder," he continued. "There's rape," he stated. "There's murder and rape." Then he paused to gather himself. "And then there's the unequivocal carnage of a Rodney Alcala–style murder and rape."

Barcomb then declared that he did not believe Alcala should get life without the possibility of parole. Speaking to the judge, Barcomb said, "None of his victims were ever afforded that grace."

Barcomb concluded his victim impact statement with these words, "Give up your dead, Rodney. All victims, all states, all occurrences. Own your truth."

Many people in the courtroom were unable to hold back tears.

After the judge thanked him, Barcomb slowly took his seat, head down, tears streaming down his cheeks.

Next to speak on behalf of the victims was Anne Michelena, Georgia Wixted's sister.

Michelena began by reading a letter her mother had written to one of Georgia's friends after the murder. In the letter,

Georgia's mother said that when the coffin was brought into Our Lady of Malibu, where Mass was celebrated, she met the coffin at the door. "The official said I should go in and sit down. That was nixed. I'd walked with Georgia for twenty-seven years, and I'd walk the last mile with her." Mrs. Wixted wrote that she had been in St. John's mental health unit after her daughter died, and had been on sick leave since. "Days are long and lonesome. My thoughts are continually on Georgia. Good times and that ghastly night. I don't think she'd be proud of me, but I can't accept or adjust to this. It's sort of a vegetating life."

Michelena then read a letter from her brother, written on March 28, 2010. "First, I would like to thank the court for the opportunity to testify during the sentencing phase. It was extremely painful, physically and emotionally, to relive the events of December 1977, but I drew some measure of satisfaction to look my sister's killer in the eye and state for the record what my feelings were as I cleared and cleaned my sister's horrifically bloody apartment.

"What I did not have an opportunity to describe are two things. First, living for the better part of twenty-five years with absolutely no clue as to who did this savage crime—twenty-five years of birthdays, Christmases, weddings, picnics, and yes, even funerals; natural events in the family life circle.

"The question was always there and asked by friends and family members, 'Did they ever find out who Georgia's killer was?' Twenty-five years of reliving that terrible time and always the same answer, no.

"Second, living the past seven years knowing who this savage beast was, but not being able to see him brought to justice. . . . No amount of justice can replace the years of life that Georgia was denied. No amount of justice can give my now deceased mother back her sanity nor displace the sad emotions our whole family will have forever.

"I unequivocally believe that the jury's recommendation on March 9, 2010, that [Alcala] should be put to death is a just sentence.

"Respectfully submitted, Michael G. Wixted."

Then Anne spoke of her own quarter-century-long ordeal. "The night of December 16, 1977 . . . my whole world was ripped apart. My life could not be put back together again.

"In addition to taking care of my anguished mother, I had to somehow make a life for myself out of the pieces that were left. For twenty-five years, I looked over my shoulder, never knowing who or what I was looking for. I never felt safe."

After describing the holidays that would come and go and that "I could not share with Georgia," Anne said, "I could never again listen to 'I'll Be Home for Christmas.'" She continued, "I never imagined that she would not be there for my wedding. I would give anything if she could meet my husband and see my son."

Like the others, Michelena asked herself aloud, "Who would do that to her? There would be no answers for over twenty-five years. That is an eternity to wait for someone you love, but I never gave up hope.

". . . Even after the DNA miracle that happened seven years ago, I am still left with the question of why? Why her? I will never know why he picked her for one of his victims.

". . . No one should have to die the way my sister did. No one should have to suffer that way. . . . Rodney James Alcala is a reason to use the death penalty, a good reason. We need to make sure that there can never be a chance for him to even be considered for parole. So I am asking that he receive the recommended death penalty."

And with that, emotionally spent Michelena slowly walked to her seat.

Gina Satriano then told the court that the next victim impact statement would be about Charlotte Lamb. "Robert Samsoe has graciously offered to read a letter from Charlotte Lamb's family, written by Lamb's sister, Carolyn Adkins."

Samsoe began. "My name is Robert Samsoe. Throughout this trial, we have learned that Charlotte Lamb and Robin have become sisters. So I'm reading this now as a brother of Charlotte Lamb." He then proceeded to read the letter from Carolyn Adkins (née Lamb).

"From the moment the dreadful news of our sister's death came, over thirty years ago, there has been a giant hole in each of our lives. She was the fourth child born in our family of eight children. I was eight when she was born and I well remember a tiny bundle with golden blond hair and a sweet smile.

"When the news came, my knees turned to jelly and I simply collapsed. For days, sleep would not come. I prayed that her suffering was short-lived. Our mother had to be hospitalized due to dangerously high blood pressure. Claudia, four years younger than I, battled a maddening fear of men. . . . The ripple effect of her loss has taken a toll on each family member. We've been robbed of hearing her cute laugh when she'd call at least once every month and chat for over an hour. We've been robbed of receiving her newsy notes and letters expressing her sincere interest in each of our lives. We've been robbed of the loss to our children, who will never know the continuing love of their aunt, Shug.

"Now that we're thirty years older, we remaining sisters wonder how many children she might have had and if they would have had her delicate features, her small hands, perfect teeth, and oh, yes, her golden hair. Would they have had her love of animals . . . would they have had the same compassion for the less fortunate?

"We'll never know the answers to these questions. That giant hole created when she was taken from us will never be filled, but we do have memories of a sister who graced our lives with decency and beauty for a while. Our only comfort rests in the hope of seeing her in a far better place and of hearing that cute little laugh once again."

After the judge thanked Samsoe for reading Adkins' letter, Satriano called Dedee Parenteau, Jill's sister, to address the court.

In a gentle yet strong voice, Dedee spoke: "During this

trial, the question has been asked, 'Is your memory as clear today as it was thirty years ago?' Yes, it is. I remember the weather the day I learned that my precious sister Jill was gone forever. It was one of those hazy June days. It was hot and uncomfortable. I hate days like that. They remind me of that day.

"I remember my mother meeting me at the apartment manager's door. She looked so pale, so weak, so helpless, and in such disbelief. I'll never forget the look on her face . . . and her sobbing uncontrollably over losing her youngest daughter.

"I remember my father . . . two days later, standing at the window alone, tears streaming down his cheek. That was the first time I ever saw my father cry.

"At one point, my father told my mother, let's move back home to Minnesota. Maybe it would be better. . . . My mother convinced him that wherever they went, the pain of losing Jill would follow. Nothing would end this nightmare.

"When I returned to work, I learned to count the hours just to make it through the day. . . . My older brother was also devastated. To this day, he does not talk at all about Jill.

"My father died fourteen years ago. My mother died last November. When I was going through my mother's house, I found my father's wallet. Inside there were pictures of my brother, myself, and Jill. . . . There was also a newspaper clipping from July 12, 1980. The title of the article read, 'Convicted Murderer Faces Burbank Strangling Charge.' My father carried that in his wallet for seventeen years, until the day he died.

"My family would sometimes talk about Jill, things about her we remembered. How beautiful, kind, and gentle she was. Funny little habits she had. She always seemed upbeat and happy. A friend of hers once said Jill had a smile that could bring down the house.

"We spoke of her often, but we never spoke about what happened to her.

"Rodney Alcala seems to have a loving relationship with his sister, although I don't believe he is capable of love. I wonder how he would feel if his sister was murdered like he murdered my sister Jill.

"People think you're over it, doing okay, just because you don't display your sorrow. You're never over it. . . . I think of how Jill must have felt safe in her apartment, in her own bed. Then this evil monster appeared. She fought for her life. The terror she must have felt. It sickens me, breaks my heart, knowing the last face that she saw in her life was of this monster. I will never understand why she had to die that way.

"She was twenty-one years old. She had her whole life ahead of her. . . . Rodney Alcala prevented that. . . .

"My wish is that somehow, she and my parents have been looking down and watching all that has transpired. I wish my parents could know that after thirty years, this has finally been somewhat settled. . . .

"If there is a hell, I hope Rodney Alcala burns eternally. I wish he would experience the terror that he put his victims through. He is truly a devil who does not belong on this earth."

As Dedee spoke, the collective sorrow of the testimonies was clearly visible on the people in the courtroom, many of whom sobbed quietly, uncontrollably.

When Dedee finished her statement, Leila Otery, a longtime next-door neighbor of the Parenteau family, spoke. She stated that she and "Mayme Parenteau used to talk over the fence for thirty-nine years. She was a very stoic woman, keeping her grief to herself. Did that mean that she grieved any less? Of course not. . . . I told Mayme, before her mind began deteriorating, that I wanted to come to court and look Alcala in the eye. . . . Perhaps Mayme's dementia was a blessing in disguise, so she wouldn't have to relive the horror of that fateful day.

"Mr. Alcala, I suspect it's a blessing that your mother is not here today to witness this. I feel sure she died with a broken heart."

* * *

Next called was Anne Ericsson, a close friend of Dedee Parenteau.

Ericsson said that she had waited over thirty years to tell the court the horrific pain "you have caused my family with the savage murder of Jill Parenteau.

"Jill's sister, Dedee, has been my best and dearest friend for over forty-one years. The day that you murdered Jill was one of the worst days of our lives . . . and it never goes away. . . .

"Going to her parents' house and see[ing] the pain that they were in was agony." In speaking about Jill's father, Cliff, she said, his daughters were "the apple of his eye. The loss of Jill, his baby girl, and then to bear his and her mother's unbearable pain was difficult to watch. . . .

"Your silence during this court proceeding regarding Jill's murder screamed to me that you are guilty of this heinous crime. We didn't need blood evidence to prove it. Your absolute silence became your admission that you did that.

"You are worse than a rabid pit bull. At least someone can see a pit bull coming. You just sneak around and destroy innocent, unsuspecting, trusting lives for the fun of it. . . .

"Jill doesn't get to play Ping-Pong, exercise, use the computer, write to friends, have conversations with family and friends, watch movies, but you do. . . .

"My dear friend Dedee was so afraid of coming to court and being in the same room with you, her only sister's murderer. I told her that you couldn't hurt her any more than you already have. . . . We are here to represent Jill and make sure that justice is served for the short-lived life of Jill Parenteau.

"It takes a very weak man to do what you have done. . . .

"I am not God, nor am I your judge or jury. My only hope is that you burn in hell for eternity for what you have done. . . .

"It has been said that your eyes are the windows of your soul. Looking into your eyes during this trial, you have no soul."

And with the words "no soul" ringing in the attendees' ears, Ericsson said she would now read a letter from Janet Jordan, who was unable to attend the trial.

In the letter, Jordan wrote that she and Jill were co-workers who "quickly became friends. . . . We were young with our whole lives ahead of us. I was only 19 and sometimes Jill seemed like a big sister to me. She had a way of kindness that was almost protective. I remember how excited she was to move into her apartment. . . . I will never forget the day she didn't show up for work . . . all the while, we were thinking she must have stayed out really late after the Dodger game and overslept.

"As clearly as I remember this morning, I remember knocking loudly on her door and her not answering. I remember hearing the phone ringing in the living room. . . . I ran to the landlord's place to let me in. Rounding her bedroom corner and seeing her lying naked and bloodied on the floor is as clear a picture today in my mind as it was at that moment over thirty years ago. . . .

"I remember calling 911 . . . I was in a daze, somehow thinking she was just sick and this couldn't be what it looked like, but yet knowing something godawful happened. . . . It was years before I could close my eyes and see something else. That monster didn't just take my friend that day in June, he took something from me, too. My strength and my spirit. I am so angry that I didn't get to have her friendship for life. I know that if I met her today, we would be friends. . . .

"I grew up quickly that day and learned the meaning of loss and hate all at the same moment. [Alcala] doesn't deserve this time and attention. He deserves to die, and, frankly, in the most horrific way possible, in a much more painful way than we are talking about here."

Kathy Franco, another friend of Jill Parenteau, spoke next. She said that in 1979, she and Jill were best friends. "We saw each other almost every day . . . Jill was smart, funny, and nice. She was shy and reserved if she didn't know you well. . . .

"One night, Jill and I met Rodney Alcala at the Handle-bar Saloon. We were there with a group of our friends and he really made no impression on us. . . . We never even discussed him beyond agreeing he was a little dorky. I honestly don't think I would ever have thought of him again if I hadn't recognized him in the group of pictures Detective Bowers asked me to look at.

"On June 14, I didn't hear from Jill and she wasn't at work . . . Perhaps she fell in the shower or didn't put her glasses on and somehow hurt herself. Either way, I'd be there to help her. And then one of the officers told me she was dead. It was incomprehensible. A part of me was gone. . . .

"I was naïve to the circumstances of her death. This trial has shown me a depth of such disturbing proportions. . . . There is no escaping the knowledge of the horror, pain, and torment that my friend endured. . . . My heart breaks to think of my beautiful, sweet friend scared and suffering in pain. . . .

"I feel that Rodney Alcala has been lurking in the background of my life since Jill's death. I wonder how we could have spoken with him and not known he was so dangerous. . . .

"I have so many questions that will never be answered. Why Jill? Did she do something, or say something, or was it her hair or her height? Or if she hadn't come home that night, would he have gone away and never come back? Why does he kill people? What made him this way? . . .

"I hope that the verdict and sentence will be upheld and that we all can find peace."

After thanking Franco, Gloria Allred, well-known victims' rights lawyer, said she would read a letter on behalf of Taranne Robinson, Robin Samsoe's sister. Allred said that she was representing both "Taranne and Marianne Connelly, who is the mother of the victim."

Allred then asked Connelly if she would read her statement first, which Connelly did.

Her voice shaking, Connelly began: "As the mother of Robin, my beautiful daughter, I want to call the defendant . . . a cold-blooded, evil, mass-murdering monster that should have died years ago.

"Losing my precious Robin was the worst tragedy of my life, and knowing the defendant tortured his victims makes it even harder to accept. What I am grateful for is the fact that my little twelve-year-old Robin stopped him from taking any more lives. . . .

"I hate him for the pain he has caused me and so many people, but I have prayed about this and I'm giving this hatred all to God because I've let this feeling consume me for thirty-one years and I'm not giving this kind of power over me anymore to the defendant who murdered my daughter.

"I noticed in court that not one single person was there in support of the defendant. That may be because the defendant disgusts me and everyone else.

"Losing Robin, we lost so many things. We didn't get to see her grow up, graduate high school or college, have a dance career, get married, have children. Who knows what her future could have been if she was able to live life as she did to the fullest? He took her life, her future, and our joy. . . .

"In closing, I just want to add this thought. I know where my little Robin is now, and that's heaven. She never again has to face the defendant because he is the devil's own and I hope and believe he will rot in hell. I just pray that I live long enough to watch him executed. . . . I only wish I could be the one to administer the injection. . . .

"The defendant made my precious baby a hero while he will be known as a murderer. This world needs more children like my Robin, but never again another murderer like Rodney James Alcala."

At this point, not one single eye was dry in the courtroom.

After Connelly walked slowly back to her seat, Allred read the letter from Taranne: "My sister Robin was a very loving and compassionate person, even at twelve. She loved God and was such a mama's girl. I loved Robin immensely. I miss her more than words could ever express. . . . Robin has been a positive force in my life and has made me want to reach out to others to make a difference for my kids, my family, and the community. . . .

"I beg the courts to please give the defendant the death penalty again for the third time. . . . God bless you all."

Robin's brother Robert Samsoe spoke next. "I'm here for the third time," he said. "I don't have anything prepared, so I'm just going to say it from the heart.

"Robin was the biggest part of my life. She was my best friend. . . . Not only did the death of Robin destroy our family, I not only lost Robin, I lost my brother for a while, I lost my mom for a while. I lost my hope.

"Rodney, I hope you don't sleep at night. I hope you have dreams of us coming after you because if there is a heaven and justice, that's what I'm going to do when I die: haunt your dreams. . . .

"Hopefully, we don't have to do this again. . . . Maybe after thirty-one years, Robin can rest."

After the judge thanked Samsoe, he asked, "Does that complete the statements by members of the victims' families?"

Satriano said, "Yes, it does."

"Any statements by the people?

Murphy said no.

"Mr. Alcala?"

"No, Your Honor."

Then, after having listened to ninety minutes of victims' families' heart-wrenching remembrances, the judge spoke directly to Alcala and formally read him his death warrant.

"It is the order of this court that you shall suffer the death penalty, said penalty to be imposed within the walls of the state prison at San Quentin, California. . . .

"You are remanded to the care, custody and control of the sheriff of Orange County to be by her delivered to the warden of the state prison at San Quentin. . . .

"Further, this is to command the warden of the state prison of the state of California at San Quentin to hold in your custody the said Rodney James Alcala pending the decision of this cause on appeal, and upon the judgment herein becoming final, to carry into effect the judgment of said court at a time and on a date to be hereinafter fixed by order of this court . . . at which time and place you shall then and there put to death the said Rodney James Alcala in the manner and means prescribed by law."

The judge ended by saying "Done in open court on the thirtieth day of March, 2010."

However, Judge Briseño was not quite done. He quickly added, "I want to make a few comments. It's my normal practice not to say anything after having read a judgment or sentence, because the sentence speaks for itself. But I wanted to acknowledge the family members who are present during the proceedings. . . .

"As you have voiced in very eloquent terms," he said looking out over the courtroom, "we would like to think that our courts can . . . make [people] whole, but as you can see, passage of time does not abate the loss and your sense as to how immoral the taking of life was. It's exceedingly difficult, but we thank you for your presence and cooperation with the court."

The judge then commented on the violent lyrics in the song "Alice's Restaurant" that Alcala played to the court during his closing statement in the penalty phase of the trial. Although the song was written as a lengthy satire on the Vietnam War, Alcala played only the section of the song containing the lines "I wanna kill. Kill. I wanna, I wanna see, I wanna see blood and gore and guts and veins in my teeth. Eat dead burnt bodies. I mean kill, kill, kill, kill."

"In '68 and '69, I was in Vietnam," continued the judge, who was clearly affected by the victims' impact statements as well as disturbed by Alcala's overall behavior in court, "so I was not listening to protest songs. But the words, the tone, the violence contained in that song that he played to the jury told me that this is Alcala's national anthem, this is his thought. This is the state of his mind, this is his feeling, this is who he is, when he took life. That's my personal assessment."

The victim impact statements were over. The families

and friends of the deceased had had a chance to speak publicly about their loved ones, themselves, and Alcala. They had had their day in court, but they would never, ever have closure. A heart torn by grief can never be mended.

Judge Briseño then adjourned the court, and Alcala was taken away in shackles and handcuffs.

Alcala would become the seven hundred and second inmate on San Quentin's death row.

Outside the courtroom, several jurors, clearly exhausted and emotionally drained, spoke to reporters. They felt confident they had done the right thing in recommending a death sentence for Alcala—and they were also relieved the trial was finally over. They reported feeling exhausted by the relentlessly disturbing testimony and the sideshow of Alcala acting as his own lawyer.

"These were horrendous crimes," said one juror. "There was an overwhelming feeling to render a verdict of justice to show our sympathies to the families."

"I am a father and a husband," said another. "Seeing [the victims] gave us the strength to do our duty."

One juror noted, "Alcala's arguments were very insulting. He basically called us killers."

"This trial will have a lasting effect on me," said one. "I don't think any of us will ever forget this."

Directly after the trial, Robin's mother visited her daughter at the Huntington Beach Good Shepherd Cemetery. Bending down to kiss the gravestone, Connelly told her daughter, "We won." Before leaving, she said a prayer, ending with "Keep her safe until I get there. Amen."

The gravestone did not have a date of death for Robin but instead read, "Born again June 20, 1979," an acknowledgment and affirmation of Robin's deep religious beliefs.

The afternoon the verdict came down, the Web site for the *Orange County Register* posted more than one hundred photos Alcala had taken over the years, mostly of young girls and women. The Huntington Beach Police Department had originally obtained more than 1,700 photos from Alcala's storage locker in Seattle, and now the authorities were releasing many of these photos because they believed they might lead to the identification of more missing persons and more victims.

According to the *LA Times*, detectives were withholding hundreds of photos because they were too "sexually explicit." Some of the photographs showed nude females engaging in sexual acts, and some of the women in the photos appeared to be unconscious. The girls' clothing and hairstyles typified the seventies. Some shots were taken outdoors and seem to be of free-spirited females. Others, however, showed pensive, brooding, and blatantly uncomfortable girls.

Knowing that the photographs were taken by a now-convicted serial murderer made the lens through which one viewed the photographs far different than if they had simply been taken by an amateur photographer with no special baggage other than camera equipment. Knowing that, by viewing the pictures, you were seeing through a killer's eyes was creepy if not downright macabre.

Matt Murphy said the Orange County DA's office wanted to make sure each of the females in the photographs was alive. "We'd like to locate the women in these pictures," said Murphy. "Did they simply pose for a serial killer, or did they become victims of his sadistic, murderous pattern? . . . I can't imagine for a million years that we've got him for the only murders he's done."

The *Orange Country Register* gave a phone number at the Huntington Beach Police Department for anyone with information to call. The police received over a hundred calls within two days. Many of the callers said they recognized themselves. The callers hailed from states including Connecticut, New Hampshire, California, and Washington.

One woman who called in, Liane Leedom, now a psychologist in Connecticut, said she had lived next door to Alcala in Monterey Park and was his friend in June 1979—the month and year that Alcala was later accused of having killed Samsoe. Alcala had taken a portrait photo of Leedom then, and when his photos were released by the police, Leedom recognized her younger self in the collection. Leedom told the police that Alcala once drove her to work and invited her to go to his house to see all his photographs. He said he wanted her to pose for him. She said she was flattered. "I was a seventeen-year-old girl and I said, 'Oh, a professional photographer wants to take my picture! Of course, I'll do it,'" she recalled.

Leedom believed that she might have become Alcala's next victim—if it hadn't been for an observant neighbor. She saw Leedom leaving Alcala's car and told Leedom's parents, who then told Leedom she could never see Alcala again. "I was super-lucky," said Leedom.

Cynthia Libby, now forty-eight, also called in after seeing herself in photos numbers 111, 185, and 193. Libby was just sixteen when she dated Alcala. He was an amateur photographer, she recalled, who one time drove her to a secluded canyon in Southern California. "I could do anything I want to you, and no one would know," Libby recalled Alcala telling her. She didn't think he was being serious and simply laughed it off. Some thirty years later, after she saw herself as a happy young girl in the photos, she wondered why she was spared being his next victim.

The answer was simple, although Libby didn't know it at the time and thought she had simply been stood up. Alcala didn't show up for his next date with her because he was in jail, having been arrested for killing Robin Samsoe.

As of fall 2010, no new missing persons or victims have been discovered in the Alcala photos. But many of the women and girls remain unidentified.

Chapter Ninety

After the trial was over and Alcala had received his death sentence, Matt Murphy offered his opinion of Alcala as a defense attorney. "Thankfully, he was terrible," said Murphy. "A lot of sociopaths think they are smarter than their attorneys, smarter than everybody. These guys obsess about facts and lose sight of the big picture. Intellectually, they are smart, but they are never as smart as think they are. Trying cases is a skill, like swinging a golf club. It sometimes takes years to perfect. So, just like [Ted] Bundy, Alcala was absolutely terrible, and he even studied law.

"The key to trying cases is trying to figure out what the jury is wondering, thinking, wanting to know, and needing to know. . . . And sociopaths are incapable of empathy, of feeling what another person feels, and thinking the way another person thinks. That's why they have no clue what a juror wants or needs to hear. That's why Alcala did a terrible job in his role as a defense lawyer."

Commenting on Alcala's playing of "Alice's Restaurant" to the jury, Murphy pondered, "What was he thinking? In his mind, he was trying to guilt them. In his mind, the way he sees the universe, the earth revolves around him; the sun revolves around earth. He is the center of God's creation. [Serial killers] are all like that. Half of the jury was confused and others were wildly offended."

Although Alcala behaved like a sociopath in court, Murphy said Alcala was surprisingly easy to deal with on the occasions they had one-on-one contact outside the courtroom. On a personal level, Murphy said of Alcala, "He and I got along fine. But I did wish him the death penalty because I dealt with [the victims'] families. That's the real contact. The families endured so much for so long, and you see and feel the grief that they have held for thirty years.

"All the victims' loved ones dealt with the anger and tragedy in their own ways," continued Murphy, "and they all used different strategies to power through the trial and go on with their lives.

"You could see that Dedee Parenteau has become more skilled at coping but it never goes away," said Murphy. "She has this winning, cutting sense of humor. But you know how deeply it pains her.

"The Samsoe family was destroyed by this murder. You see ripple effects. . . .

"Charlotte Lamb was so stunning and gorgeous, as beautiful as a girl can get, and you hear about her chasing dollar bills and how much she loved animals. And her friend, Fraracci, came on the stand and just broke down crying—the imprint she left thirty years later. He probably never met another woman in his entire life like her. So you get this imprint when you talk to people who knew her."

Murphy said it was impossible to work on the Alcala case without developing affection for the victims' families. "Through the way they talk, you meet the victims' shadows, and you get a feeling about who they were on a soul level," he said. "And then you look at the photos and you know what he did. And then you look at his background and see he wasn't ever friggin' abused. The victim[s] didn't do anything that caused this. Alcala liked doing this. Combine that with the horror of what these women went through. He liked to torture. He would let them come to, strangle them, and let them come to again, and see the horror in their eyes, see them suffer the physical pain. All five victims in this case.

"It is a rarity in my job. Not all the victims are so nice. I deal with drug dealers. Some people put themselves in a position of vulnerability, but every one of these people [victims] was a really genuine good person. An eight-year-old and a twelve-year-old beautiful girl, and you look at what he did, again and again and again." After pausing for a moment to reflect on the horror, Murphy said a death sentence was highly appropriate in this case. "I would pull the switch myself," added Murphy, "and wave goodbye to my friend Rodney as he went under.

"Death is better for victims' families than living on Death Row," commented Murphy. "The single most important thing about him [Alcala] is that it is all about him. When a woman witness came on the stand, Alcala would ask her to stand up and approach the posterboard, then say she could sit down; then say he forgot something, could she walk over again: he forgot to ask her something. He didn't ask Fraracci or the police or any man to do this. It's about control.

"When Rasch [Alcala's defense investigator] came in with his two female assistants," continued Murphy, "Alcala had sat next to him for four months and had no interest in talking to him, but he took great interest in the assistants. Alcala would say, 'I want you to get this for me. I want you to get that for me.'

"The most important thing for Alcala is control. The second most important thing is control. That's why he does things in the first place. But the fact that his life is going to end on someone else's time scale, that eats at him. He doesn't have control. And that is huge.

"And that is worth it all."

PART
XVI

PART

XVI

Chapter Ninety-one

With his long track record of crimes and convictions, Rodney Alcala has spent most of his adult life in prison. During that time, his actions have been pondered by experts, and he has been interviewed by countless specialists. The mind-set of a serial killer is so different from a normal person's that any attempt to understand Alcala's worldview is a bit like peeking into the brain of an alien being. Nonetheless, it is the job of detectives, criminal profilers, and forensic experts to attempt to understand and even predict the behavior of dangerous offenders like Alcala. This work not only aids in the capture and conviction of serial killers but also may help the public avoid encounters with such predators.

After Alcala had been convicted and sentenced (again) to death row in 2010, Mark Safarik, formerly of the FBI's Behavioral Science Unit, weighed in on the particular and peculiar personality of Rodney Alcala.

According to Safarik, Alcala had an MO that allowed him to get close to girls and women. "He used his skills in photography to disarm them, and then he used their vanity against them to not only gain access but to lower their inhibitions and get them into a situation where he was alone with them—all without any force. It was a perfect setup for him." Once he got his victims alone, he would unleash his violent side.

"He has no empathy for his victims as human beings," continued Safarik. "For him, they are simply objects to be used to satisfy his cravings, and when he was done with them, they were simply disposable trash."

Safarik believed that Alcala was driven by emotional and psychological needs that no doubt arose early in adolescence. Somewhere along the way, violence, sexual arousal, and certain behaviors became fused together in his mind. He developed paraphilia, a psychosexual disorder marked by atypical and extreme sexual urges, fantasies, and behavior involving objects, suffering or humiliation, children, or other non-consenting partners. He also engaged in paraphilic behaviors that fed these needs and developed fantasies to satisfy his emotional urges. "At some point, the fantasy was not enough and he crossed over into acting out," said Safarik. "He very likely acted out at first with consenting partners until that did not do enough to satisfy his needs."

Safarik pondered the variation in the ages of Alcala's victims: from age eight to thirty-two. "Alcala's selection of both children and adult women is interesting," he said. "In the unit, we called guys like this that have multiple age and gender victims 'trysexuals'; that is, they will try anything sexually whether it's a male, a female child, or an elderly woman.

"Alcala is more educated and smarter than most serial killers," said Safarik, "and I think this is always confusing for the public because their belief is that he could have done anything with his life yet he chose to be a killer."

Noted expert on serial killers and former leader of the Bronx homicide task force, Vernon Geberth also weighed in on Alcala.

According to Geberth, the enormous stash of photographs that Alcala had personally taken of women, young girls, and even young men—and that he had hidden in a Seattle storage locker—was cause for serious concern. Although many of the shots featured fully clothed subjects in candid and seemingly harmless poses, others were sexually suggestive and some depicted sexual acts. Alcala's history of sexual violence and murder, combined with the fact that he felt the need to hide the photographs, suggested they might depict other unknown victims. "That information alone," said Geberth, "would certainly indicate that this offender was much more prolific a killer than at first thought. These types of offenders are 'collectors.'"

Geberth described Alcala as having a "malignant narcissistic personality disorder with the following co-morbidities: psychopathy and sexual sadism." In essence, he added, Alcala is a "human predator," and Geberth thought it highly unlikely that the total number of his victims had been accounted for.

Veronica Thomas, a forensic psychologist hired by the prosecution to interview Alcala, also weighed in on the now three-time convicted murderer.

Thomas felt that Alcala was a keen observer of the environment and had a "keen sensitivity for those who were vulnerable. Thomas admitted that Alcala "did have some 'normal' interpersonal relationships—with his sister and her kids and with a girlfriend." However, she added, "this did not seem to be what made him feel alive. It was part of his disguise. I think Keith Ablow, M.D., described these people as 'aliens in human suits.' They look and act like the rest of us on the outside, but on the inside they are highly idiosyncratic and egotistical. Most of them are highly organized and narcissistic. The intelligent ones like Alcala, Bundy, and BTK can slip in and out of the 'normal' world very easily."

In thinking about Alcala, Thomas surmised that he could possibly be bisexual. "Alcala was indiscriminant in his choice of sexual objects, although he chose each object for a different reason. The things we know that he has done to women and female children may also be things he has done to boys and grown men."

Thomas believes many serial killers, including Alcala, enjoy being interviewed by psychological specialists. "People like Alcala are highly organized, intelligent, and articulate," she noted. "They see the forensic interview as their time to shine and explain their beliefs and feelings that motivate their behavior. The capacity for empathy with these people is nonexistent, so they speak about the victims as if they were reading a book."

Asked whether or not she felt Alcala was evil, Thomas replied, " 'Evil' is not a psychological term and difficult to objectify. I believe that evil is a moral description, and if you think of people in terms of their ability to put themselves in the shoes of their brother or sister or feel the sadness or pain of hunger or torture, then Alcala is evil. He does not have the capacity to empathize with others. His degree of inhumanity, which was determined by his biology, psychology, and environment, reflects a constant predatory attitude.

"To me, evil characterizes a particularly perverse mind that has *no* capacity to feel like others and thereby acts like a monster. That is Rodney Alcala."

Chapter Ninety-two

Because of his appearance on *The Dating Game* in 1978, Alcala is often referred to as the *Dating Game* killer. Viewers today have different reactions to Alcala's performance after watching a tape of the show, which is readily available on YouTube and other Internet video sites. Some people say that Alcala looks and acts like a creep, while others are disturbed by how unremarkable he seems—at least, within the context of a tongue-in-cheek 1970s game show that was filled with sexual innuendo. When CNN asked noted criminal profiler Pat Brown to analyze Alcala's appearance on *The Dating Game*, she observed that Alcala "was aware that he could say things that were considered sexy and funny and the [bachelorette] would like that. He had watched the game before, so he learned some tricks. But a psychopath's true nature comes seeping through."

In hindsight, what Brown found most notable was Alcala's ability to compartmentalize and to hide his true nature on camera. "When you go back and look, what's most fascinating is that he had already committed a crime. Raped a little girl. Here is a man portraying himself as a desirable young man when he is a violent sexual predator of children."

Brown believed that Alcala revealed his true identity off the stage when he was with the other bachelors. She told CNN, "He is showing his psychopathic personality in the green room. He wasn't acting at that time. Those were his enemies, and he had to beat them to get the girl and he wanted to win. . . . His ego was riding on it."

Jed Mills, who appeared as Bachelor Number Two on the same episode of *The Dating Game*, was quoted in an article by Christine Pelisek in *LA Weekly* that he had had an almost immediate aversion to Alcala: "Something about him, I could not be near him. [On the show] I am kind of bending toward the other guy to get away from him, and I don't know if I did that consciously. But thinking back on that, I probably did."

Mills said that Alcala may have appeared charming to Bachelorette Cheryl Bradshaw, but he was the complete opposite in the show's green room, where contestants hung out before the show. As it turned out, however, Bradshaw decided not to go on her date with Alcala, telling the producers of the show that she just didn't feel comfortable with him. She found him "creepy."

"He was quiet, but at the same time he would interrupt and impose when he felt like it," Mills said. "And he was very obnoxious and became unlikable and rude and imposing, as though he was trying to intimidate. . . . He got creepier and more negative. He was a standout creepy guy in my life."

Mills continued, "The more time has gone by, the creepier it gets, because it kind of sinks in slowly. What this guy did, it's hard to express. Just talking about it, I get a tightness in my stomach."

Armand Cerami, who also appeared on *The Dating Game* with Alcala, as Bachelor Number Three, told 10News.com that he never thought twice about Alcala until friends e-mailed him decades later and told him that Alcala was on trial for the murder of five females. "And I'm looking at this and I'm not even believing what I'm seeing. I was three feet away from a serial killer. My God!"

Cerami said he has no sympathy for Alcala. "Just being around somebody who would do something like that, you want to take him out and boil him in olive oil. Let's just say that I hope he gets what's coming to him. Quickly!"

Chapter Ninety-three

Both Marilyn and Art Droz played major roles in identifying Rodney Alcala as Robin Samsoe's killer in 1979. Marilyn was the police artist who created the composite sketch of Alcala based on young Bridget Wilvert's description. Marilyn's husband, Art, was the detective who first spotted Alcala on *The Dating Game*. Plus, Art had extensively interviewed Dana Crappa, the key witness at Alcala's first murder trial—the witness who initially seemed too frightened or too guilt-stricken to talk about what she had seen—but who ultimately linked Alcala and his car to Samsoe and the location where her body was discovered.

"Alcala's case has been a major part of our family for thirty years," said Art. "Both of us testified in the first trial. In 1980, Marilyn was eight and a half months pregnant with our son when she testified.

"Our son is now a police officer for another agency. He's known about the Alcala case from the time he was a child. This past year [2010], I took him to the trial for the reading of the jury verdicts.

"Robin's case was on the line for a third time. Listening to the verdicts being read and seeing the reactions of the family members of all the victims was a heart-pounding experience. I think that was the only time that I got emotional in the case. At that time, I was not doing the investigation but was just a spectator and it was thirty years after the case.

"That was a special day for us. I may be too old to re-member my name when we do the fourth trial, but I will never forget this one."

Reflecting on his interviews with Crappa, Art Droz said, "I never dealt with any witness or victim like her before or afterward in my career, and I've spoken to thousands of wit-nesses and victims of major traumatic violent crimes and in rape cases. It was like talking to a tight piano wire. She never relaxed. She never got conversational. There would be moments where it appeared that she was going to talk, but then she'd shut down."

Of course, at the time Droz had no way of knowing that his sessions with Crappa would feature large in Alcala's later appeals.

"During Alcala's appeals and appellate cases," stated Art, the defense made a big issue over Crappa's interview with me. At that time in police work, doing hypnosis with wit-nesses and victims of crimes was fairly new. I had attended two training seminars and had done a few cases with victims and witnesses prior. However, one aspect of hypnosis is that the person must be in a *relaxed* state and must be *coopera-tive*. It takes work to get to that point. It's not something we can do secretly to a witness.

"I never attempted to do any hypnosis whatsoever with Crappa. It would have been wrong to attempt it under those circumstances, and again, it requires a lot of cooperation from the witness. One thing [is] for sure, the witness must be willing and have provided an account of what they saw and heard so that a comparison can be made before and af-ter any hypnosis. We would first had to have a statement from her. We never did.

"Alcala's defense included a psychiatrist who stated that even though I did not purposely try to hypnotize her, it sort of just happened by the way I spoke to her. And thus, I tainted her. Wow, what a crock! First of all, Crappa never ever relaxed one minute during our interviews. Like I stated, she was a piano wire. She drove us nuts.

"If I had that kind of talent to inadvertently hypnotize

someone by talking to them, I would have had my own Las Vegas show. And if [I had hypnotized her], I would have been prohibited from interviewing anyone else in my police career.

"I always believed that Crappa saw Alcala kill Robin, or saw him push her into that area, like she testified, and later returned and saw the body and could not live with it mentally because she did not try to stop it and told no one about it. . . ."

Marilyn Droz had had a very different experience with her key witness in the case. Twelve-year-old Bridget Wilvert had been eager to help investigators find the man who had been photographing her and Robin at the beach. By listening to Bridget carefully and drawing on her memory, Marilyn had created the composite that led police to Alcala.

Summing up her feelings about her work, Marilyn Droz stated, "I have worked with over five thousand victims and witnesses in the thirty-plus years I have been doing this job. I remember lots of the people I have worked with, but certainly not all. Often, cases tug at my heart and I can only hope I can make the process of doing the drawing a positive thing for the person. I believe it gives a victim an opportunity to take back some control in their lives as they participate in the investigative process."

In this case Marilyn Droz's sketch did that and more. The composite was so good that it triggered multiple people to call in identifying Alcala as the man in the picture. Without the composite, it is likely police would *never* have linked Alcala to Samsoe's murder.

Chapter Ninety-four

One of the most disturbing things about Alcala's history is how easily he fit in with a variety of roles—student, tenant, boyfriend, camp counselor, co-worker—despite openly having what by today's standards is a rather suspicious hobby: photographing underage girls.

Sharon Gonzales, who worked with Alcala at the *Los Angeles Times* starting in 1977, remembers thinking that Alcala was unusual but not threatening. In an interview with *LA Weekly* she stated, "I was young then. If I had more sophistication, I might have questioned some of the photographs he so proudly displayed in his portfolio. Especially those of young girls. They were naked. . . ."

Gonzales continued: "I was neither smart enough nor mature enough to realize that I was actually viewing child porn." Obviously, others at the *LA Times* weren't, either, even when Alcala started flashing homemade child porn around their water cooler. "There were other people in the department who were in their 40s and 50s. The [*Times*] supervisor at the time—she saw it. Instead of having an immediate negative reaction, we thought he was a little different. Strange about sex—but nothing more."

Chapter Ninety-five

When Matt Murphy, senior deputy DA in Orange County, was assigned to the third Samsoe trial in 2003, he had been working in the Orange County DA's homicide unit for nine years. Alcala's case would be the one hundred and seventh murder case that he would bring before a jury.

Even with his wide-ranging experience with homicides and murderers of all stripes, the Alcala trial was one of a kind. "Alcala was the only case I had with five victims," said Murphy. "The number of victims and the degree of cruelty makes Alcala's trial stand out."

In an hour-long interview with this author, Murphy berated a justice system that seemed more concerned with the rights of criminals than with the rights of victims or the reasonable punishments for offenders. "Alcala never should have been released in 1974," said Murphy. "Under today's laws, he never would have been." Murphy elaborated in an interview with *LA Weekly*, saying, "The seventies in California was insane as far as treatment of sexual predators. Rodney Alcala is a poster boy for this. It is a total comedy of outrageous stupidity."

In the interview he also spoke disparagingly of the Ninth Circuit Court of Appeals. "They reversed this thing twice," Murphy said. "When [the Samsoe case] landed on my desk, it had been gutted by Rose Bird, gutted by the Ninth Circuit. It was very difficult, but we now had the additional LA cases."

In speaking about how the trial for all five victims got to be held in Orange County, Murphy recounted: "Steve Cooley was the LA district attorney. We went to a meeting up there, and I asked his permission to try the cases in Orange County. They could have kept the cases in LA and it would have been a pure LA case, and it would have been a feather in their cap. They had a political opportunity to get a big headline-grabbing win on a serial killer, but instead they realized that the right thing to do would be to do all cases together. By putting all cases together, they all get stronger.

"I was tremendously impressed with Cooley. He understood. He did the honorable thing."

Murphy felt confident that Orange County was the best place for the trial. He had prosecuted death penalty cases before Judge Briseño previously, plus the Samsoe murder *had* to be tried in Orange County, since that was where the original convictions had been reversed. Murphy was sure that if the cases were consolidated in Orange County, he would get convictions on all five.

"They sent Gina Satriano down to help us," said Murphy. "She handled the LA cases. Gina's style is different from mine, but as it turned out, we worked well together. She is detail-oriented, and I'm not. We got to be really good friends. We were together for six years on the case, and it went all the way to the California Supreme Court to get cases combined."

When asked how he prepares for homicide cases, Murphy said, "You have to learn every single detail about every person and absorb it and make it part of you, and then you have to take the whole breadth of it and boil it down. You have to craft it, like a writer. Success in trial means you've got not to be a lawyer but be a person. . . .

"I try to relate to a jury as much as I can. I look them in the eye. In closing arguments, I raise my voice. I point right at the defendant. I try to breathe fire and ask the hard questions.

"In my opinion, the whole trial boils down to closing arguments and cross-examination. If you are good and somebody is lying, you will expose them."

Murphy said that his goal in trying any case was to have the jury feel the sense of outrage that he felt about the victims. "You want the jury to hit into the grief and the true gravity of what happened. It's easy for a lot of people to wash it off." Before the average American has graduated from high school, Murphy noted, he or she will have "witnessed" seventeen thousand murders on television shows like *Law & Order.* "On a certain level, you get desensitized. I have to bring them [the jurors] back to the real world so they see the victim as a person who had hopes and dreams, just like they do."

When asked his impressions of Alcala, Murphy said that he was evil in a "Ted Bundy way": charming, with a sense of humor, and reasonable. In terms of the trial, Alcala was often easier to deal with than some of his own colleagues. "I could see, after spending ten minutes with him, why women would get into his car," said Murphy. "Although he is a very cold sociopath—not a lot in the way of emotions—if you met him on the street, you'd never know in a million years that he was capable of what he did."

Because Alcala was not only the defendant but also acting as his own lawyer, Murphy had numerous meetings with him outside the courtroom. "Gina and I had to engage him," said Murphy. "We had to give him a sense that we were being fair and respectful, and for someone on death row, someone who has been told what to do all the time, he was eager to talk.

"We talked about death row a lot," continued Murphy. "The guy next door to him for four years on the row was Skylar Deleon [whom Murphy sent to the row in 2004, after convicting him of the murders of Thomas and Jackie Hawks, whose bodies were never found but on whose yacht Deleon was on as a prospective buyer]. And deputies told me Rodney was giving Deleon pointers about death row—how you get this going for you; how to get in this yard. Alcala liked Skylar. . . . I think they will be in the same yard—which is another interesting thing. I asked Rod what happens with these guys who are dangerous to the staff and people, and his response was: 'For the nonviolent guys like me, we wind up in the softie yard and the others spend a lot of time in the adjustment center.' Rod doesn't consider himself to be violent. And in his world, he *is* nonviolent. As long as eight-year-olds are not there."

Murphy stated that in his opinion, Alcala "is definitely bisexual. In the sixties and seventies, Alcala told people he was gay, plus he also had lots of photographs of young boys. And he made a statement to Monique Hoyt that he buried a boy."

According to Murphy, Alcala did what he did because he liked doing it. "He got a sexual charge and he liked the cruelty. He liked inflicting pain on strangers. That was his deal." Alcala wasn't interested in hurting people he knew well. "He didn't do it on the girl he dated," added Murphy. "It was the thrill of breaking in and controlling strangers.

"He had a full-blown perversion. There is a huge sexual component to this man, and he was able to hide that in his normal interactions. But Alcala is an extreme version. On top of that, he is an evil human being in his ability to be cruel and to fully, genuinely enjoy it.

"If he were ever released, he would do it again in a New York minute."

Murphy admitted that he doesn't win cases alone. "I have a ton of help. I work with paralegal, Dena Basham, who walks on water. We have been together for sixteen years. I couldn't have the successes I have without her. She organizes thousands of pages of police reports, coroner's reports, crime scene photos, autopsy photos, and all recorded media on every case. She provides me with trial notebooks as well as anticipating what I need before I even ask for it."

Also, continued Murphy, "an investigator is assigned to me full-time. Her name is Lisa Hunter. She is awesome, a police officer. She identifies and finds all the witnesses on every case without fail, which was definitely a challenge on this case, as we were dealing with some witnesses from over forty years ago. She coordinates them for trial by maintaining contact until trial, which can sometimes take years."

Murphy said, "In addition to their formal job descriptions, the true role of Basham and Hunter are as intergral members of a close working team. They participate in every aspect of the trial itself, from overall strategy to the details of what questions should be asked on cross-examination. They offer their ideas on everything from what photos to include in the closing argument to which witnesses would be most effective to illustrate any given point. Every trial is a team effort, and every win is a result of the hard work of all three."

When Murphy was asked how he is able to deal with such heinous murders and such depraved individuals, he said that as a balance to his work, he surfs.

"I try to get out just about every morning," he said. "I sit out in the water, a pod of porpoises sits in the bay. Paddling away from land, I am off North America and I see the hustle and bustle—and I relax. I am away. It gives me a sense of perspective. It balances me out."

Chapter Ninety-six

Huntington Beach police officer Steve Mack was the lead detective on the Samsoe case when Alcala's second conviction was overturned in 2003. As the senior homicide detective, he stayed on the case for five more years, until he retired in 2008. During that time, among other things, Mack had a beach towel, a shoe, and some jewelry that was in evidence taken to be tested for DNA, including an earring in Alcala's "trophy pouch" that ultimately connected Alcala to Charlotte Lamb. At that time, the Huntington Beach police department still had Alcala's car, so Mack had it towed to the sheriff's crime lab for DNA testing.

Mack realized how good Alcala was at gaming the system when, while Alcala was in custody and a pretrial date was set for two or three months later, "Alcala would come in and request that the date be changed, giving one excuse or another. Really, it was just so he could get out of jail for a while."

The first time Mack had any real contact with Alcala was when two New York detectives came to California and together the three got a court order for a bite impression from Alcala. When Mack and the detectives brought in the dentist and he took a plaster mold of Alcala's teeth, Alcala didn't resist. He was compliant. He didn't argue.

"But he did manage to irritate the NYC detectives," recalled Mack, "saying, 'I'm surprised it took you so long to come out here.' But then he refused to say another word to them."

Watching Alcala during the trial, Mack said that Alcala was very effeminate in his movements. "He would use his hand and brush his hair back, and I got to thinking, based on other photos I saw, that he probably had homosexual tendencies."

Mack said, "Alcala is the most prolific killer I ever had to work with. He's not the scariest. I had a robbery homicide case. The man shot and killed the store clerk. Looking into [the killer's] eyes, it was truly scary. Alcala is not physically imposing or scary. He couldn't take on a man. Taking on women, he is a coward."

Speaking of the trial, Mack said, "Matt and Gina did an exceptional job. Gina is very outgoing, not reserved. All of the victims' families loved her. They hugged her every day. They couldn't wait to talk to her every day. They all adored Murphy, too, and recognized what an outstanding job he was doing. He nearly brought the entire court to tears."

Concerning Alcala's ability as a lawyer, Mack said, "Although Alcala has a high IQ, he's not very smart. He was unprepared and unsure of himself. He was way outgunned. He represented himself so he could control the situation. He had had competent lawyers, but they wouldn't do what *he* wanted done so he asked to represent himself. Judge Briseño was so patient. He went out of his way to let Alcala defend himself and tried to explain many intricate points of law to him."

Speaking about his years as a detective, Mack said, "The amount of devotion to cases is different from case to case. Burglary is entirely different from working homicide. If your house gets broken into, at the end of the day, I can leave that.

"If you have any conscience at all, when working homicide, while you are trying to enjoy family time, the case is always there. You keep a notebook or tape recorder handy. . . .

"A detective needs tenacity and drive to solve a case. We

work for God and for the victim. We are the victim's voice. We try to give the victim's family some closure."

Mack believes that the death penalty is appropriate for Alcala but sadly, he said, "This is not Texas. Worse is the exorbitant amount of time Alcala has to sit on death row, the automatic appeals, the channels to take it to the Supreme Court."

Mack took the Alcala case—and the Samsoe murder in particular—personally. "This one sticks out because of Robin. You look at her photo and say, 'Who could harm this girl?'" Mack felt particularly outraged that someone could come to Huntington Beach and kidnap and murder a young girl. And the fact that the case was overturned by "Rosie [Bird] and the Supremes" was a huge insult.

Remembering a particular moment in the Samsoe case, Mack said, "On December 17, 2004, a street located less than a mile from where Samsoe had been abducted was named Alcala Drive to fit with the Spanish theme of the neighborhood. Alcala is a university town near Madrid and is also the name of a busy street in the capital.

"When I heard about the street sign, I took it personally. It offended my senses. I didn't want Robin's mother to ever find out that street was named Alcala."

Mack eventually contacted the developer of the high-end residential neighborhood. He tried to get the street renamed after Robin, but because of the Mediterranean theme of the development, the developer couldn't do it. The developer did, however, immediately rename the street.

"No one in the city of Huntington Beach wanted anything to do with the name Alcala," said Mack.

Chapter Ninety-seven

In 2010, detective Steven Hodel thought back on that August twelfth day in 1971 when he arrested Alcala for brutally raping eight-year-old Tali Shapiro. Quoted in Christine Pelicek's article "The Fine Art of Killing," which appeared in *LA Weekly* on January 21, 2010, Hodel recalled that Alcala had been on the lam for three years—living in New York and New Hampshire—after giving police the slip at the scene of the crime in West Hollywood. Remembering Alcala's capture, Hodel said, "My impression was that it was his first sex crime, and we got him early." After the arrest, Hodel believed "society is relatively safe now."

Then, Hodel stated, "I had no idea that in two years [he would be out] and continue his reign of terror and horror. . . . It is such a tragedy that so much more came after that."

(In 2003, Hodel would become famous for penning the best seller *Black Dahlia Avenger: A Genius for Murder*, a true-crime book that fingered his own father as the murderer of twenty-two-year-old Elizabeth Short, as well as from seven to twenty others, after the LAPD was unable to solve the crimes.)

Chapter Ninety-eight

During his fifteen years on the bench, from 1978 to 1993, now retired Orange County Superior Court judge Donald McCartin had sentenced nine murderers to death. "I was doing my job," said the judge, now eighty-two. "It didn't bother me one bit."

However, the judge exclaimed, "Zero for nine!" The men he sentenced to die for their crimes, including Rodney Alcala, have yet to see the inside of San Quentin's gas chamber. "None of them has even come close to being toasted. They're probably all going to outlive me. That makes me mad."

All of Judge McCartin's cases were either reversed or delayed by the appeals court.

McCartin doubts that any of the men he sent away will *ever* be executed. Over the past thirty years, four hundred murderers were put to death in Texas, but over the same period of time, only thirteen death row inmates were executed in California.

When asked about Alcala's claims of innocence, McCartin said, "Hogwash! He's as guilty as anybody who has ever come through this department."

PART
XVII

Chapter Ninety-nine

Over the years, police in New York City had been looking into two cases that they believed Alcala was tied to—the murder of Cornelia "Michael" Crilley in 1971 and the murder of Ellen Hover in 1977. In the case of Crilley, who had worked as a flight attendant and been murdered in her brand-new apartment, the MO was very similar to the murders of Georgia Wixted and Jill Parenteau in Los Angeles. All three victims were found nude or partially nude in their apartments. All three had been raped, suffered severe trauma to the face, and been strangled with nylon stockings. Two of the victims had been severely bitten on their breasts during the attacks.

And there was one more similarity: It took two decades to nail Alcala for the crimes, but police had found forensic evidence linking Alcala to Crilley's murder. Alcala's DNA was a match to DNA found in fluids on Crilley's body.

In 2010, in an interview with this author, Leon Borstein recalled Michael Crilley, his girlfriend, some thirty-nine years after her death. An assistant district attorney at the time, he had been on the scene when police discovered Crilley's body, and the loss continues to haunt him. Borstein, a distinguished-looking, dignified man, spoke in a soft voice and with a hint of nostalgia as we sat in his New York City law office.

"She was everything a man could want. This occurred forty years ago, and I am still affected by it. I was crazy about her at the time. . . . I was devastated by her death."

Borstein said that he got married a year after the murder. "Every year, I would go to the cemetery, for maybe three years [until] I realized that it was probably not good for my relationship with my wife. So one year I stopped stone cold. I realized it could take over my life and leave me back in time forever."

In early 2000, a friend called him and told him that authorities had found a DNA match from saliva on a bite mark left on Michael's body. "I was pleased that they got a match," he said, and then paused. "I was told he wrapped panty hose around her mouth."

In spite of the DNA evidence that police say implicates Alcala, he has never been charged with the murder of Michael Crilley. Borstein said he doesn't want a trial for Alcala for Crilley's murder. "He's already convicted. Why waste time and money?"

In thinking back on his girlfriend, Borstein said, "Michael will never grow old. She remains as beautiful, lively, and perfect as she was then."

As for the Ellen Hover case, Alcala has long been the prime suspect. In fact, Larry Welborn, *OC Register* journalist, started in 2011 that his October 20, 1979 article proves he was the first to put in writing that Alcala was "the principal suspect in [the] earlier slaying [of Hover] in New York in 1977." Hover vanished in 1977 from her Manhattan apartment, during a brief period of weeks when Alcala was known to have visited New York and passed himself off under the alias John Berger. Although Alcala admitted to having been with Hover on the day she disappeared—and a witness reported having gone with Alcala to the same remote spot where Hover's body was found dumped—Alcala was never charged with Hover's murder.

No forensic evidence has ever been found linking Alcala to Hover.

Bruce Ditnes, one of Hover's boyfriends, still calls her "the love of my life." In an article on OCRegister.com, he is quoted as saying, "She was extremely intelligent, graceful, demure and refined. She was very pretty . . . with a voluptuous body. . . . Even though she tried to dress conservatively, she could stop traffic. . . . It's not surprising she stood out and was noticed by Alcala."

In 2010, the authorities in California gave the NYPD a batch of photographs taken by Alcala that they believed dated from the time he lived in or visited New York. Much like the photos released to the press by the Huntington Beach Police Department, the New York photos primarily depicted young women. It was hoped that the NYPD might match some of the people in these photos to cold cases, involving missing persons or even homicides. When the NYPD balked at releasing the photographs to the public, Hover's surviving relatives were livid.

"They should be in every newspaper, on TV, and on the Internet," Sheila Weller, a cousin of Ellen Hover, told the *New York Daily News.*

Soon after this outcry, the photographs *were* released to the public, and the NYPD asked citizens to call their tip line if they knew anyone in the pictures. "It is rare that someone kept trophies of the women he came into contact with. . . . I am grateful to the *Daily News* for calling attention to the pictures," Weller said. "He is one of the biggest serial killers in the country. His trophy photos should be out in the open."

Within a day of the photos being displayed, a woman named Judy Cole, living in North Carolina, told police she recognized herself in photo number 169—showing the face of a young girl with her arms thrown behind her head. When she was nineteen years old in the late 1970s, Cole had met Alcala in Manhattan, and he had persuaded her to pose for him on the roof of a building. "He was very charming," Cole remembered. "I should have known better."

Maybe Cole is right. She should have been more careful, more wary of strange men with cameras and flattering ways. But then again, Cole shouldn't blame herself. Alcala preyed upon the young and vulnerable. He preyed upon their trust. The blame falls squarely on him.

Chapter One Hundred

Rodney Alcala's crimes were brutal and horrific. When police arrested him in 1979 and charged him with the murder of Robin Samsoe, it put a stop to his wanton killing spree. Alcala has not been out of jail since, and the last murder he committed was more than thirty years ago. Nonetheless, the violence he perpetrated created shock waves. These tremors still rock the lives of his surviving victims, his victims' loved ones, and the many police and court officers who witnessed horrors that can never be forgotten.

Alcala's 2010 conviction—for the murders of Robin Samsoe, Georgia Wixted, Jill Barcomb, Charlotte Lamb, and Jill Parenteau—at least brought some closure to their survivors. But it can never undo their suffering or the traumas they have endured.

In talking about the impact that Alcala's 2010 trial had on her life, Dedee Parenteau said, "I'll never have Jill back, but I do feel a sense of relief. I'm happy for Jill and the other girls that they got justice." As for the murder itself, Jill's death put a tremendous hole in her life. "My life changed dramatically," said Dedee.

Tali Shapiro, now fifty years old, said that she was a carefree eight-year-old skipping to school one day, and the next day she was a completely different person. In a recent interview, Shapiro said, "I was never carefree again. Alcala should have been put away forever for what he did to me. I don't believe I was the first," she said, "because he was too smooth."

Anne Michelena, Georgia Wixted's sister said of the trial, "I've waited thirty-three years for this. It was really hard to hear what happened to my sister, but this feels like a sense of relief."

Carolyn Adkins, Charlotte "Shug" Lamb's oldest sister, said of the trial, "This was more grievous than the original news of Shug's death, due to learning more about the details. Being the oldest sibling, I've always been able to hold up pretty well, but I was surprised by my own lack of control over my emotions. I couldn't stop crying for days and asked, 'Is this what a nervous breakdown feels like?' During the worst times, my dear husband, Jerry, would pull up a chair and sit beside me for as long as it took. Every time I'd see Shug's picture on television, the crying would start again. Finally, only with God's help, I was able to quiet my emotions to some degree, but life will never again be 'normal' for any of us."

Robert Samsoe was thirteen when Robin was killed. Her death, he said, ended his childhood. "Instead of playing with little Hot Wheels cars and G.I. Joes, I learned to take care of mom. My high school was ruined. My mom to this day can't deal. She went from being a very strong woman to a puddle of water some days."

Robert said he barely went to Huntington Beach High that fall. Instead, he sat in the park all day and wrote letters to Robin. "I went to school twenty-three days that year."

Talking about herself, Robin's mother, Marianne Connelly, said, "Grief is such a selfish emotion. When you have pain, you can't imagine anyone else having it. So sometimes you aren't the easiest person to live with."

Connelly said that in the years since Robin disappeared, the nightmares never stopped and that just keeping herself and her family together was a Herculean task. "Robert felt guilty for years," she said. "He was supposed to have gone to the beach that day with Robin, but instead he decided to go surfing." Connelly said that she had told her son to go ahead, that Robin would be fine.

Connelly said she keeps Robin's smiling photographs all around her home. Robin's old dolls are positioned throughout the house, too, to keep Robin's memory alive. Connelly said that she began to volunteer to help other crime victims, believing that Robin would have wanted her to do that.

Talking about the therapy she tried in an effort to heal, Connelly said that the therapist told her she would never get past the death until she could forgive Alcala. "But, my God, how could I?" The therapist suggested she write Alcala a letter in prison to help her with her grief. She said she wrote a seven-page letter telling him how he had ruined her life. "It didn't make me feel any better, and I never sent it to him."

Connelly said she had to take off months from work while attending trials and court hearings, leaving her family in a precarious financial situation. Robert concurred: "My mom hasn't had gainful employment since Robin, and she was a worker." During the 2010 trial, Connelly told reporters that her home had gone into foreclosure.

Each of the Barcomb siblings had a special remembrance of Jill.

To her youngest brother, Michael, Jill was the older sister who played catch with him, showing him how to pass a football. She was a great athlete, and fast enough to have run in girls' track had she chosen to do so.

Joey remembered Jill playing "hacky sack" with him in front of the house. Her petite frame and manual dexterity made her the awe of onlookers as she aggressively played and volleyed the sack back and forth.

Kelly remembered Jill teaching her how to roller-skate at the skating rink. Jill was gifted. Sometimes Jill would skate up from behind or hold her hand while she gained her balance.

To younger sibling Kimie, Jill was the sister who took her to the city swimming pool and would sometimes spend her babysitting money on treats for her younger brothers and sisters at Dave's market. Kimie said that Jill made sure they were taken care of before she ever bothered to spend any money on her self.

Younger brother Brian, who had a superb singing voice, treasured the uniqueness of the year he made all-county choir. He was proud to watch Jill magnificently play the trumpet and Maurice the trombone, when they also earned coveted seats at the all-county event.

To older brother Maurice, Jill was the sister who threw newspapers for him on his paper route when he had fractured his wrist. Jill didn't complain at all: She just wanted to help.

Older sister Marlene treasured the memories of their youthful innocence together, especially making mud pies in the backyard. Marlene helped Jill learn how to ride a bike. Marlene and Jill often walked to and from school together.

To Debbie, Jill's gift of song was what made preparing for her wedding so romantic and dreamy. Jill had a beautiful voice, and Debbie remembered how Jill had practiced singing the Carpenters' "We've Only Just Begun" as a possible choice for the ceremony.

To oldest sister Alice, out of all her sister's, Jill was the one she entrusted to serve as Godmother to her only daughter at her formal christening. Jill's compassion was what she wished to pass along to her daughter.

In the late 1970s, after Jill's death, Jill's parents opened their own business, Beaver's Diner, in Oneida. Jill's death awakened in them the desire to pursue their dreams while they were still able to. They were only too painfully aware that the future was uncertain.

Bruce Barcomb recalled that it was 2005 when he received a postcard in the mail from the LAPD. "When I called them, they told me, 'We believe that we identified your sister's killer via DNA.'" Barcomb stated that "tears of joy came down my cheek."

After that, Barcomb decided to write to Alcala in jail. "I wrote to Alcala four times. . . . I implored him to tell the truth: 'I'm a serial killer. This is what I did.' Give up the victims." He hoped that Alcala would confess and spare the victims and their families—including his own elderly mother, who was undergoing chemotherapy—the ordeal of going through a murder trial with all its gruesome detail.

In his letters, he told Alcala that even cannibal Jeffrey Dahmer expressed remorse for his crimes, and that Ted Bundy had assisted police in solving some of his killings.

With bitterness along with resignation, Barcomb said, "Alcala never wrote me back."

Today, Rodney Alcala sits on death row at San Quentin. His death sentence and conviction for five murders are under appeal.

Since 2006, no one on the row in California had been put to death.

PART XVIII

Chapter One
Hundred and One

On September 23, 2010, an article on OCRegister.com by Larry Welborn stated: "The crime spree and 31-year legal odyssey of serial killer Rodney Alcala, who was sentenced to death by an Orange County judge earlier this year, will be featured on CBS news *48 Hours Mystery* in its season premier episode on Saturday."

The one-hour episode, "The Killing Game," was aired on Saturday, September 25, 2010, documenting "serial killer Rodney Alcala's 40-year odyssey of rape, murder, and eluding justice." It was producer Harold Dow's last episode before his untimely death.

In the episode, Officer Camacho recalled that while he was on patrol on Sunset Boulevard on September 25, 1968, he got a call to investigate a suspicious sighting of a little girl and man going into an apartment. When Camacho got there and knocked on the door, he saw "an evil face at the window." The man wouldn't open the door, and Camacho kicked it down. "The image will be with me forever.

"A body. A lot of blood. White Mary Janes. . . . We determined she was dead. Her throat was constricted by a ten-pound steel bar." But then, he continued. "She was gagging, trying to breathe." After realizing she was alive, he said to himself, "Okay, I figured, one for the good guys."

In 1972, Alcala pleaded guilty to child molestation and received one year to life. Camacho was "flabbergasted" when the parole board let him go after thirty-four months.

Steve Hodel, lead detective on the case in 1968, was also interviewed. In his opinion, Alcala "was a snake charmer." People didn't want to believe that a talented student could commit a brutal crime. Commenting on the decision to release Alcala after serving thirty-four months for the Tali S. crime, Hodel said that it had "catastrophic consequences."

Bridget Wilvert spoke about her friendship with Robin Samsoe and that day when she and Robin were having their pictures taken on the beach by a "professional" photographer; then being reprimanded by Jackye Young for allowing that to take place; and later saying goodbye to Robin, who took her bicycle so she wouldn't be late for ballet.

That was the last time she, or anyone else, saw Robin.

Marianne Connelly spoke to Dow. She appeared tired and very sad. She said that, to her, the name Rodney Alcala "means evil. It means horror. It means pain and a lot of anger." Speaking of her daughter, Connelly said, "She was probably the most loving child a mother could have." Robin's brothers agreed. Tim spoke about how she knit the family together and Robert called her his best friend.

Connelly recalled the day she learned the police had found Robin. She asked if she could go and see "her baby." The police said no. Connelly asked why.

"Because it took us three days to identify her," they said.

Still not understanding what the problem was, Connelly said, "How many little girls with long blond hair disappear that it took you three days?"

The officer "shook his shoulders and tears were coming down his face, too. He said, 'There was *no* hair.' "

Beth Kelleher was twenty-two years old when she met Alcala in the spring of 1979. Speaking to Dow, she said that she thought "his photography was good." Most of his photographs were of young girls. Kelleher said she was in love with Alcala at the time. She said she had absolutely no reason to think Alcala was involved in Samsoe's disappearance: his personality didn't change during the days the media barraged the public with images of Robin. But, admitted Kelleher, she had no idea where Alcala had been on June 20.

The episode documented the day Alcala was arrested, July 24, 1979, for the Samsoe murder, and the subsequent search of his Seattle locker. Huntington Beach Detective Patrick Ellis remarked that, by the time of his arrest, Alcala had completely changed his appearance and cut his long curly hair.

Lori Werts spoke of the pictures of herself that were found in the Seattle locker and how Alcala, the photographer, had told her that she would be in a magazine. "That'll be cool," she thought.

Throughout the episode, Matt Murphy filled in the timeline between the speakers. He said that he believed that just like Alcala convinced Tali to get in his car, he most likely convinced Robin, also an innocent twelve-year-old, who was late for ballet class.

Murphy reported on the 1980 trial, in which Alcala was convicted and sentenced to death. But soon after, the California Supreme Court reversed the decision and ruled that Alcala had not received a fair trial.

The episode documented the fact that Alcala was tried again and convicted a second time and sentenced to death. But again the verdict was thrown out.

Then, Dow said, in 2003 the case again fell to Matt Murphy. Murphy said it was difficult to prepare for the trial at first, because when the higher court reversed the earlier conviction, it ruled that a lot of evidence was inadmissible ["when they reversed it, they also removed a substantial amount of evidence."] However, Murphy continued, they soon got a huge break—DNA.

"The DNA technology . . . pointed to . . . one person only . . . Rodney Alcala," said LA County Deputy DA Gina Satriano.

Murphy realized that he now had hard evidence that not only had Alcala viciously murdered Samsoe, but he was "the serial killer that we always suspected him to be." Murphy observed that the evidence against Alcala was not *only* DNA, but that his MO fit a pattern: all victims were sexually assaulted, left naked, posed, severely beaten around the head, and strangled with ligatures.

Murphy and Satriano talked about how they joined the cases—the two counties, LA and Orange, had never shared a murder case before.

And it was the best decision they could have made.

Speaking of Alcala's miscalculations in not only representing himself but also focusing only on the Samsoe case during his 2010 trial, Satriano said that "Alcala had no idea how to challenge" the scientific evidence.

Murphy said, "Alcala does absolutely one-hundred percent deserve to die for what he did."

During the penalty phase, Tali Shapiro introduced herself to Murphy and said she was was alive because of a "guardian angel." But, she asked, "why in the world are there so many other victims when it was a known fact of what he did to me?"

In bringing the show to a close, Dow said that the "saga of Rodney Alcala's murderous odyssey still hasn't ended." He explained that, after Alcala's conviction, Huntington Beach police released photos recovered from Alcala's Seattle storage locker of more than one hundred young women. Authorities hoped to identify them and to, "learn if Alcala claimed still more victims."

Speaking of the photographs, Detective Ellis said, "We just don't know . . . who's alive and who's not. Maybe just maybe there's another victim out there, or victims, someplace. . . ." Ellis asked anyone with information to call him at the Huntington Beach Police Department.

"There are four other murders in New York that have been linked to Rodney Alcala," said Murphy. He expressed confidence that the New York police "will get the job done."

Conelly's words closed the show. She said, "I want him to die here" in California and not in any other state where he had killed. She said that if she could outlive Alcala by at least one day, "I could die a happy woman."

* * *

On March 17, 2010, host Dr. Phil McGraw devoted one of his *Dr. Phil* episodes to "Snapshots from a Serial Killer," featuring Rodney Alcala. On the show, several of Alcala's "victims" spoke: Tali Shapiro, Bruce Barcomb, Robert Samsoe, and Marianne Connelly.

The narrator of the show began by displaying photographs of Jill Barcomb, Robin Samsoe, Charlotte Lamb, Jill Parenteau, and Georgia Wixted. He then told the audience that none of these young women would be on the show today because each one had been "raped, tortured, brutalized, and then murdered." He said that none of this should have happened. His conclusion: "The system failed these women."

"The mission of today's show is to make noise about this problem. But first let's take a look at the latest on serial killer Rodney Alcala, who investigators say may be the most prolific serial killer in U.S. history."

Tali was interviewed first. She stated that she had been to court three times and that she was alive because of guardian angels and the Good Samaritan "that was in the car . . . against every fiber in his being thought he was doing the wrong thing and followed me and called the police and they broke down the door . . . . Maybe I'm here now to speak for others that can't speak. . . ."

Robert Samsoe stated that Alcala was out on bail when he attacked his sister. "I am so angry at our system. . . . The fact that he was out on bail for raping a fifteen-year-old for $10,000 [bail]." In disgust, he continued: "My sister's life was worth $10,000 because he was out on bail." He said he missed Robin "every day, every night."

McGraw asked Connelly whether she had, in fact, brought a loaded gun in her purse to the courtroom. She confirmed that she did so because Alcala "kept blowing kisses at me across the courtroom" and she simply couldn't bear it.

However, she never pulled the gun out of her purse because "Robin's hand on my wrist. . . . All of a sudden, I smelled her shampoo and I felt this warmth on my hand and couldn't get my hand out of my purse."

McGraw wondered aloud how Alcala could have been let out of prison, when he, McGraw and anyone else who studied forensics, knows "you can't rehabilitate a sexual offender in seventeen months."

The show ended with the unequivocal belief that "the system is broken." Former FBI profiler and NBC and MSN-BC's chief analyst Clint Van Zandt said that there were probably hundreds of cases in which sexual predators are on the streets, re-offending. "We need a one-strike law. We need to say if you offend against a child, a woman, a man in a sexual—in a violent sexual manner, you're going to jail and you are not going to get out of that jail, and that's what this country needs."

If only there had been a one-strike law in the early 1970s. Then Jill Barcomb, Georgia Wixted, Charlotte Lamb, Jill Parenteau, Robin Samsoe, Cornelia Crilley—and many many other young, beautiful, innocent, and special daughters and sisters and mothers—would have lived to grace those close to them with years of friendship and love.

Chapter One Hundred
and Two

Alcala's involvement with the justice system seems to be the story that never ends.

In 2010, Cyrus Vance Jr. opened a cold-case unit in Manhatttan. Among the cases the officers were given to review were the deaths of Cornelia Crilley, TWA stewardess, and Ellen Hover, aspiring musician and socialite.

After working on these cases, the detectives soon realized they had put together enough evidence to convene a grand jury to hear the details. And the details were all about Rodney Alcala.

On January 26, 2011, several New York and California newspapers reported that Alcala, now sixty-seven, had been indicted by a Manhattan grand jury for the murders of Cornelia Crilley, murdered in 1971, and Ellen Hover, murdered in 1977. The indictment came down in spite of the fact that Rodney Alcala was already sitting on death row in California. Among the people testifying at the grand jury hearing was the lead detective on the Crilley case some forty years earlier: Frank Donnelly, now retired.

Ellen Hover's first cousin, Sheila Weller, who has written often about her cousin's death, was quoted in the *New York Post* on Saturday, January 29, 2011, as saying, "I applaud Manhatttan District Attorney Cyrus Vance Jr. for not letting the redundancy of five death penalties—along with any fiscal concerns over the coming prosecution—keep him from understanding that every single murder victim deserves her own justice."

When Leon Bornstein, Crilley's boyfriend at the time of her murder, heard the news of the indictment, he had a different reaction from that of Weller. Borstein is quoted in the *New York Times* as saying that he did not see the point of prosecuting Alcala. "All it does is entertain him, and it doesn't do anything for us. He gets to fly out to New York, meet with his lawyers, sit in a courtroom for days on end. It certainly alleviates the boredom of sitting in a jail cell."

Patrick Ellis, the Huntington Beach police detective who was in charge of the investigation of Alcala's third Orange County trial, was quoted by Larry Welborne in the *Orange County Register* as saying that the New York indictments were "excellent news. It will help give closure to the family of those two women and it will hold him responsible for the murders of those women.

"If it was my daughter and mother who were murdered, I definitely would want him prosecuted," Ellis added. "You can't put a dollar sign on human life."

Ellis is still receiving phone calls from people who believe they recognize a loved one or acquaintance from among the photos in Alcala's photo gallery. "We still get four or five a week. It could happen tomorrow, you never know."

As of the publication of this book, exactly when Alcala will be extradicted to New York remains an unanswered question. But no doubt about it, Alcala will once again be in the spotlight he so fervently seeks.

Alcala's is truly a story that never ends.